PILGRIMS,

COLONISTS,

AND FRONTIERSMEN

AN ETHNIC COMMUNITY IN TRANSITION

Alex Simirenko

THE FREE PRESS OF GLENCOE
COLLIER-MACMILLAN LIMITED, London

TO EDITH AND DON

Preface

AMERICA is unique among the nations of the world in the number of ethnic communities that make up its population. From 1820, when the first ethnic census was taken, to 1960 more than forty million persons (primarily adults) immigrated to the United States. The great tide reached its peak in the period from 1890 to World War I. In some years the immigrants numbered from one and a half to two million annually. Alien in speech and customs, the immigrants crowded into the cities, where they were estranged both from the American environment and from other immigrants.

American sociology came of age in the period when the immigrant problem was at flood tide. When such major scholars as W. I. Thomas, Florian Znaniecki, Robert Park, R. McKenzie, Ernest Burgess, and Louis Wirth turned their attention to the urban world, they began researches that raised sociology from a mere discipline based on second-hand materials gathered by historians into a study that required gathering of first hand facts. Competition, conflict, and assimilation of immigrant groups from the various countries of the world posed perhaps the most pressing problem for American cities. It was only with the study of the immigrant and his problems that sociology effectively evolved as a research science.

This early period saw the first steps taken toward an effective theory of the immigrant, as well as toward empirical research into the facts of his life. Particularly under the leadership of Park, the examination of areas of settlement by immigrants (sometimes called natural areas) and of the movement of immigrant groups in and out and through them was undertaken. This research was incorporated eventually into the systematic arguments that compose ecological theory. Park and Stonequist also followed earlier leads by Thomas and Znanicki into study of the types of adjustments and individual psychological orientations that accompanied the changing relations of the immigrant to American life as a whole. This study led to typologies of immigrants like Thomas and Znaniecki's Bohemian, Philistine, and Creative Men and was synthesized in the Park-Stonequist theory of the *marginal man*.

While the pioneering researchers were preoccupied with the forms of assimilation of the immigrant and his social problems, the study of the immigrant community *per se* was largely forgotten. Looking back and appraising his own classic study of the Italian immigrant community, William Foote Whyte summarizes the state of sociological research prior to 1936:

It is hard to realize now how rapid has been the development of sociological and anthropological studies of communities and organizations since 1936, when I began my work in Cornerville. At that time nothing had yet been published on W. Lloyd Warner's "Yankee City" study. I had read the Lynds' *Middletown* and Carolyn Ware's *Greenwich Village* with interest and profit, and yet I began to realize, more and more as I went along, that I was not making a community study along those lines. Much of the other sociological literature then available tended to look upon communities in terms of social problems so that the community as an organized social system simply did not exist.[*]

With the passing of time, as the problem of assimilation of the immigrant receded into the background, students of social science became increasingly attracted to research into the social structure of the ethnic community. Such interests are embodied in the work of William Foote Whyte, W. Lloyd Warner and his distinguished associates, as well as in R. A. Schermerhorn's theoretical concern with

[*] William Foote Whyte, *Street Corner Society* (Chicago: University of Chicago Press, 1955), p. 286.

the formation of the ethnic community. Publication of the translated works of Max Weber dealing with the "guest" or "pariah" community also tended to stimulate sociological research in this direction.

From the point of view of the present study, the most significant break in the theory of the ethnic group since the days of Thomas and Znaniecki, Park, and Stonequist is to be found in Don Martindale's *American Social Structure*. Martindale has freed the theory from its narrow dependence upon first-generation American-born reactions to immigrant parents and from the problems of individual marginality. The theory of the immigrant community has been developed and reconceptualized in terms of the general theory of community.

Since one of the primary objectives of the present study is to subject this revised theory of the ethnic community to empirical test, it will be useful to outline the theory briefly. Martindale has argued that a community is a total way of life, a set of groups and institutions sufficient to bring a plurality of its members through the cycle of a normal year and the cycle of a normal life. The set itself is continually being renewed, as well. He has presented evidence that the primary principles of community formation are stability, consistency, and completeness.

Martindale has argued that various secondary principles are also at work and that two of them are basic to the formation of the ethnic community: extra-community closure and extra-community innovation. That is, an ethnic community forms only when a majority community permits a group of aliens to take up a way of life in its midst (extra-community innovation). At the same time, an ethnic community does not ordinarily form unless the majority community tends to deny full reception to immigrants (extra-community closure). The majority community allows the immigrant to come in, but it treats him with reserve and suspicion. There is thus a dominant combination of receptivity and prejudice toward the alien plurality. The immigrant tends to respond to the new environment with a combination of adjustment to the wider community and simultaneous withdrawal into a partially separate group within it. The ethnic community is a semi-withdrawn subcommunity.

Some element of the alien group's former culture or institutions usually becomes the focal point of the community in the new land. Most often the ethnic church serves as a community center in a way that was unnecessary in the homeland. Around it a whole array of institutions may form: parochial schools, labor unions, cultural societies, specialty restaurants, foreign-language newspapers, burial societies—a complete system of institutions constituting a total way of life.

The present study, an extensive revision of my doctoral dissertation, examines the dynamics of social and cultural change that accompanied the formation and transformation of the Minneapolis Russian community. The members of this community came from Slavic peasant villages in the Austro-Hungarian Empire when the national loyalties of the people in that region were still in the process of crystallization. Shortly after their arrival in the United States, the members of the Minneapolis community identified themselves with the Russian nationality and the Russian church. It was the first such American community to change its allegiance from the Uniate Church to Russian Orthodoxy, and it was for fifteen years the first and only training center for Russian Orthodox clergymen in the United States.

The Minneapolis Russians formed their community within the framework of the majority society. To these Pilgrims (as they will be called in the present study) sons and daughters were born who displayed many of the characteristic traits of the marginal man caught between two worlds. They worked out their conflicts, however, and in turn produced children. At present, members of the third generation are beginning to take key positions in the community.

In this book, the responses primarily of the first and second generations to the ethnic community and to the wider Minneapolis society are examined in terms of class, status, and power. A variety of hypotheses have been developed concerning these variables in terms of the ethnic community outlined above.

It has been my good fortune to carry out my researches under optimum conditions. Among teachers at the University of Minnesota who have encouraged me each step of the way and given freely of their counsel are Professors John Sirjamaki, Roy G. Francis, Elio

Preface   (xi)

D. Monachesi, George B. Vold, and John Forster. To Professor Don
Martindale, who directed my program, I wish to acknowledge my
great debt for his constant help and encouragement at all stages of
the work. I received assistance and cooperation from many individuals inside and outside the Russian community. Rev. Vladimir
Borichevsky, Rev. Leonard Soroka, Rev. John Dzubay, Dr. and Mrs.
Henry Jerabek, Mrs. Susan Murray, Mrs. Dora Green, Gary Miller,
Constance and Mary Tarasar, Natalie Brinda, Patricia Pilkey, Sonia
Reshetar, and Roberta Weinard were especially helpful. Professor
and Mrs. Wassilij Alexeev were most generous in putting me in
touch with the Minneapolis Russians, and I should like to thank
them for all they have done for me. My colleagues in the Department of Sociology at the University of Minnesota—Mary Adams,
Noel Iverson, Roger Krohn, Ronald Althouse, Balwant Nevaskar,
and Tom Philbrook—contributed much to the improvement of the
study.

Professor Carl W. Backman of the University of Nevada assisted and encouraged completion of the project. Dean Thomas
O'Brien of the Graduate School and the Graduate Research Committee at the University of Nevada provided funds for the processing
of the gathered data. Rev. Alexander Shmemann, editor of the *St.
Vladimir's Seminary Quarterly,* has given permission to reproduce
previously published data. For typing the manuscript I am indebted
to Mrs. Alma Smith and especially to Miss Louise P. Olsen, whose
editorial work was particularly appreciated. My wife, who assisted
and encouraged me during the whole work, deserves my very special
thanks. While I received help from all of these friends and colleagues, I alone should be held responsible for any errors.

ALEX SIMIRENKO

June 1963

Contents

(xiii)

Contents

List of Tables

(xv)

PILGRIMS, COLONISTS, AND FRONTIERSMEN

1 The Theory of the Ethnic Community

STRANGERS OR GROUPS of strangers in the United States have been viewed from many different perspectives. They have been described as aliens, immigrants, minorities, races, refugees, ethnic communities —even, in Weber's terms, as "guest" or "pariah" communities. In this study, the term "ethnic community" indicates that we are interested in the uniqueness of the community, rather than in problems of ethnicity or problems of groups *per se.*

The community represents a complete way of life. American society is made up of many communities (some writers say "subsystems" or "subcultures") of varied degrees of integration and intensity of social life. The definition of "community" used here is that of Robert M. MacIver:

Wherever any group, small or large, live together in such a way that they share, not this or that particular interest, but basic conditions of a common life, we call that group a community. The mark of a community is that one's life *may* be lived wholly within it, that all one's social relationships may be found within it. . . . But civilized communities, even very large ones, are much less self-contained. We may live in a metropolis and yet be members of a very small community, because our interests are circumscribed within a narrow area.[1]

(1)

The term "ethnic" signifies the unique base upon which the immigrant community is formed and continues to operate. The uniqueness of the ethnic community centers on the minority status of aliens who seek to preserve a distinct way of life within the framework of the majority community. Two major principles operate in the formation of the ethnic community: selective receptivity by the majority and partial closure by the minority.[2]

One precondition for the creation of a minority (ethnic) community within a majority community is the ability of the stranger to offer services to the majority community. For example, most Slavic immigrants to the United States arrived at a time when an emerging American industrialism had created extensive demands for unskilled labor. The Slavs were admitted into the majority community to perform menial and back-breaking labor at the height of the industrial expansion in the 1890s.

But the presence of strangers with a unique way of life in the midst of the majority community has often seemed to threaten the way of life of the majority. The more appealing the stranger, the greater may be the threat he represents, since his existence proves that other solutions to life's problems are possible. In any case, strangers are usually looked upon with a mixture of curiosity, interest, fear, resentment, hostility, or prejudice. At the same time, they are tolerated for the services they render.

This combination of hostility and tolerance favors the segregation of the strangers into semi-isolated communities of their own. In the meantime, strangers in a new land may find that their lives become meaningless unless they can bolster themselves through association with their countrymen. Such pressures from the majority community engender conscious efforts at self-help among the strangers themselves, and the ethnic community is born.[3]

In the 1920s, Bogardus attempted to measure majority prejudice toward various minority groups. His "social-distance scale" attempted to determine differential acceptance of minority group members. Later studies added to understanding of differential acceptance.[4]

Bogardus and his students also showed that members of minorities are sensitive to the acceptance or nonacceptance of their groups by the majority.[5]

Gerth and Mills called attention to correlations between the acceptance of minority groups within American society and changes in the political relations of the United States with their home countries. During the Second World War, for example, the Greeks and the Slavs enjoyed greater acceptance than previously, while the Germans, Japanese, and Italians suffered increasing hostility and prejudice. To retain a favorable position within the majority community, many individuals from the latter groups joined the armed services to prove their loyalty to the majority community. After the war, with the changing circumstances of the cold war the position of the Germans, Italians, and Japanese improved, while the position of the Slavic and Chinese groups declined in turn.[6]

The strangers themselves, however, are not always eager to embrace the majority member and his values. Mikhail K. Jeleznov (M. K. Argus) vividly described the attitudes of Russian Civil War refugees in New York in the 1920s:

One could get along in New York exclusively with the Russian language —one still can—and we saw no need to waste time on learning the extremely difficult barbaric tongue of the natives, whom we viewed with a mixed feeling of contempt and pity. Poor ignorant creatures, they have lived in this country for such a long time and have not yet learned how to speak Russian![7]

Max Weber saw the partial closure of the Jewish community since the Babylonian exile as the self-imposition of commensalism, connubium, the celebration of the Sabbath, circumcision, and other traditional practices. The Jews succeeded in segregating themselves into a unique community difficult for outsiders to penetrate.[8] Hughes argued that the location of the minority within the majority community underlies mutual awareness that they belong to different worlds:

An ethnic group is not one because of the degree of measurable or observable difference from other groups; it is an ethnic group, on the contrary, because the people in it and the people out of it know that it is one; because both the *ins* and the *outs* talk, feel, and act as if they were a separate group.[9]

The Significance of Status Relations

Gerth and Mills conceived of the formation of ethnic communities as "status phenomena." To them a minority "refers to a status group based on descent, whose members are denied status equality with nonminority people, irrespective of individual achievements."[10] Weber's concepts of "closed" and "open" social relationships supplied major theoretical distinctions for understanding the significance of status differences in the creation of communal relationships. An open social relationship is one in which the "participation in the mutually oriented social action . . . is . . . not denied to anyone who wishes to participate and who is actually in a position to do so." The closed social relationship is one in which "participation of certain persons is excluded, limited, or subjected to conditions."[11]

In Weber's view, many significant social relations are closed for rational reasons. Men tend to monopolize access to material and spiritual satisfactions, but "if the participants expect that the admission of others will lead to an improvement in their situation, and improvement in degree, in kind, in the security or the value of the satisfaction, their interest will be in keeping the relationship open." There are various means by which closed social relationships may guarantee monopoly positions to individuals and groups within society. They may be completely open to attainment by competitive struggle; various rules and regulations may ration and distribute these positions; or they may be permanently appropriated by certain individuals or subgroups of society. According to Weber, "the last is a case of closure within, as well as against, outsiders." Weber has argued that in "the case of many relationships, both communal and associative, there is a tendency to shift from a phase of expansion to one of exclusiveness."[12]

The ways by which outsiders may be excluded from participation in a community's social advantages vary widely. For the most part, the transition from an open to a closed social relation is gradual. A whole series of conditions for participation may be laid down short of complete closure. Extreme permanent closure is illustrated by cases in which particular rights are reserved to an individual by birth in a particular household, clan, or family. Weber isolated three principal motives for such closure: to maintain quality, as in such communities as ascetics or monastic orders, religious sects, and organized groups of warriors; to maintain consumption advantages, as in the self-sufficient village community; to maintain acquisition advantages, as in such trade monopolies as guilds and ancient monopolies of fishing rights. The first motive is usually combined with the other two.[13]

The significance of these formulations by Weber, Gerth, and Mills is found in their location of status advantages at the core of the ethnic structure. In comparison with the majority community, the ethnic community's advantages may be slight. Yet an ethnic group may monopolize access to certain values for its members, by denying it to members of other ethnic groups or less fortunate individual members of the majority community. The same formulation holds true for the majority community, since the majority may be even more eager to protect the greater advantages secured through regulation and closure.

Weber's ideas also explain the disintegration and transformation of many ethnic communities in the United States. Members of ethnic communities acquire skills by which they obtain advantages in the majority community. Through fulfillment of various regulations, qualifying tests, periods of probation, and possession, they are able to achieve positions inaccessible to the new arrival to the country.

THE SOCIAL STRUCTURE OF THE ETHNIC COMMUNITY

The ethnic community develops its own way of life around whatever institution holds greatest promise of keeping the community together. Like many other ethnic communities in the United States, the Russian community in Minneapolis transformed its church into such a central institution. Studies of Russian immigrants in other parts of the United States confirm the importance of the church as a unifying institution.[14]

No other institution available to the Russians is strong enough to institute a partial closure in the face of the majority community and unite the minority into a purposeful body. In the heterogeneous environment of the American city, Russians have had great difficulty in establishing a labor union, a newspaper, or a political party as a dominant institution. They have rarely become numerous enough to be a locally dominant political force. They have rarely, if ever, dominated a single industry as the Jews, for example, dominate the garment industry. Finally, being predominantly of peasant origin, the Russians have lacked an elite who could establish intellectual institutions as a dominant form.

The ethnic community's distinct way of life is preserved by a system of stratification. Individuals with prestige, influence, and authority within the community protect and sanction its cultural uniqueness. Initially the ethnic community clings to the same system of stratification that obtained in the country of origin.

Jeleznov acutely isolated the system of stratification initially dominant among the post-1918 Russian refugees in the New World. While many persons who had formerly enjoyed authority and prestige performed menial tasks in America in order to make a living, their status remained high within the Russian ethnic community. A former general turned taxi driver, a former professor forced to work as a night watchman, a former writer became a housepainter, or a former actress established as a charwoman—all were familiar in early Russian-American circles. In the eyes of immigrant Russians, they retained the aura of their pre-Revolutionary positions. Jeleznov called this phenomenon a kind of "inverted democracy."

Jeleznov also observed a phenomenon he described as "perennial youth" among Russian refugees. The artists who left Russia in their youth remained "young" all their lives in the eyes of their compatriots; an able actress who was never able to perform in the United States also remained "young" in the eyes of the Russian community, despite her actual age. In short, there occurred a sort of psychological fixation on Old-World social relations.

According to Jeleznov, the habits, language, tastes, and personal lives of the Russians tended to remain static from the time they left Russia. Members of the Russian community who attained high positions in American society—foreign policy consultants, for example—

but who had not held equivalent positions in the mother country were subject to pity and consolation! It was the money one had in the old country that counted—not the status one achieved in the new.[15]

Equivalent to this freezing of old world status distinctions are certain processes among other Russian immigrants. The majority of Russian immigrants were of peasant origin. Among such immigrants the freezing process took the form of maintenance of Old-World kinship systems and Old-World village loyalties.

Since Old-World conditions forced the poorest peasants to emigrate, there were few representatives of the peasant elite among immigrant groups. The maintenance of a stable Old-World stratification system proved to be especially difficult for them, since the major index of peasant status was possession of land—difficult to achieve in the American city. Village craftsmen coming to the United States were often able to secure semi-skilled positions envied by immigrants from peasant families of greater prestige. Still, back-breaking tasks in the new country had some effect on stratification. The accumulation of possessions, highly important as an index of one's position among the peasants in the Old World, rapidly became accepted as a basis of prestige in the American environment. It forced the restructuring of the old system of stratification among former Russian and Slavic peasants.

WORKING HYPOTHESES

It is hypothesized that the original system of stratification in the ethnic community tends to disintegrate with the rise of the second and later generations—and that the economic and professional advancement of these new generations bring about cultural dispersal as well as assimilation into the larger American community. The theoretical basis of the first hypothesis has been sketched earlier in this chapter. That for the second has been supplied by Karl Mannheim, Hans Gerth, and C. Wright Mills.

Mannheim believes that culture is accumulated less by individuals than by the "continuous emergence of new age groups" who look at their heritage with fresh eyes and take fresh approaches to old problems. Fundamental changes (or so-called "fresh contact") in any society take place in two forms: change in the structural social relations of a society and change from one generation to another. The second is "potentially" disruptive, since a new attitude toward the cultural heritage may develop.[16]

Given the social differentiation of an ethnic community, a whole array of theoretically possible types of marginal man can arise. Gerth and Mills distinguished four major types of personality produced by the ethnic community. A member of a minority may seek status either by employment of the status symbols of his minority or by employment of the status symbols of the majority. These symbols may be used either within the ethnic communty or within the majority community. According to Gerth and Mills, "within each of these four situations there are many possible varieties and types of men and women." They contend, however, that the majority of Jews in the United States are in none of these situations, that they seek status among both groups and with the symbols of both."[17] Gerth and Mills were primarily interested in the personality characteristics of present-day ethnic types and were not attempting to explain the process by which this internal differentiation takes place or its effects upon the ethnic community. Only the new generations of the ethnic community can successfully claim status advantages utilizing the status symbols of the majority. It is important, thus, to fuse the generation concept of Mannheim with Gerth and Mill's ideas of employment of status symbols. From this fusion flows the second working hypothesis.

THE TRANSFORMATION OF THE ETHNIC COMMUNITY

In *The Social System,* Talcott Parsons declares that "a general theory of the processes of change of social systems is not possible in the present state of knowledge." He argues that such a theory would necessarily have to be based on complete knowledge of the laws by which the social system operates, knowledge that we do not have at the present time. In general, however, Parsons claims that two types of change may affect the social system: It may disappear through the "dissoluation of the boundary-maintaining system and its assimilation to the environment," or it may transform itself into something new.[18] The disintegration of the community is thus attributed by Parsons to the dissolution of boundary-maintaining closure operating from within and from without the community.

Baltzell accounts for this dissolution when he distinguishes between two types of learning process—socialization and acculturation. Socialization pertains to the assimilation of the subculture into which an individual has been born; acculturation refers to learning about other subcultures with which one has had little experience. According to Baltzell, the problems of the second-generation member of an ethnic community are essentially represented by the culture conflicts emerging as a result of his acculturation into American society.[19]

Commitment to an ethnic community is represented by the ratio between the two learning processes: socialization and acculturation. Those prepared to sever their relations with the ethnic community and dissolve the boundary-maintaining closure will necessarily be those who have adopted the goal and value system of the larger American society and are able to function with the symbols and styles of life acceptable to it.

Status relationships, according to Gerth and Mills, always involve at least two people, "one to claim it and another to *honor* the claim." These claims to status "are expressed in all those mannerisms, conventions, and ways of status levels."[20] An ethnic-community member who successfully raises claims to recognition in the wider American society but fails to raise claims in his ethnic community will not remain in the ethnic community for long. Other members of the same ethnic community may simultaneously raise successful claims in both the wider society and in the ethnic community, thus remaining in a marginal situation, clinging to the ethnic community while dividing loyalty between it and the wider society. Mannheim has pointed out, however, that

. . . membership of an organization lapses as soon as we give notice of our intention to leave it; the cohesion of the community group *ceases to exist* if the mental and spiritual dispositions on which its existence has been based cease to operate in us or in our partners; and our previous class position loses its relevance for us as soon as we acquire a new position as a result of a change in our economic and power status.[21]

The result of the process in which members of an ethnic community strive for access to the advantages of the wider society is the breakdown of closure of the ethnic community. With the opening up of opportunities in the outside world for the new generations of the ethnic community, the process of disintegration is set in motion. Many American-born members of ethnic communities undergo "anticipatory socialization," as it has been called by Merton,[22] acquiring the values of the wider American society even while remaining within the ethnic community.

The Study of the Transformation of the Minneapolis Russian Community

The present study of the Minneapolis Russian community seeks to test hypotheses concerning the formation and disintegration of the ethnic community drawn from the theories of Weber, Gerth, Mills, and Martindale. These theories place major emphasis on internal and external closure and monopolization of advantages and privileges made possible by such closure.

Theoretically, existence of the ethnic community is endangered when the boundaries (which are sometimes even physical in nature as in the medieval ghetto) are gradually liquidated and the values of the majority community are acquired by the minority members. In America, the privileged positions of the majority have never beeen completely closed to outsiders. The new generations born within the minority community have found it possible to acquire the skills by which, if they wish, they can gain access to advantages from which their parents and grandparents were excluded.

Thus the new generations of the ethnic community possess improved access to the advantages of the majority community. Those who leave the ethnic community have acquired the means to claim the prestige values of the majority community. They have also improved their class positions over those of their parents or of others remaining in the community. As Weber pointed out and Mannheim, Gerth, and Mills reaffirmed, the "class position is an objective fact, whether the individual in question knows his class position or not, and whether he acknowledges it or not."[23]

The study of the Russians in Minneapolis focuses on intergenerational social stratification according to "objective" criteria. Social stratification is composed of several distinct dimensions. Weber recognized three major dimensions—class, status, and power. People with common access to wealth occupy the same class situation. Those who share social honor or esteem belong to the same status group. Parties and pressure groups are made up of persons with a common interest in gaining power.[24] Gerth and Mills have isolated occupation as an additional dimension, similar to Weber's distinction between the "property class" and the "acquisition class," to pinpoint in a more specific way the source from which the wealth comes. Gerth and Mills, however, point to the decline of the independent entrepreneur and the subsequent decline of the property class in modern American society; occupation thus remains the one basic reliable measure of class position.[25]

In this study the dimensions of class, status, and power will be kept distinct. While one member of an ethnic minority severs his connection with the community, he may be gaining access to majority community values of status and class. At the same time he may be forced to relinquish access to power in the community he is leaving. In the wider American society, dominated by the influence of mass media and large institutional power, he may well become relatively powerless. Others who leave the ethnic community may sacrifice financial strength and economic security in order to obtain deference from the wider community. There are various other ways in which these three variables may be separated or combined.

Two distinct Russian communities are present in the Minneapolis area. One is composed of the "old" immigrants who formed a community at the turn of the century; the second consists of a group of "new" political Russian refugees who came to the United States between 1949 and 1951. The "old" community is further subdivided into the immigrants and their children born in the United States.[26] This "old" community is the subject of our investigations.

We shall use the "generation unit," as described by Mannheim. Mannheim maintained that, while the generational phenomenon is ultimately based on biological rhythm, the social process itself creates generational distinctions that are sociologically more meaningful for the analysis of social change. For this reason, Mannheim distinguished between three basic generational groupings: the generation location, the generation as actuality, and the generation unit.[27] The generation location refers to the location of individuals within a generation determined by biological rhythm. The fact that individuals are born and live in a society in the same historical time does not mean that they all will share "in the common destiny." According to Mannheim:

We shall therefore speak of a generation as an actuality only where a concrete bond is created between members of a generation by their being exposed to the social and intellectual symptoms of a process of dynamic de-stabilization.[28]

Under specialized conditions, an actual generation may be subdivided into two or more "generation units" when individuals experiencing common social and intellectual influences nevertheless respond to them in different fashions:

The generation unit represents a much more concrete bond than the actual generation as such. Youth experiencing the same concrete historical problems may be said to be part of the same actual generation; while those groups within the same actual generation which work up the material of their common experiences in different specific ways, constitute separate generation units.[29]

Mannheim holds these three generational distinctions "indispensable for any deeper analysis" of social change.

If we speak simply of "generations" without any further differentiation, we risk jumbling together purely biological phenomena and others which are the product of social and cultural forces; thus we arrive at a sort of sociology of chronological tables, which uses its bird's-eye perspective to discover fictitious generation movements to correspond to the crucial turning-points in historical chronology.[30]

Mannheim's ideas may be illustrated with the generational profile of the "old" Russian community. The formation period dates
from the 1880s to the First World War—a thirty-year span. Many individuals were born within the community early in its formation. By
1900, some of these American-born individuals had already entered
the labor market. Meanwhile, other European-born age-mates were
still arriving in Minneapolis. The American-born citizen had more in
common with his age-peers arriving from Europe than with people
from the wider American society. The Minnesota census shows them
entering the same manual occupations as their European-born peers
or their own fathers. Their social existence was tied in with the
destiny of the Russian community. They formed, in Mannheim's
terms, a "generation as actuality," and they responded to their common experience as a single "generation unit."

American-born members of the old Russian community long retained the language of their fathers and identification with their
European heritage. Children born in the United States from mixed
marriages also shared a common outlook with their European peers.
The opportunities opened as a result of the breaking down of ethnic
closure marked a change in the social destiny of a later generation.
The responses to these opportunities were, however, uneven. Some
individuals took the opportunity to leave their ethnic community and
joined the majority community, while others preferred to remain
within the ethnic community. This actual generation of the Minneapolis Russian community divided itself into two distinct generation
units.

Objectively speaking, there are now three differently located
generations in the "old Russian community" in Minneapolis: those
born at the turn of the century—some in Europe and some in
America but sharing equal social destinies, nevertheless; their children, most of whom were born in the United States of foreign-born
and mixed parentage; and the grandchildren. The grandchildren are
now in adolescence. Some have finished college, others are still
attending, while others are still in high school. Since my study is concerned with family units (for more adequate comparison among the
cases), the youngest generation of Minneapolis Russians was not
studied.

Our investigation centers upon three groups of Russians in the Minneapolis area: the generation of "old" people within the Russian community; a generation unit of their children who remain—sometimes reluctantly, sometimes enthusiastically—within the Russian community; and a second generation unit composed of children who have left the ethnic community.

If one were to construct specific typologies within the Russian community, he could divide these three groups into specific personality types. The first group uses the symbols and styles of the ethnic community to claim status solely within the ethnic community. This group, the "Pilgrims," represents the founders of the community who try to preserve the community they helped to create. The second group, while remaining within the community, already makes claims both in terms of the ethnic community's symbols and in those of the majority community; this group is secondarily directed to the wider society. They may be labelled the "Colonists," representing those who are reluctant to venture outside the community. A third group has broken its ties with the community, though perhaps retaining occasional kinship ties to the community. This group operates within the wider American society with the symbols and styles of life of the majority, claiming recognition only within the majority community. It can be called the "Frontiersmen," representing those venturing alone for personal advantage without sharing the disadvantages or advantages of the established ethnic community.

RECAPITULATION

The argument may be expressed diagrammatically:

Table 1—Units of the Old Russian Community and the Dimensions of Study

Generational Units	Model Personalities	Dimensions of Study
Unit I The First Generation	The Pilgrims	Class Status Power Acculturation

Unit II

Second Generation Conservatives	The Colonists	Class
		Status
		Power
		Acculturation

Unit III

Second Generation Radicals	The Frontiersmen	Class
		Status
		Power
		Acculturation

Three generational units of the old Russian community of Minneapolis will be studied in their dimensions of class, status, and power. The general hypothesis that the ethnic community is formed by the process of closure in terms of an ethnic principle serves as foundation for *two working hypotheses* (see page 7 above), which will specifically guide the study: *The system of stratification in the ethnic community is gradually destroyed with the rise of the second and later generations; the economic and professional advancement of the second and later generations brings about cultural assimilation with and dispersal among the members of the majority community.*

The study of the three generational units—the Pilgrims, the Colonists, and the Frontiersmen—in terms of three stratification dimensions should show a gradual displacement of values from those of the minority toward those of the majority community. *Hypothesis 1* predicts a displacement from the stratification of the ethnic community to that of the majority community. *Hypothesis 2* predicts a displacement from the values of the ethnic community to those of the majority community.

NOTES

1. Robert M. MacIver, *Society* (New York: Farrar & Rinehart, Inc., 1937), pp. 8–9.
2. Don Martindale, *American Social Structure* (New York: Appelton-Century-Crofts, Inc., 1960), pp. 377–96.
3. *Ibid.*, pp. 394–5.
4. Emory S. Bogardus, *Immigration and Race Attitudes* (New York: D. C. Heath & Co., 1928); see also J. P. Guilford, "Racial Preferences of a Thousand American University Students," *Journal of Social Psychology*, II (May, 1931), 179–204; and David Katz and Kenneth Braly, "Racial

Stereotypes of One Hundred College Students," *Journal of Abnormal and Social Psychology,* XXVIII (October, 1933), 280–90.

5. Bogardus, *op. cit.,* pp. 13–29; also see R. Zeligs and G. Hendrickson, "Racial Attitudes of 200 Sixth-Grade Children," *Sociology and Social Research,* September–October, 1933, pp. 26–36.

6. Hans H. Gerth and C. Wright Mills, *Character and Social Structure* (New York: Harcourt, Brace & Co., 1953), p. 334.

7. M. K. Argus, *Moscow-on-the-Hudson* (New York: Harper & Bros., 1948), p. 3.

8. Max Weber, *Ancient Judaism,* trans. and edited by Hans H. Gerth and Don Martindale (New York: The Free Press of Glencoe, 1952), pp. 336–55.

9. Everett C. Hughes, "Principles and Rationalization in Race Relations," Everett C. Hughes and Helen MacGill Hughes, *Where Peoples Meet* (New York: The Free Press of Glencoe, 1952), p. 156.

10. Gerth and Mills, *op. cit.,* p. 325.

11. Max Weber, *The Theory of Social and Economic Organization,* trans. by A. M. Henderson and Talcott Parsons (New York: The Free Press of Glencoe and The Falcon's Wing Press, 1947), p. 139.

12. *Ibid.,* pp. 139–141.

13. *Ibid.,* pp. 141–3.

14. See Jerome Davis, *The Russian Immigrant* (New York: The Macmillan Co., 1922); Jerome Davis, *The Russians and Ruthenians in America* (New York: George H. Doran Co., 1922); George Martin Day, *The Russians in Hollywood* (Los Angeles: University of Southern California Press, 1934); Pauline V. Young, *The Pilgrims of Russian-Town* (Chicago: University of Chicago Press, 1932); and Lillian Sokoloff, *The Russians in Los Angeles* (Los Angeles: University of Southern California Press, 1918).

15. Argus, *op. cit.,* pp. 11–12, 19–20.

16. Karl Mannheim, *Essays on the Sociology of Knowledge* (London: Routledge & Kegan Paul Ltd., 1962), pp. 293–94. Recent work on the nature of age groups and their relationship to social structure has been performed by S. N. Eisenstadt, *From Generation to Generation* (New York: The Free Press of Glencoe, 1956).

17. Gerth and Mills, *op. cit.,* p. 326.

18. Talcott Parsons, *The Social System* (New York: The Free Press of Glencoe, 1951), pp. 482, 486.

19. E. Digby Baltzell, *Philadelphia Gentlemen* (New York: The Free Press of Glencoe, 1958), pp. 63–4.

20. Gerth and Mills, *op. cit.,* p. 315; see also C. Wright Mills, *White Collar* (New York: Oxford University Press, 1951), p. 241.

21. Mannheim, *op. cit.,* p. 289.

22. Robert K. Merton, *Social Theory and Social Structure* (New York: The Free Press of Glencoe, 1957), p. 265; see also Seymour Martin Lipset and Reinhard Bendix, *Social Mobility in Industrial Society* (Berkeley: University of California Press, 1959), p. 257.

23. Mannheim, *op. cit.,* p. 289; Gerth and Mills, *op. cit.,* p. 313.

24. Max Weber, *From Max Weber: Essays in Sociology,* Hans H. Gerth and C. Wright Mills, trans. and eds. (New York: Oxford University Press, 1946), pp. 180–95.

25. Gerth and Mills, *op. cit.*, pp. 307–14; Weber, *The Theory of Social and Economic Organization, op. cit.*, p. 424.

26. Alex Simirenko, "The Social Structure of the Minneapolis Russian Community," *Proceedings of the Minnesota Academy of Science for 1959,* XXVII (1960), pp. 79–86

27. Mannheim, *op. cit.*, pp. 290–1, 302–4.

28. *Ibid.*, p. 303

29. *Ibid.*, p. 304

30. *Ibid.*, p. 311.

2 Methodological Problems and a Design for the Study of Stratification Change

THE RUSSIAN COMMUNITY of Minneapolis came into existence in the 1880s. There has been time for a second generation to grow up. Since World War II, a new wave of immigrants has arrived from Russia, forming its own distinct community. Consequently, two sociologically distinct Russian groups can be identified in Minneapolis: the "old" community of 930 family units and a group of "new" or recent immigrants of over fifty families.

The old group is subdivided into generation units among the original immigrants and their children. This study centers upon the old ethnic community, with its intergenerational system of stratification, and those former members who have broken ties with the community.

Maintenance of the ethnic community within the majority society is facilitated by the partial closure to which the ethnic community is subject from both within and without. In American society, such closure is not permanent but takes the form of a series of standards for which the first generation of the ethnic community is, for the most part, unable to qualify. This group finds itself outside the competition for many advantages offered by the majority community. The second and subsequent ethnic generations appropriate the symbols and styles of life of the majority community and are permitted to compete for its typical objectives.

One can establish a series of minority types, which represent distinct degrees of adjustment to both the ethnic and the majority communities. Three distinct Russian types have been observed:

1. The Pilgrims, who are the old people within the Russian community anxious to preserve the established life of the community.
2. The Colonists, members of the second generation who find themselves torn between incentives of membership in the majority community and a persistent loyalty to their parents' way of life.
3. The Frontiersmen, those in the second generation who have made the break with their ethnic colleagues to seek their individual fortunes within the majority community.

This study attempts to test six hypotheses about these three types:

A. A general improvement of class is discernible as one moves from the Pilgrims, to the Colonists, to the Frontiersmen.
B. An improvement of status within the ethnic community is discernible, as one moves from the Pilgrims to the Colonists.
C. The basis of status is transformed as one moves from the Colonists to the Frontiersmen. Pilgrims and Colonists find status within the ethnic community; the Frontiersmen increasingly find it outside the ethnic community.
D. As one moves from the Pilgrims to the Colonists, an increase in power is discernible.
E. As one moves from Colonists to Frontiersmen, the basis for power is shifted, and a drop in comparative power is evident.
F. As one moves from the Pilgrims to the Colonists to the Frontiersmen, a general increase in acculturation to the American community is observable.

A number of methodological problems are posed by these hypotheses. They may be classed roughly in two major categories: technical and procedural. The technical problems consist in the development of instruments adequate to isolate and quantify the major variables involved in changes in social stratification. Once such technical instruments have been established, it will be necessary to develop a procedural design to test the hypotheses themselves. The present study draws, for solution to the first problem, upon a number of classic studies conducted by American sociologists in the field of stratification. The techniques developed by F. Stuart Chapin, W. Lloyd Warner, William H. Sewell, and August B. Hollingshead are particularly important.

THE TECHNIQUES OF STRATIFICATION STUDY

F. Stuart Chapin The pioneering venture into techniques of stratification study in the United States was made by F. Stuart Chapin in the early 1920s at the University of Minnesota. Assuming that behavior of individuals belonging to each social class is intimately connected with various objective features of the corollary style of life, Chapin sought a reliable and objective way of measuring class and status differences. He explored the possibility of developing a scale of social status based on items in the family living room. In justifying this proposal, he made three basic points:

1. The living room represents the center of the family's interaction.
2. The living room displays cultural and material acquisitions of the family, reflecting its "objective" socio-economic status.
3. Claims for status by the family are most likely to be presented in the living room, which contains the "proper" display of cultural articles.[1]

Chapin warned, however, that his scale should not be looked upon as a final or universal instrument. It was finally standardized only for American urban homes of that particular period (the 1930s) in a particular place (the Midwest), where social and cultural changes would make periodic revisions of the scale necessary if it were to continue to be of use.[2]

The social-status scale was initially standardized for sixty-seven Negro families in the Minneapolis area whose relative status was rated by their friends and neighbors. The ratings were then correlated with various items of actual living-room equipment. The scale was then (1926) tested on St. Paul families and revised. Meanwhile, other Chapin students worked on its standardization in Indianapolis. The scale emerged in its standardized form in 1930.[3] In 1943, Chapin's scale was analyzed by Louis Guttman, who believed it was an adequate and valid instrument when used as intended by Chapin.[4]

In the 1930s, Chapin began developing a complementary scale to measure participation of a family or an individual in various organizations in his community. While the earlier scale was primarily intended to measure the social status and class of a family, the social-participation scale was intended to measure relative influence in community affairs. The highest ratings on the scale were received by persons who served as officers of particular organizations or as members of committees.[5]

William H. Sewell   Chapin's work was extended by his student, William H. Sewell, who developed standardized scales for the measurement of socio-economic status among Oklahoma rural families.[6] Dissatisfied with the cumbersome length of his original scale, which prevented its greater application, Sewell worked up a brief but valid measure of the socio-economic status of rural families that could be used with limited funds and limited time.[7] Belcher and Sharp shortened and revised Sewell's scale still further to meet demand for a more applicable instrument in the field of rural sociology.[8] In the 1950s, two major studies used living-room equipment as a measure of socio-economic status: Chapman's study in Liverpool and Davis's in Cambridge, Massachusetts.[9]

W. Lloyd Warner   The best known and most controversial student of stratification in the United States is the anthropologist, W. Lloyd Warner. Assuming the unidimensionality of the socio-economic classes, Warner sought to measure them by quantifiable and statistical procedures.

Warner's studies of Yankee City and Jonesville mark stages in his development of techniques for the study of stratification. Turning from his field research among Australian aborigines, Warner argued that the phenomena of stratification were subjective. To him the most essential single fact in all communal relationships is that all people judge one another and accept or reject each other's company on the basis of their particular values and styles of life. Warner found that wealth does not necessarily confer higher honor. He argued that, although a banker, for example, will not be found at the bottom of the system of social stratification, he will not always be guaranteed the highest position. The only true estimate of a person's standing must therefore be derived through examination of the judgments that community members make about each other. Warner's definition of social class followed his assumptions:

By class is meant two or more orders of people who are believed to be, and are accordingly ranked by the members of the community, in socially superior and inferior positions.[10]

In this period, Warner not only believed that people's judgments were alone important in the system of stratification, but he also tended to assume that judgments pronounced "unconsciously" were of greater influence in determining status within the community.

Such ranking was frequently unconsciously done and for this reason was often more reliable than a conscious estimate of a man's status.[11]

In her analysis of Warner's assumptions in this early period, Ruth Rosner Kornhauser delineates three main emphases:

1. Essentially subjective approach to the study of social stratification.
2. Primary concern with the prestige dimensions of stratification.
3. Warner's resulting assertion that his strata were empirically existing entities.[12]

In the third volume of the Yankee City series, however, in the reported study of ethnic groups, Warner and his associates began to incline toward more objective indices of status. Both a residential status scale and an occupational scale were developed. Each scale was divided into six distinct values.[13]

Objective and subjective indices of a person's socio-economic standing were finally combined in Warner's studies of Jonesville. The subjective indices of status were studied by the so-called method of "evaluated participation," or the "E.P." Even here an attempt was made to check personal judgments of community members against objective criteria like membership in various organizations and clubs. Nevertheless, the use of the method of evaluated participation forced Warner to reassert his earlier assumptions that individuals within the community are "explicitly and implicitly aware of the ranking and translate their evaluations of such social participation into social-class ratings that can be communicated to the investigator."[14]

The objective method developed by Warner was called the "index of status characteristics," or the "I.S.C." It consisted of four seven-point scales that measured the differentials of occupation, source of income, house type, and dwelling area. By totaling the results from the four scales, the investigator converts his statistical score into the relative standing of the individual. The investigator may, if he wishes, combine or compare his results on the I.S.C. with the results derived by the E.P.[15]

The major theoretical problem associated with Warner's methods —the E.P. and I.S.C.—has been pointed out by Martindale: Warner is able to discover only the combination of class and status factors operating within American communities.[16] The investigator using Warner's approach is inclined to ignore the elements of social power that are present in *every* community.

August B. Hollingshead Hollingshead was closely associated with Warner, and his early work bears some similarity to Warner's. His most recent work, however, is removed from conceptual kinship with Warner. Hollingshead's ideas on social stratification evolved in three stages:

1. A subjective approach to the study of stratification in Elmtown's Youth.
2. Attempts by the investigators to standardize and give weights to the objectified scale in *Social Class and Mental Illness.*
3. Reduction of his previously standardized three-factor scale to two factors since 1957.

In *Elmtown's Youth*, the study performed at Jonesville, thirty-one judges rated 535 families among five distinct strata. Relatively little disagreement in ratings was reported. There were seventy-four families about whose status 75 per cent of the total disagreement was found. The examination of these families showed that either a whole family or some of its members were socially mobile. Of them, 85 per cent were upwardly mobile. It was therefore difficult to get a unanimous decision from the raters.[17]

A more difficult task awaited Hollingshead in his study, *Social Class and Mental Illness*. A sample of 5 per cent of households drawn from the New Haven area and its suburbs numbered 3,383 households. This meant that the researchers could no longer depend upon judges from the community to rate all the residents in the community. As a result, an objective instrument called the "index of social position" was devised to solve the problem at hand. Two sociologists served to validate and create the instrument. Hollingshead and Jerome K. Myers, who, it is claimed, were "familiar with the community's social structure," have studied closely the 200-question schedules of the interviewed sample of 552 families. Independently of each other they separated these families into five strata according to criteria each of them chose. They found that their perception of the existing socio-economic classes in the community coincided in 96 per cent of the cases. After the rating, they agreed that their judgments were primarily affected by three criteria: residence, occupation, and education. To establish the weights to be given to these three indices, the investigators intercorrelated them with judgments made about each family.

The index of social position was established upon the total score of three scales: a six-point place of residence scale, a seven-point occupational scale, and a seven-point educational scale. The residence scale was assigned six weight points, the occupational scale nine weight points, and the educational scale five points. The assumption was that the home and its location reflect the style of life of the family, occupation reflects "the skill and power associated with maintenance functions in the society," and education reflects the "tastes of the family."[18] As with Warner's methods, the index of social position was employed to discover a person's class and status position.

In 1957, Hollingshead published his latest "two factor index of social position."[19] It was developed to meet demand for an "easily applicable procedure to estimate the positions individuals occupy in the status structure of our society."[20] The earlier index could only be utilized when ecology and residence areas were closely studied. To avoid the need for such long-term studies and to permit application of the scale in areas other than New Haven, Hollingshead developed the new index on the basis of education and occupation scales, using the previous scale to validate it.

In the two-factor scale, the occupation carries a weight of seven, and education a weight of four. Hollingshead states his assumption that occupation measures not only prestige, skill, and talents but also relative manipulative power. It may be agreed that some occupations reveal such relative power, yet it is doubtful that the seven-point scale offered by Hollingshead could ever reveal the power of a ward heeler, for example.

Education is assumed by Hollingshead to determine tastes, attitudes, and "similar behavior patterns." Again, his scale is not likely to elicit valid responses, especially from the higher status groups. Graduate professional training is given the highest rating, thus disqualifying men like Rockefeller while nevertheless claiming to distinguish a style of life.

Despite problems associated with the two-factor index in its application to the wider American society, it may be an excellent short measure of relative individual standing in some communities. It may be particularly applicable in the studies of American ethnic communities. The differentiation and upward social mobility of members of ethnic communities is achieved primarily through acquisition of education and concomitant occupational achievements. Styles of life and class membership are reflected for the most part by the two indices of education and occupation.

It is evident from this review of the various students of stratification that, despite problems of one sort or another, a comparatively rich array of techniques has been developed for such study. All these sources have been consulted in the compilation of the scales employed in the present study. In some respects, however, my scales differ from all of those reviewed.

STRATIFICATION SCALES EMPLOYED IN THIS STUDY

The most important deficiency of these various techniques for stratification study is their tendency to lump together variables that are best kept separate. In one way or another, they fuse class and status, class and power, or all three variables. Furthermore, the distinctness of the ethnic community is lost when the problem of ethnic alienness or acculturation is treated merely as a modality of status.

In this study, the comparison of socio-economic traits is conducted according to the three dimensions of stratification as outlined by Weber—class, status, and power. The concept of acculturation is based on Baltzell's definition, in terms of relative learning and acceptance of American goals and values. The study involves objective comparisons between the statuses of the three groups. The final comparisons will be conducted according to the four scales developed for this study: the class scale, the status scale, the power scale, and the acculturation scale.

The scaled responses to each individual question within each scale will be reported and discussed; only then can full scale comparisons be made. Separate discussion of each item is deemed necessary, because each scale has been developed for the measurement of the Minneapolis Russian community and cannot be taken as a perfectly weighted instrument, as many of the established short scales claim to be. No scales have yet been devised to measure the distinct dimensions of class, status, and power. Instead, we have a number of scales that attempt to measure the combined socio-economic status of various groups and communities. In the present attempt to outline roughly a comparative difference among the standings of the three groups, the larger number of different items in each scale should lend the measure greater reliability and exactness.

Each of the four different measures contains a number of component five-point scales. The Mandel social adjustment scale served as the major model for the development of the present scales.[21] The use of the five-point scale in this study is facilitated by the fact that the results may be further cross-validated by the use of Hollingshead's two factor index, the scores of which are geared to discrimination among the five classes. The cross-validation will be performed at the end of the study. The specific scales and the precoded questionnaire used in the interviews are given in the Appendix.

DESIGN FOR THE STUDY OF THE CHANGING DYNAMICS OF THE RUSSIAN COMMUNITY OF MINNEAPOLIS

The procedural problem falls logically into two parts: a general description and a sampling in terms of the study design.

The Russian community of Minneapolis is made up of the institutions, which serve to organize the social behavior of its members; the logical prerequisite of any more extended study is therefore a general description and structural analysis of the whole. Since no previous historical studies of the Minneapolis Russian community have been made it has been necessary to satisfy this prerequisite from basic source materials, unofficial documents, and a series of personal interviews with members of the Russian community. The researcher's previous studies have been of considerable assistance in this task.[22] The findings on the history and structure of the Minneapolis Russian community are reported in Chapters 3, 4, and 5.

The special problems for which the present study was designed also involve establishing a study design to isolate the inner dynamics of change. The main requirements of the study design are fixed by the theory of ethnic community change and a number of practical considerations. Our theory requires that samples be drawn from the three major subdivisions of the old Russian community—Pilgrims, Colonists, and Frontiersmen.

Various practical considerations determined the selection of cases (the sampling) from among these groups. The selection of cases within the three groups proved to be extremely difficult. Statisticians suggest that in studying a homogeneous population "greater precision can be achieved with fewer cases."[23] Furthermore, since many comparisons concerned possessions, the decision was made to gear the precoded questionnaires to the family unit. It was also decided that interviews would best be conducted with the wives, since they would be more likely to be at home and available for the forty- or forty-five-minute interviews.

In the selection of cases, two specific problems had to be overcome: The Pilgrims had to be separated from the Colonists, and the Frontiersmen had to be located within the larger American society. Both problems were further complicated by the fact that we tried to locate only married couples for the study. For cases within the Russian community, reliance was placed on a "Financial Report" of St. Mary's Church from December, 1959, listing all the dues-paying members, and on the 1959 church register supplied by Father Soroka.

To locate Frontiersmen, we relied upon the city directory and information given by interviewees. The selection and number of cases were based on our estimate of the population inside and outside the community. The following breakdown of the membership of St. Mary's Church in 1959 was taken from the Financial Report:

Table 2—St. Mary's Church Membership, 1959

	Number	Percentage
Families	618	66.5
Lone men	118	12.7
Lone women	170	18.3
Unclassified men	16	1.7
Unclassified women	8	.9
Totals	930	100.1 (due to rounding)

It was decided that we should attempt to interview 10 per cent of the married population. Double or mixed sampling procedure as defined by Parton was used to select the cases from the Pilgrims and the Colonists. Each column of names in the financial report was given a number for each name that represented a family unit. This distinction was possible because of the difference in dues—$16 for

families and $11 for a single person. For each column, one-half-inch
cardboard squares were cut out, and each square was given a number
from one to forty—according to the number of family names in
the particular column under sampling.

A total of seventy-five names was drawn. As expected, only nine
appeared with any certainty to be first generation. To compensate
for this inadequate number of cases, a search for all the known
names in the first generation group was made in Father Soroka's
register, which was unsatisfactory in many respects, as many "official"
documents are. The search yielded forty-two additional names, which
seemed fairly certain to be of the Pilgrims group. By random selection, twenty-five of these names were added to the other seventy-
five names.

A somewhat similar procedure was used on a different problem
by Hollingshead and Redlich during their study of *Social Class
and Mental Illness*. While studying the class distribution of the
New Haven population, they took a sample of 3,383 addresses from
the city directory and added to it "a listing with 225 households
living in the poorest areas. This was done to compensate for the
known underlisting of addresses by the city directory in these areas."[24]

To locate the Frontiersmen, a small search was made in the city
directories using the fifty most typical communal names. (The results
of the search are cited in Chapter 6.) By comparing the names listed
in the 1959 Financial Report with those in the 1959 City Directory,
it was discovered that out of 240 Russian family units in the city
directory as many as 150 were also listed in the Financial Report.
There were thus ninety families who did not belong to St. Mary's
Church. Not all of them, however, could be included in a list to
be used for the selection of cases. Some had the same first and last
names as those listed in the Financial Report, and it was sometimes
impossible to establish which of two families was a member of the
Russian community. At times, this problem was solved with the aid
of the telephone directory. Eventually, seventy-four names were
collected for use in the sampling procedure.

The decision was made to select twenty-five cases from this list
and twenty-five from the questionnaires as the interviews were being
conducted. During the interviews, as many as eighty-six families

were established as having left the community. Again, not all of these names could be used. Some of them came too late in the study, contributed in interviews with other Frontiersmen, and a few duplicated already known names from the city directory.

Fifty-eight names were finally brought together, from which the cases were selected. The procedure was to select four or five cases as soon as twenty new names had been accumulated.

Our total sample of 150 thus consisted of seventy-five taken from the Financial Report and twenty-five each from the church registry, the city directory, and the interviews.

THE INTERVIEWING

With the precoded questionnaire it was felt that several persons could participate in the interviewing without significantly influencing the respondents' answers. It was especially desirable to have people from the community doing the interviewing of community members. Eight college students, including the investigator, did the interviewing. Among the interviewers, one information session was held first, followed by a series of meetings and telephone conversations to clear up minor problems of decision-making. The interviewers were advised, where there was the least hesitation about how to code the material, to indicate it on the questionnaire and to contact the investigator immediately when there was any serious problem.

Most interviews were conducted during July and August. It was expected that during this season, it would be impossible to reach many of the sample. The number was not expected to reach great proportions, however. From 150 selected names, 105 were interviewed. The results are summarized in Table 3.

Table 3—Interviewing Results

Groups	Selected	Interviewed
Pilgrims	34	29
Colonists	66	42
Frontiersmen	50	34
Totals	150	105

In the Pilgrim group, two cases were discarded, since the heads of both families had died within the year prior to the interviews; one man was in the hospital, and his wife could not be interviewed; and two refused to be interviewed. The majority of the un-interviewed Colonists and Frontiersmen could not be reached. In at least two cases, the addresses could not be found; in many others, the families were gone, presumably on vacation. Still others were either preparing to leave for vacation or had just returned and had no time to spare. The greater proportion of successes in locating and interviewing the Pilgrim group has been explained by the findings of the study. The Pilgrims preferred to remain at home during their vacations, while the Colonists and Frontiersmen were determined to travel.

RECAPITULATION

Significant contributions to the measurement of social stratification in various communities and groups have been made by Chapin, Sewell, Warner, Hollingshead, and their students. The subjective method for studying status by soliciting judgments from neighbors was fairly successful in the study of a small homogeneous community in which the members knew each other or were familiar with a family's standing. The study of social stratification in a large city, however, renders this procedure unreliable. The numerous subcommunities within a heterogeneous city tend to survive without ever coming in contact with one another. Students of stratification must therefore develop objective methods for distinguishing among strata: display of material possessions, style of life, wealth, occupation, membership in and sometimes control of exclusive or open associations, and so forth.

In this study of the Russian community, it is hypothesized that maintenance of the ethnic community is made possible by partial closure from within the community and also from without. The closure is achieved by a series of regulations that the first generation of an ethnic community is unable to meet. The second and consecutive generations become familiar with skills and symbols by which to penetrate the closure. Through greater differentiation within the ethnic community and appropriation of the symbols of the majority community, a whole series of ethnic types tend to develop. Within the Minneapolis Russian group, there is a predominance of three types: Pilgrims, Colonists, and Frontiersmen. It is hypothesized that each successive type will be placed in a specific class, status, and power position, as measured by the three scales, and will also show greater acculturation into the general American society, as measured on the scale of acculturation. The scales employed to measure socio-economic standing in this study are aimed at differentiating among a family's class standing, status, and power; they represent modifications of techniques evolved from Chapin to Hollingshead. In the methodological design of the present study, 105 members of the three groups were interviewed with the aid of a precoded questionnaire.

NOTES

1. F. Stuart Chapin, *The Measurement of Status by the Use of the Social Status Scale* (Minneapolis: University of Minnesota Press, 1933), p. 3.
2. *Ibid.*, p. 4.
3. F. Stuart Chapin, "Scale for Rating Living Room Equipment" (Institute of Child Welfare Circular No. 3 [Minneapolis: University of Minnesota, January, 1930]).
4. Louis Guttman, "A Review of Chapin's Social Status Scale," *American Sociological Review*, VIII (June, 1943), 362–8.
5. F. Stuart Chapin, *Social Participation Scale* (Minneapolis: University of Minnesota Press, 1938); and revised *Social Participation Scale*, (1952 ed., Minneapolis: University of Minnesota Press, 1952). For further literature on Chapin's scales by the author, see "The Measurement of Sociability and Socio-Economic Status," *Sociology and Social Research*, XII (January–February, 1928), 208–17; "A Quantitative Scale for Rating the Home and Social Environment of Middle Class Families in an Urban Community," *Journal of Educational Psychology*, XIX (October, 1928), 99–111; "Socio-Economic Status: Some Preliminary Results of Measurement," *American Journal of Sociology*, XXXVII (January, 1932), 581–7; *The Social Status Scale* (Minneapolis: University of Minnesota Press, 1933; revised in 1936); *Contemporary American Institutions* (New York: Harper & Bros., 1935), pp. 373–97; *Experimental Designs in Sociological Research* (New York: Harper & Bros., 1947), pp. 41–50, 58–84.
6. William H. Sewell, "The Construction and Standardization of a

Scale for the Measurement of the Socio-Economic Status of Oklahoma Farm Families" (Technical Bulletin No. 9 [Stillwater: Oklahoma Agricultural Experiment Station, 1940]); and "A Scale for the Measurement of Farm Family Socio-Economic Status," *The Southwestern Social Science Quarterly*, XXI (1940), No. 2, pp. 125–37.

7. William H. Sewell, "A Short Form of the Farm Family Socio-Economic Status Scale, *Rural Sociology*, VIII (1943), No. 2, pp. 161–70.

8. John C. Belcher and Emit Sharp, "A Short Scale for Measuring Farm Family Level of Living: A Modification of Sewell's Socio-Economic Scale" (Technical Bulletin No. T-46 [Stillwater: Oklahoma Agricultural Experiment Station, September, 1952]).

9. Dennis Chapman, *The Home and Social Status* (London: Routledge & Kegan Paul, 1955); and James Allan Davis, "Living Rooms as Symbols of Status: A Study in Social Judgment" (Unpublished Ph.D. thesis, Harvard University, January, 1955).

10. W. Lloyd Warner and Paul S. Lunt, *The Social Life of a Modern Community* ("Yankee City Series," Vol. I [New Haven: Yale University Press, 1941]), p. 82.

11. *Ibid.*

12. Ruth Rosner Kornhauser, "The Warner Approach to Social Stratification," in Reinhard Bendix and Seymour Martin Lipset, eds., *Class, Status, and Power* (New York: The Free Press of Glencoe, 1953), pp. 226–7.

13. W. Lloyd Warner and Leo Srole, *The Social Systems of American Ethnic Groups* ("Yankee City Series," Vol. III [New Haven: Yale University Press, 1945]), pp. 39, 59.

14. W. Lloyd Warner, Marchia Meeker, and Kenneth Eells, *Social Class in America: A Manual of Procedure for the Measurement of Social Status* (Chicago: Science Research Associates, 1949), p. 35.

15. *Ibid.* The major findings of the Jonesville studies are reported by Warner and his associates in *Democracy in Jonesville* (New York: Harper & Bros., 1949).

16. Don Martindale, *American Social Structure* (New York: Appleton-Century-Crofts, 1960), p. 451.

17. August B. Hollingshead, *Elmtown's Youth: The Impact of Social Classes on Adolescence* (New York: John Wiley & Sons, Inc., 1949), pp. 25–45.

18. August B. Hollingshead and Frederick C. Redlich, *Social Class and Mental Illness: A Community Study* (New York: John Wiley & Sons, Inc., 1958), pp. 32, 387–97. See also August B. Hollingshead and Frederick C. Redlich, "Social Stratification and Psychiatric Disorders," *American Sociological Review*, XVIII (April, 1953), 136–70.

19. August B. Hollingshead, *The Two Factor Index of Social Position* (New Haven: August B. Hollingshead, 1957).

20. *Ibid.*, p. 2.

21. Nathan G. Mandel, "Mandel Social Adjustment Scale Manual" (Minneapolis: Department of Psychiatry Research, University of Minnesota, 1959). Used with permission of the author.

22. Alex Simirenko, "Aspect of the Social and Ideological Adjustment of

the Russian Community in Minneapolis," (Unpublished M. A. thesis, the University of Minnesota, 1958); and "The Social Structure of the Minneapolis Russian Community," *Proceedings of the Minnesota Academy of Science for 1959,* XXVII (1960), 79–86.

23. Mildred Parten, *Surveys, Polls, and Samples: Practical Procedures* (New York: Harper & Bros., 1950), pp. 233–4.

24. Hollingshead and Redlich, *Social Class and Mental Illness,* p. 32.

3 The Founding of the Minneapolis Russian Community

In 1940, the Northeast Neighborhood House of Minneapolis celebrated its twenty-fifth anniversary. To publicize the celebration, a public letter written by Mrs. C. C. Bovey was circulated, which read in part: "In that section lives our most interesting group of eighteen nationalities as shown by the alien census of 1918. These peoples have brought many old world cultures to our American nation." Perhaps most significant were the closing remarks of her letter: "You will enjoy learning more of this worthwhile but almost unknown group of our city." The statement reflected the characteristic attitudes of the majority of Minneapolis residents toward the northeast section, which has traditionally been inhabited by low-status men and women from Central and Eastern Europe. It was in this section that the Russian community was formed in the 1880s.

THE FIRST ARRIVALS

Those who formed this Russian community arrived from the peasant villages of the Carpathian Mountain region in the Austro-

(37)

Hungarian Empire. They came at a time when the crystallization of national loyalties in Central and Eastern Europe was under way. The loyalties of these immigrants were distributed among several nationalist movements. The majority of the immigrants coming to Minneapolis from this Austro-Hungarian region identified themselves with Russia and affiliated with the Russian Orthodox Church. To the other national groups in Minneapolis they became known as Russians and were treated accordingly.

The founder of the Russian community in Minneapolis was George Homzik, who arrived in 1877 at the age of twenty-four.[1] In 1879, he settled in Ward 1, in the northeast section near the Mississippi River. In 1881, he married a newly arrived girl (Pauly) from his home village. They settled at 614 Ramsey Street, and by 1905 they were raising a family of ten children—eight girls and two boys. George Homzik rose from common laborer in 1895 to the position of watchman in 1905.[2]

The second Russian arrival in Minneapolis was Theodore Sivanich, who came to Minnesota in 1880 at the age of twenty-five and settled in Ward 1 in 1887. Frank Masley arrived in northeast Minneapolis in 1881, and John Borris in 1882.[3]

The new arrivals proved to be energetic and successful promoters of Minneapolis to their countrymen in Europe. By 1884, there were four or five families and a small number of single men in the community.[4] From that time forward, the number of people in the community multiplied rapidly. Most of the new arrivals retained ties with their European home villages—most of the immigrants came from three villages—usually Beherov, Komlos, or Stebnik in what is now Czechoslovakia.[5] As a consequence, a homogeneous community was formed.

Because of the background of the people, it is difficult to piece together a demographic picture of their numbers. The census reports have listed them as Austrians, Hungarians, Bohemians, Slovaks, Czechoslovaks, Russians, and even Polish.[6] Many who were reported as Russian were of Russian-Jewish background. George Homzik himself was reported as Hungarian in the Fourth Census and as Austrian in the Fifth Decennial Census of Minnesota. Members of the Russian community are thus distributed throughout several nationality categories. (See Table 4)

The common background of the immigrants and their uniqueness in the Minneapolis community have permitted an approximate estimation of their ecological position in Minneapolis throughout the past seventy years. It was necessary merely to trace representative names of members of the community in the Minneapolis city directories. The results of this study are reported in Chapter 6.

Table 4—Population of Foreign Birth and Foreign Parentage in Minneapolis*

	1890a,b	1900	1910c	1920c	1930	1940a	1950
Total ethnic population	66,362	63,711	202,486	243,187	183,941	64,149	152,695
Austria	603	698			2,557	1,564	3,470
Czechoslovakia	706	231	3,022	5,246	5,302	1,503	4,590
Hungary	271	306	385	329	343	401	910
Russia	1,019	793	946d	3,363	5,766	4,481	6,360
Poland	392	432	8,129	10,689	8,325	3,637	7,785

* U.S. Bureau of the Census, *U.S. Census of Population: 1890*, Part I, (Washington: Government Printing Office, 1895), p. Cl i.
U.S. Census of Population: 1900, Vol. I, Part 1, (Washington: Government Printing Office, 1901), pp. 762–3.
U.S. Census of Population: 1920, Vol. II, (Washington: Government Printing Office, 1922), pp. 1007–8.
U.S. Census of Population: 1930, Vol. III, Part 1, (Washington: Government Printing Office, 1932), p. 1222.
U.S. Census of Population: 1940, Vol. II, Part 4, (Washington: Government Printing Office, 1943), p. 175.
U.S. Census of Population: 1950, Special Report P-E No. 3A, (Washington: Government Printing Office, 1954), p. 3A-79.
[a] Foreign born by country of birth.
[b] Hennepin County.
[c] Reported by mother tongue.
[d] Persons speaking Hebrew were erroneously included in the Russian category.

THE PIONEERING PERIOD, 1882–1896

The development of the Minneapolis Russian community proceeded through four specific periods or stages: the pioneering period (1882–1896); the heroic period (1897–1917); the readjustment period (1918–1941); and the modern period (1942 to the present).

Each period presented special problems to community members.

The first Russian immigrants settled in northeastern Minneapolis near the Mississippi River and Seventh Avenue.[7] By 1890, some families had begun to build homes in the vicinity of Fifth Street and Seventeenth Avenue. Of the fourteen Russians listed in the 1890 city directory, four resided near Seventeenth Avenue.

The men were employed as unskilled laborers in the rapidly expanding industries of Minneapolis—in flour mills, the lumber industry, and railroad shops. In a partial persistence of peasant traditions, the land areas around the immigrant houses were kept under cultivation, primarily for vegetable gardens. The immigrants also kept their own poultry and livestock, and the majority had their own cows. The more prosperous were even able to afford horses.[9]

As early as 1882, an attempt was made to solve the problem of religious affiliation. The immigrants had been baptized as members of the Eastern Rite Roman Catholic Church, popularly called the Uniate Church. The Uniate Church had been established in 1596 by a portion of the Eastern Orthodoxy clergy in what is now the western Ukraine. These clergymen accepted the Roman pope as their head in return for rights to continue, with some small modifications, the traditional Greek Orthodox rites. They also retained the right to marry before entering the priesthood. Since they already had ties with Roman Catholicism, the Minneapolis Russians first attempted to establish ties with the Polish Catholic Church near where they lived. Contact with the Polish community proved unsatisfactory, however, serving mainly to sharpen awareness of their cultural differences. Religious and linguistic barriers between the two groups seemed insurmountable.[10]

In 1884, the community invited the priest from the first Uniate Church in the United States—in Shenandoah, Pennsylvania—to visit Minneapolis. The priest, Rev. John Volianski, held a church service and administered the sacraments in the home of one of the parishioners. Rev. Volianski urged the community to build its own church. For this purpose, the colony in 1886 chose Peter Cook to be its church elder. At the same time, lots for the church were purchased from Patrick Morgan. In the following two years, money was collected for construction. The building was constructed by the parishioners themselves and was dedicated in 1889 in honor of St. Mary, the Protectorate, by Rev. Volianski. The first resident pastor of the church, Rev. Alexei G. Toth, arrived on November 27, 1889, from the Uniate diocese of Prague.[11]

In 1889 the community, which now totalled eighty-nine members, included fourteen families and a number of single men.[12] With such a small number of income-earning parishioners, many of whom were sending money home to support their families, the financial situation of the church and the community remained in a critical state. The first brotherhood of the community was therefore formally organized on June 3, 1888, to supervise the financial affairs of the community. It was initially composed of twenty-one members and was called the Independent Russian Orthodox Church Society of Saints Peter and Paul of Minneapolis. Shortly after his arrival in Minneapolis, the energetic Rev. Toth initiated the organization of a nationwide brotherhood, the Russian Orthodox Catholic Church Mutual Aid Society. The Society of Saints Peter and Paul became one of its first chapters and remained until 1910, when disagreements on the national level prompted most of the Minneapolis members to favor withdrawal.[13]

On August 15, 1893, the Society of Saints Peter and Paul filed formal articles of incorporation (No. 202800) at the Minneapolis Court House and became the first Russian benevolent society. Its aims were to support its members in sickness and want, to furnish help to widows and orphans of members in case of need, and to support and maintain the plant and clergyman of St. Mary's Russian Orthodox Catholic Church, Diocese of Alaska and North America. The official incorporated name of the society became the Greek Russian Orthodox Church Auxiliary of Peter and Paul of Minneapolis. Its first president was Sebastian Dabovich; Basil Timms was vice president, John Mlinar secretary, Michael Potochny second secretary, and Peter Cook treasurer. Monthly dues of fifty cents were levied against members, and the admission of members was accomplished by special balloting. On March, 1943, the society filed a Certificate of Amendment of the Articles of Incorporation (No. 2176604), in which the name of the society was changed to the Russian Orthodox Church Society of Sts. Peter and Paul.

Because the parish was too poor to support a priest, Rev. Toth established the first community grocery store in order to support himself and to defray the cost of maintaining the church. In 1891 he persuaded John Mlinar to take over the operation of the store, which he continued until 1919.[14]

The financial problems of the parish mounted as each month went by. In this period, sentiment toward accommodation to Roman Catholicism was strong. This sentiment was reversed, however, when the Roman Catholics rejected support and official recognition of the parish. Upon learning that Rev. Toth was a widower, Bishop Ireland of St. Paul refused to accept him under his jurisdiction.[15] Prior to this time, Bishop Ireland had refused to authorize contributions and donations to the parish by Roman Catholic philanthropists.

As a result of the isolation of the Russian community from the larger American community, as well as from other ethnic groups in Minneapolis, the parish was forced to turn to its own Slavic kinsmen for support. Solicitors traveled from Minnesota to Canada, Montana, and Pennsylvania. The most energetic and devoted of all was John Mlinar, who went to San Francisco in his search for funds. There he came in contact with the Russian Orthodox Episcopal See, which had been transferred from Sitka after the purchase of Alaska by the United States. Mlinar returned with a small contribution—thirteen ikons and an Orthodox cross. Immediately, community sentiment shifted toward Russian Orthodoxy. In 1890, the parishioners held a secret meeting, independently of Rev. Toth, at which they decided to affiliate their parish with the Russian Orthodox Church. After the meeting, delegates were sent to Rev. Toth to win his support.[16]

Rev. Toth joined his parishioners in their decision to accept Russian Orthodoxy. He became a fiery and successful missionary in the conversion of the Slavic Uniates to the Russian Orthodox Church. Because of his tireless efforts in this field, he is sometimes called the "Father of American Russia."[17]

At that time, the Uniate Church itself faced difficulties from various Roman Catholic pressures throughout the United States. William Shriver cites three major conflicts between the Uniates and the Roman Catholics: The Roman Catholic bishops, mostly of Irish or Italian descent, opposed the marriages of Uniate clergymen; the bishops demanded that Uniate parishes accept their absolute authority; the bishops demanded that transfers of title to church property be made to them. Opposition by the Uniate parishioners to any of these demands often entailed a complete break with Roman Catholicism. Many of these breaks were accompanied by conversion to either Russian or Eastern Orthodoxy.[18]

On February 11, 1891, Rev. Toth started his journey to San Francisco, where he was accepted into the Russian Orthodox Church. With him traveled Paul Podany, who petitioned in the name of the parish to be accepted into the church. Two months later, the Russian Orthodox Bishop of Alaska and the Aleutian Islands came to Minneapolis, and on March 25 took the parish under his jurisdiction. The parish that year consisted of 361 members.[19]

March 25, 1891, the day of official acceptance of Russian Orthodoxy by the Minneapolis parish, is regarded as one of the most significant dates in the history of the Russian Orthodox Church in America. The Holy Synod has always regarded the Russian Orthodox Church in America as the missionary church. It had ministered to the natives of Alaska and the Aleutians, not only teaching them the Russian language but also translating church services into their own languages. While the number of native Russian immigrants in the United States was small, there was a large potential for converts among other Slavic immigrants. Proselytizing among other Christians was not in the tradition of the Eastern Orthodox Church, but the Uniate Church had always been regarded as a temporarily misguided body, which would eventually return to the fold. The acceptance of Russian Orthodoxy by the Minneapolis community, which was the first such large-scale conversion in the United States, triggered a wholesale transfer of allegiance to Eastern Orthodoxy. It has been estimated that in 1950 the number of transfers had reached more than 225,000.[20] Davis states that the Russian Synod, supported by the Russian government, spent a minimum of $40,000 annually until the Revolution for the support of its missionary church in America.[21]

August 25, 1892, marked the arrival in Minneapolis of Paul Petrovich Zaichenko, the first teacher and choir director for the parish. He was sent by Bishop Nicholas of San Francisco. Bishop Nicholas believed that the parish school was the foundation of the present and future church.[22] Prior to the arrival of the choir director, church services were accompanied by unison singing from the congregation. Zaichenko tells of some of the difficulties that he experienced while attempting to organize an *a capella* choir:

None of the persons who were willing to partake in the singing had any prior musical experience and it was found that most of them had rough, unmusical voices of unpleasant quality; some of them had stiff throats, others had nasal tone, metallic, throaty, and harsh sounds—They all came from Sherish province of Austro-Hungary and were unaccustomed to choral singing and there was not a single man from Russia in the city of Minneapolis.[23]

He selected eight men for the choir and practiced with them six times a week. After two years of patient rehearsals, the choir finally pleased the ears of the congregation and visitors. Several years later, a mixed chorus was organized.

With the acceptance of Russian Orthodoxy, the financial situation of St. Mary's parish improved. Rev. Toth began to receive $92 a month from the Holy Synod in Russia, permitting him to give up his work at the grocery and devote full time to his ministerial duties.[24] In 1893, he was transferred to the parish of Wilkes-Barre, Pennsylvania, where he died on April 26, 1904.[25]

In 1892, the community consisted of 377 members, including 76 families and 77 single persons.[26] Little has been recorded about the actual life of the people in the community in this period, but the Fourth Decennial Census of Minnesota in 1895 gives some basic data about them. Only 152 persons were traceable as definite members of the Russian community, however. In the course of ascertaining the actual number of Russians in Minneapolis, many of their characteristics were illuminated. Thirty-one reported Russia as their place of birth, twenty-eight reported Austria, and twenty-four reported Hungary. The rest—sixty-nine—were children born in Minnesota. There were eighty-four males and sixty-eight females in the group. The median age of the males fifteen years of age or older was between thirty and thirty-four years. The median age of the females over fifteen was between twenty-five and twenty-nine years. Because of the youth of the immigrants, their families were small in size. The thirty-three families had a total of seventy-five children. The median family had two children. Only four families had five or six children.

The census also revealed the grave difficulties experienced by members of the community in finding and keeping jobs. Thirty-six men were reported as performing manual labor. Of that group, twenty-two reported to the census that in the previous year their median employment period on the job had been six months. Only two of the unskilled workers were employed throughout the year. The group also included six skilled or professional men: a painter worked four months out of the year, a band sawer six months, a carpenter eight months. The other three were employed full time: Paul Zaichenko as a teacher, Willian Cranak as a policeman, and John Mlinar, the grocer.

In an interview with John Mlinar, some information was gleaned concerning the social and recreational activities of the community members. Much time was devoted to the celebration of life-cycle events of individual members of the community. The whole community often participated in baptismal celebrations, marriages, funerals, anniversary celebrations, church holidays, and other such events. The taverns in the northeast area of Minneapolis served as male social centers. The Minneapolis city directory for 1890 lists one member of the Russian community (Peter Podany) as a barkeeper. The women, on the other hand, gathered in each others' homes to visit. The Russians' social life served to fix their cultural identity in a manner that deterred them from farming. Although they were of peasant origin, the Minneapolis Russians who tried to settle on farmsteads in North Dakota almost invariably returned to the community. Life lost much of its meaning in desolate and lonely places far from the social sphere of their ethnic group.

NOTES

1. According to the *Fourth Decennial Census of Minnesota, 1895*, he lived in Ward 1 at the address of 614 Ramsey Street. The *Fifth Decennial Census of Minnesota* gives his arrival in Minnesota, as well as in Ward 1, Minneapolis, as 1878, also at the age of twenty-four.

2. *Fourth and Fifth Decennial Censuses of Minnesota, 1895* and *1905*, Ward 1.

3. *Fourth Decennial Census of Minnesota, 1895*, Ward 1.

4. A tape-recorded interview with John W. Mlinar on January 20, 1958. He was one of the pioneers of the community.

5. Rev. John Dzubay, "The Light of Orthodoxy," the 66th Anniversary of St. Mary's Russian Orthodox Church, Minneapolis, Minnesota (Minneapolis, 1953).

6. Wasyl Halich, *Ukranians in the United States* (Chicago: University of Chicago Press, 1937), pp. 22–3.

7. Tape-recorded interview with John Mlinar.

8. George Michael Jalma, "The Church of St. Mary the Protectorate," *The Russian Orthodox Journal* XXV, No. 3 (July, 1951), 5.

9. Interview with John Mlinar.

10. *Ibid.*

11. Rev. John Nedzelnitsky, "The 50th Anniversary of the Russian Orthodox Colony in Minneapolis," *Golden Jubilee Album of the St. Mary's Russian Orthodox Greek Catholic Church* (Minneapolis, 1937), pp. 16–8.

12. *Ibid.*, p. 17.

13. "Russian Orthodox Church Society of Sts. Peter and Paul," *Golden Jubilee Album*, p. 93.

14. Rev. John Nedzelnitsky, *Golden Jubilee Album*, p. 18; interview with John W. Mlinar.

15. Interview with John W. Mlinar; see also Dimitry Grigorieff, "The Historical Background of Orthodoxy in America," *St. Vladimir's Seminary Quarterly*, V, No. 1–2 (1961), 9; P. Kochanik, *Yubileyny sbornik soyuza pravoslavnykh sviashchenikov v Amerike* (New York: 1936), pp. 84–103; and *Russky Pravoslavny Kalendar* (Pittsburgh: 1934), pp. 102–6.

16. Statement of John Mlinar, who was the principal participant in this development. The writings available on Toth describe him as the principal leader in this decision. Mlinar's account contradicts such writings. See Rev. John Nedzelnitsky in the *Golden Jubilee Album*, p. 17.

17. Paul Zaichenko, "For the 50th Anniversary of the Parish of Minneapolis," *Golden Jubilee Album* (Minneapolis: 1937), p. 43.

18. Wm. P. Shriver, *Immigrant Forces* (New York: Missionary Education Movement of the United States and Canada, 1913), pp. 180–1. See also Wasyl Halich, *op. cit.*, pp. 29, 99; and Julian Batchinsky, *Ukrainian Immigration in the United States of America* (Lwiw: 1914), p. 258.

19. Nedzelnitsky, *op. cit.*, pp. 17–8; also tape-recorded interview with John W. Mlinar.

20. Dimitry Grigorieff, *op. cit.*, p. 9; and *The Russian-American Orthodox Calendar for 1950* (Wilkes-Barre, Pennsylvania: Svet, 1950), p. 216.

21. Jerome Davis, *The Russians and Ruthenians in America* (George H.

Doran Co., 1922), p. 82. In another work, Davis cites a figure of $77,850 spent annually to support missionary activity. Jerome Davis, *The Russian Immigrant* (New York: The Macmillan Co., 1922), p. 91.

22. Rev. John Nedzelnitsky, *op. cit.*, p. 20; Paul Zaichenko, *Golden Jubilee Album*, p. 43.

23. Paul Zaichenko, "My Twelve Years of Service in Minneapolis," *Golden Anniversary Souvenir Album of St. Mary's Russian Orthodox Greek Catholic Church a capella Choir* (Minneapolis: 1941), pp. 13–5.

24. John W. Mlinar.

25. "Pastors of the Parish," *Golden Jubilee Album*, p. 33; Rev. John Nedzelnitsky, *op. cit.*, p. 20.

26. Rev. John Nedzelnitsky, *ibid.*

4 The Heroic Period, 1897–1917

MANY EVENTS in the period from the turn of the century through World War I were of major historical consequence in the progress of Russian settlements in the United States. In those years, the Russian Orthodox Church in North America made its greatest missionary gains. The Russian bishops transformed the Minneapolis Russian community into the first center of Russian religious teaching on this continent.

In 1897, the Holy Synod in Russia authorized the organization of a missionary school in Minneapolis that would offer secondary parochial education stressing religious subjects. The Synod also provided the funds to build a three-story brick school building across the street from the church. The school was staffed with three clergymen and with teachers who had been educated in Russia. Beside students residing in Minneapolis, the school boarded others from San Francisco, Pittsburgh, Chicago, and other Russian communities in North America. After graduation from the missionary school, five students were awarded special scholarships for further theological study in Russia. Later they returned from Russia to take prominent positions in Russian-American religious life.[1]

Rev. Dzubay maintains that the missionary school was an ac-

credited institution under the supervision of the Minneapolis Public
School Board. A letter received from C. A. Sorenson, Director of
Administrative Research, Census and Attendance, of the Minne-
apolis Public Schools, indicates, however, that no records exist to
show that the missionary school was under the supervision of the
Public School Board. (Letter dated March 14, 1961.)

The work and accomplishment of the Minneapolis Missionary
School have been described by one of its first students, Bishop Benjamin of Pittsburgh:

We boarded at the Minneapolis Missionary School. Its discipline taught
us to lead a regular life, to be neat and orderly; good habits that were
very useful in later life. We prayed together, studied together, ate together, and we played together. This prompted a spirit of friendship and
taught us to be unselfish.[2]

Because of the successful proselytizing activity of the Russian
Orthodox Church among the Uniates in the United States, the need
for trained personnel and priests was intensified. The establishment
of the Minneapolis Missionary School was the first step toward
satisfying this need. The second and major step was the reorganization of the missionary school into the Minneapolis Ecclesiastical
Seminary on July 1, 1905. Students at the Missionary School (there
were 122 in the final year of its operation) were sent either to the
Minneapolis public schools or the newly created Cleveland Junior
Seminary. The students in their senior year at the missionary school
formed the freshman class of the seminary.[3]

Four teachers staffed the new seminary. It was initially supervised
by Rev. Constantin Popoff, who also taught liturgies, homiletics, and
practical administration. Basil M. Benzin was teacher of divinity
and church history; Alexander Kukulevsky taught secular subjects,
except for English, which was taught by Miss Cleora Francelle
Smith. The students at the seminary varied in background as well as
in age. There were adult and married men, some middle aged, and
there were children thirteen and fourteen years of age. According
to one teacher, Basil M. Benzin, the 1905–1906 curriculum included
the following subjects:

Study of the New Testament, church history, Russian grammar, church singing, and Russian literature. The older students were put in a special group to study the practical side of the ministry, such subjects as homiletics and practical manual of administration.[4]

A teacher at the seminary, Rev. Ingram N. Irwine, an Orthodox convert from the Episcopal Church, performed the first English-language liturgies at St. Mary's church in 1905.[5] It required half a century before English-language services became an accepted practice throughout Russian Orthodox parishes in the United States.

Simultaneously with the establishment of the seminary, a new parochial school was established to help protect the children of the parish from the secularizing influences of the public schools. It was called the parish school, and the classes were held between four and six in the afternoon after the children returned from their public schools. Senior students at the Seminary assisted in teaching the parochial students. In 1908, 108 students attended the parish school; by 1912, the attendance had dropped to 72. After 1903, the parish conducted a Sunday school, which met weekly at one o'clock. Between twenty and thirty children attended the Sunday school, where they received elementary instruction in the principles of the Orthodox faith. Perhaps the most popular form of instruction in the Russian community was the evening school attended primarily by the older parishioners, who had had little or no formal education. In 1912, the evening school was attended by 144 persons from the community.[6]

The foundation of the seminary and the various other educational programs in this period of communal history clearly established Minneapolis as the Russian Orthodox educational center in North America. In 1912, the seminary was transferred to Tenafly, New Jersey, the cathedral city of the archbishop, where greater resources were available for its further development. With the outbreak of the Russian Revolution in 1917, funds from the Holy Synod in Russia were abruptly cut off, and support of the teachers became the responsibility of the individual churches. This burden was a factor in the discontinuation of the Russian parish school in Minneapolis.[7]

During the heroic period of the Minneapolis Russian community, the basic patterns of social life were laid down and organized, including even the social response to death. By 1900, the need for a church cemetery was felt. June 24, 1900, marks the incorporation date of the Russian Orthodox Cemetery Association, which purchased a burial ground for its community;[8] in 1901, a five-acre plot was purchased at 31st Avenue and Stinson Boulevard. In 1912, a chapel was built on the cemetery grounds.[9] Today, every member of the parish is entitled to burial in the cemetery at a minimal price. The cemetery is the site for the annual Memorial Day services in which the war veterans of the community participate.

The new century brought relative prosperity to the parish. Every year, many new arrivals from Europe swelled its ranks. The church structure was becoming too small for the growing membership, and pressure began to develop for construction of a new church. When a fire broke out in the building in the early morning of January 24, 1905, and destroyed the old structure, construction became unavoidable. The Minneapolis Fire Department filed the following report on the fire:

January 24—alarm received at 3:09 A.M. from the corner fire alarm box No. 192 to St. Mary's Russian Orthodox Church, 17th Ave. N.E. and 5th St. This was a two-story frame church. The cause of the fire has remained unknown. The loss amounted to $1,468.15. The amount of insurance carried by the church was $3,500.00.[10]

Plans were immediately made for construction of a new church building, which has survived. It cost the congregation $40,000, of which $1,029 was donated by Tzar Nicholas II. The building was designed by an architect named Cordelli, whose major model was a picture of the Omsk Cathedral, and completed in the summer of 1906. Most of the ikons for the new church were painted by the renowned artist-monks at the Sergeeysky Monastery in Russia.[11]

In 1907, a new threat to the community's existence appeared with the establishment of St. John's Greek Catholic Church on the corner of 22nd Avenue and 3rd Street in northeast Minneapolis. The members of this Uniate parish also came from the Carpathian districts of Austro-Hungary and had close ties with the members of the Russian community. To combat the attraction presented by the newly organized community, St. Mary's parish, under the leadership of its pastor, Father Leonid Turkevich (now the Metropolitan of the Russian Orthodox Church of North America), organized the Society of the Defenders of Orthodox Religious Life. Every male and female over twelve who was willing to protect the traditional Orthodox church services and the Orthodox way of life was accepted into the society. Only a small number of parishioners switched their allegiance back to the Uniate church.[12]

On February 25, 1907, the second largest brotherhood of the community was incorporated—the Russian Catholic Brotherhood of St. John the Baptist and Mutual Benefit Association. Russian Orthodox males between the ages of fifteen and forty-five were admitted into the brotherhood upon the recommendation of two members and a majority membership vote. Each member's family received

. . . two hundred dollars in case of death of said member, and to pay five ($5) dollars per week to each member in case of sickness or injury and to that end there shall be collected from each member the amount of fifty (50c) cents per month for the purpose of raising funds sufficient to meet the before mentioned payments. . . .[13]

On January 4, 1927, the brotherhood filed an amendment to the Certificate of Incorporation. The official name was changed to the Russian Orthodox Church Society of St. John the Baptist.

The intellectual needs of the community were satisfied by the Russian Library Society, Inc., founded in 1908, which established a library room and subscribed to many Russian language periodicals from the United States and Europe. It promoted various courses in English and in naturalization, which were taught in the evening for the benefit of adults. The teaching of reading and writing in Russian also became a responsibility of the newly established society. In 1911, the society sponsored the organization of the Theatrical Circle. In 1936, the circle became an independent organization under the name of St. Mary's Arts and Drama Club.[14]

In the heroic period of the Russian community, two female

societies were formed. The older one was organized on June 19, 1904, as an independent local organization—St. Mary's Russian Women's Society. The purpose of the new organization was twofold:

Its first aim was to instill its members with Christian charity and desire to help one another; to imbue them with the spirit of love, friendship, and good will toward their neighbors; to strengthen their devotion toward the Orthodox faith, their church, and nationality; to teach them to respect church laws and national traditional customs; to make them conscious of their duty toward the church; to urge them to help in its decoration; to have them teach their children the Orthodox religion, encourage regular attendance at church, and the preservation of Russian interests and be good loyal citizens of the United States of America. The second aim is to help its members in case of illness and other misfortunes, and in case of death, to give them an Orthodox Christian burial.[15]

The newer society, Nativity of the Blessed Virgin Mary Women's Society, organized on February 11, 1912, was the local chapter of a nationwide organization. The chief purpose of the society was similar to that of the first—to provide aid in times of accident, illness, and death.[16]

In 1913, a committee was organized to collect funds to aid the orphans of deceased members of the community. In the first twenty-four years of the committee's activity, $6,000 were used to help the widows and their children. The collection of funds for this purpose was made at Christmas and Easter festivities.[17]

The life of the Russian community, as well as of other minority communities in the northeast Minneapolis area, proceeded relatively unnoticed by the majority community. It was not until 1902 that Davison's Minneapolis Directory noted for the first time the presence of the Russian Orthodox Church in the area. The only majority community institution concerned with the problems and lives of the immigrants in the area was the Immanuel Sunday School Mission, organized by Rev. Reuben A. Torrey, pastor of the Open Door Congregational Church.[18]

Since 1899, the mission, popularly called "Drummond Hall" or "Drummond Union," had been located at 1429 2nd Street Northeast. The rapid inflow of the Slavic (predominantly Polish Roman

Catholic) immigrants into the area made it difficult to operate and sustain the Protestant mission. Various athletic and other facilities offered by the mission were eagerly accepted by the immigrants and their children, but much opposition was voiced to the compulsory attendance at the Sunday school for all those who wanted to benefit from the social services of the mission.

In 1913, the board of directors of the mission authorized the Northeast Side Survey, which was completed on October 3, 1913. The study was supervised by Dr. John J. O'Connor, Superintendent of the Minneapolis Associated Charities, and among its major recommendations was the replacement of the mission by a settlement house. Operation of Northeast Neighborhood House, under the direction of Robbins Gilman, began November 1, 1914.[19]

Cathryn Cooke Gilman, a trained social worker, helped her husband in his work at Northeast Neighborhood House until the time of his retirement in 1948. Her three-volume unpublished book remains the only available work giving an account of the life and individual problems of immigrants in the first and second decades of the twentieth century in northeast Minneapolis. The first volume contains a full summary of the Northeast Side Survey in 1913—the first complete study made in this territory.

The survey reported that the population growth of the northeast Minneapolis area between 1890 and 1910 was greater than that of the rest of Minneapolis. Increases were particularly notable among the Slavic immigrants, listed as Austrians, Poles, Russians, or Bohemians. The northeast area alone contained 7,254 people in 1910, of which 14 per cent were Slavic immigrants, most of whom lived in the First Ward. Only 20 per cent of the population in the area were native whites born of native parents.

The northeast area also had the largest illiteracy rate in the city—2,348 among 6,139 illiterates in the whole city. The 1913 Survey estimated that the Slavs made up the largest number of illiterates in this section of the city and recommended that special attention be given to their education. It also reported great hazards to health and welfare in the northeast area, listing the following pressing problems—lack of dispensary facilities, especially for tuberculosis, dental, and maternity cases; contaminated wells and poor quarantine regulations; poor, overcrowded housing, especially among the most recent immigrants.[20] Mrs. Gilman quotes two paragraphs from the Survey report in which special disadvantages of the Slavic immigrants were discussed:

Of the foreign born peoples, the Slavs have composed the largest number of dependents in their homes. This may be either because they have more difficulty in obtaining and keeping work, or because they are ignorant of the language and opportunities here, or because as a whole they are less well paid and less skilled laborers, or because there are so few of their countrymen in good positions and able to assist them . . . Practically the entire immigration of the Slavic elements at the present time is that of peasants. Many of them are used to an agricultural wage of only 18 cents a day, to landlordism, and unequal taxation. The races from Austria-Hungary in their natural clime have the largest birth rate of any of those in Europe, more than 43 per thousand, but owing to the economic conditions, have such a large death rate that the net increase is less than that of any country of Europe, except France.[21]

The opening of Northeast Neighborhood House brought with it the establishment of a whole array of services and opportunities for underprivileged Slavic and other national groups. They included cooking and sewing classes, a gymnasium, games, and a story hour; piano, violin, and choral lessons; an infant clinic, an employment service, a library, and many other facilities. At first the workers at the Neighborhood House faced a special difficulty in overcoming the distrust and suspicion of the immigrants. The free services of the House were so unbelievable that the children of the neighborhood nicknamed it the "Nut House."[22]

Mrs. Gilman also vividly summarizes the major problems faced by the immigrants at the opening of the Settlement House:

Recent immigration, lack of occupational skills, exploitation, depressed wages, irregular employment, illiteracy together with general insecurity, heightened by a lack of native education and the inability to speak the English language, intensified the difficulties of the everyday, ordinary living conditions of the majority of the clientage of the settlement. . . . Laborers who could not understand English were subjected to discrimination, exploitation, and misunderstanding. Some employers in industries used agents, immigrants of a few years previous, to recruit newly arrived men and women for work, and to supervise them on the job. There were regular scouts used to spot the "newcomers" and to enlist them for a price that was split two ways. Evils of a serious character grew out of the system. The placement agents and the supervisors in industry often took advantage of the ignorance of the newcomer and in collusion with unscrupulous superintendents or "straw bosses", in shops, mills, and factories, extorted excessive payments to get and hold the job. Frequent discharges and re-employment increased the incomes of those guilty of the practice.[23]

The employment data for the Russians quoted earlier from the Fourth Decennial Census of Minnesota (1895) casts some light on employment problems of the immigrants at the turn of the century. The fifth and last Decennial Census of Minnesota in 1905 did not include a question on the length of employment. In that census, 567 persons were traced as coming from the Minneapolis Russian community. There were 325 males and 242 females in the group, of whom 296 gave Austria as their country of birth, twelve Russia, and one Poland. Two hundred forty-nine children were born in Minnesota and nine in other states. The median age of men over fifteen years old was thirty years; the median age of women over fifteen was between twenty-five and twenty-nine years.

The 1905 census indicated an already increasing occupational differentiation within the Russian community; 166 males were found in the unskilled labor category, five of whom were American-born adults who had reached maturity within the community. Nineteen men were found in other than unskilled jobs: a minister, an American-born printer, two saloonkeepers, a bartender, two machinists, two painters, a cabinet maker, a railroad fireman, a grocer, a mechanic, a clerk, four coopers, and one merchant. Eleven women were employed in domestic and other unskilled jobs, three in clerical positions, and one was, with her husband, joint owner of a saloon, where she worked.

This census tended to support the evidence of the Northeast Side Survey on overcrowding among Slavic immigrants. The average home in the Russian community housed 9.7 people. Homes held from three to twenty people, the median number being eight. Additional data in the 1905 census confirmed the fact that most members of the Russian community were recent immigrants. Of the 197 foreign-born males, the median Russian had spent four years in residence in the state of Minnesota. Out of 115, the median female member of the Russian community had spent as many as seven years in Minnesota.

On August 6, 1916, the first feature article on the life of the Minneapolis Russian community appeared in *The Minneapolis Sunday Tribune*. The story, written by May Wyon Rogers, contained photographs of St. Mary's Church, girls in native costumes, two native dancers, and a married woman in costume. The article was entitled "Our New Americans." The story reported that 350 families made up the Russian colony. It said that many of the men worked in railroad shops as laborers, a few kept stores, while fewer still worked at skilled trades. The article reported that members of the Russian community resided mainly around 5th Street Northeast between 10th and 18th Avenues. The article stated that St. Mary's Orthodox Greek Catholic Church was maintained by the Holy Synod in Russia and was the center of culture and thrift. It noted that the church contained a literary society, a women's society with 150 members, and a political club—and that opposite the church stood a parochial school in which seventy children were taught the Russian language, Russian history, and the English language. An active evening school of English and citizenship classes was also reported.[24]

The heroic period in the life of the Russian community ended with the Russian Revolution, when support of the parish priests and teachers had to be assumed by the parishioners themselves. The loyalties that had bound them to the Russian government and the Russian people had to be restructured. A new era was beginning.

NOTES

1. Paul Zaichenko, "For the 50th Anniversary of the Parish of Minneapolis," *Golden Jubilee Album of St. Mary's Russian Orthodox Greek Catholic Church* (Minneapolis: 1937), p. 44; Rev. John Nedzelnitsky, *Golden Jubilee Album*, p. 20; Rev. John P. Dzubay, "Orthodoxy in America" (Minneapolis: 1955), pp. 8–9.

2. Bishop Benjamin, "St. Mary's Russian Orthodox Church and the Parish of Minneapolis," *Golden Jubilee Album,* p. 71.

3. Rev. Constantin Popoff, "Memories of St. Mary's Parish in Minneapolis," *Golden Jubilee Album,* p. 71.

4. *Ibid.;* and Basil M. Benzin, "My Recollections of the North American Ecclesiastical Seminary, 1905 and 1906," *Golden Jubilee Album,* p. 83.

5. *Historical Magazine of the Protestant Episcopal Church,* Ethelbert Tabbot issue (June, 1955), 165–8.

6. Popoff, *op. cit.,* p. 71; Nedzelnitsky, *op. cit.,* p. 21.

7. Nedzelnitsky, *op. cit.,* p. 26.

8. Certificate of organization of the Russian Orthodox Cemetery Association (Unpublished document Manuscript Division, Minnesota Historical Society).

9. Nedzelnitsky, *op. cit.,* p. 26.

10. Annual Report of the City of Minneapolis for the Year 1905, courtesy of Mr. Earl W. Eggers from the Minneapolis Fire Department. (Letter dated February 24, 1961.)

11. Popoff, *op. cit.,* p. 73; Nedzelnitsky, *op. cit.,* pp. 25–6.

12. Nedzelnitsky, *op. cit.,* pp. 22–4; Rev. Vasily Kolesnikoff, "The Parish of Minneapolis Thirty Years Ago," *Golden Jubilee Album,* p. 86.

13. Articles of Incorporation of the Russian Orthodox Catholic Brotherhood of St. John the Baptist and Mutual Benefit Association, Document No. 457307; Certificate of Amendment of Certificate of Incorporation of Russian Orthodox Catholic Brotherhood of St. John the Baptist and Mutual Benefit Association, Document No. 1398984.

14. "The Russian Library Society of Minneapolis, Inc.," *Golden Jubilee Album,* pp. 115–7; "St. Mary's Arts and Drama Club," *ibid.,* p. 125.

15. "St. Mary's Russian Women's Society," *ibid.,* p. 103.

16. "Women's Russian Orthodox Church Society," *ibid.,* pp. 107–9.

17. "St. Mary's Orphans Committee," *ibid.,* pp. 118–9.

18. Cathryn Cooke Gilman, "Neighbors United through Social Settlement Services at the North East Neighborhood House, Minneapolis, Minnesota, 1914–1948," 3 vols. (Unpublished manuscript, Minnesota Historical Society, courtesy of Mr. Logan Gilman), p. 1.

19. *Ibid.,* pp. 1–3, 22–3, 49–50, 72.

20. *Ibid.,* pp. 38–47.

21. *Ibid.,* pp. 48, 56–7.

22. *Ibid.,* pp. 125–8.

23. *Ibid.,* pp. 185, 252.

24. May Wyon Rogers, "Our New Americans," *The Minneapolis Sunday Tribune,* August 6, 1916.

5 Readjustment and Adaptation to the American Milieu

THE OUTBREAK OF WORLD WAR I and the lineup among world powers must have been experienced with a new self-consciousness by the Minneapolis Russians. After all, as Russia and the United States were linked in a world conflict, so the Russian community of Minneapolis shared its day-to-day destiny with the wider metropolitan community. When individuals from the Minneapolis Russian community served in World War I, they were comrades in arms with their old-world countrymen. Then in 1917, the Russian Revolution radically cut many of the traditional ties, and financial support from the homeland was withdrawn from the Minneapolis Russian community.

THE PERIOD OF TRANSITION, 1918–1941

The sacrifice of some of its members on the battlefields of Europe forced the Russian community into a new awareness of, and kinship with, the majority community. With the Russian Revolution, the

(61)

community had to reorient itself to self-reliance and local loyalty. The Revolution was not the only influence. The period was also marked by the rise of the second generation, the majority of whom were born in the United States, sons and daughters of the early immigrants.

The loyalty of the Russian community to the United States was evinced in the enlistment of seventy-four of its young men in the United States armed services when World War I began. The community prided itself on its purchases of Liberty Bonds and its efforts to organize Red Cross chapters. In October, 1918, the Russian community held dedication ceremonies for its service flag at which Minnesota Senator Frank L. Palmer and Congressman W. I. Norton were principal speakers.[1] One of the seventy-four boys, John Loss, died from wounds inflicted in battle in France. For him and for Polish Stanley Edward Kaniewski, the Kaniewski-Loss Post No. 1852 of the Veterans of Foreign Wars in northeast Minneapolis was named. The following communication was received from Adjutant Masica of the Kaniewski-Loss Post:

Our V.F.W. Post was originally named the Slavic Post. The members who organized this post were in great majority from Northeast Minneapolis and from Polish and Russian and Carpatho-Russian origins. It seemed fitting to re-name the post after a member of each ethnic group who gave their lives in the actual battle area.

John Joseph Loss—born in Dubovu, Saros, Austria-Hungary in December 25, 1895. Enlisted in U.S. Army on February 26, 1918, at Minneapolis, Minnesota. Employed as a mechanic-laborer in woodturning plant. Served in Company A 352 Infantry and Company C 130 Infantry, 33rd Division. Foreign service was rendered in France. He died from wounds received in action in Verdun and Argonne Forest battles. Wounds were received on November 10, 1918, and he died on the same day. His body was shipped home in a military bronze casket and he is buried in the St. Mary's Russian Orthodox Cemetery in the Loss family plot. Highest rank attained, Private 1st Class. Nearest relative still living in Minneapolis, a brother, Joseph Loss, and a sister, Mrs. Adam Klisch.[2]

In 1919, the younger generation of the community organized the Platon Club. The aims of the club were specifically stated:

At that time there were two distinct elements in the congregation, one being composed of those who migrated here from Europe, and the other of those who were born in this country. All the congregation affairs were governed by the element from abroad, the American born youth shared no responsibility and took no active interest or concern in the affairs of the congregation. In order to improve the situation and derive the benefits from the active support of the American born youth, the Platon Club was organized April 3, 1919.[3]

In 1922, partly in response to the activities and challenges of the Platon Club, the middle-aged, European-born generation of the community organized a new Russian-American club. The club members stressed unity, cooperation, and mutual assistance in case of need among all the members of the community.[4]

A number of conflicts broke out among members of the community in the 1920s under the compulsions of readjustment to new conditions. In the middle 1920s, St. Mary's parish was torn by strife over the question of communal property. According to Russian tradition, the church property belongs to the church diocese. The dominant sentiment of the community, however, was in favor of incorporation of the parish into an economically independent body. The articles of incorporation of the St. Mary's Russian Greek Catholic Church were filed on June 1, 1927. The incorporation document was signed by William Kokesh and John R. Reshetar. Paul Jaroscak, a young lawyer and the first professional among the American-born Russians, served as the notary public.[5]

This and other disagreements within the community culminated in the departure of thirty families from St. Mary's to set up their own independent church. Starting in 1926, services at which Father Paul Tkach officiated were held in the homes of the parishioners. Father Tkach served on a half-time basis, traveling between Minneapolis and Holdingford, Minnesota. In 1932, the dissenting congregation built its own small church on Central Avenue and 44th Street in Columbia Heights. It was named Sts. Peter and Paul Russian Orthodox Church. In the 1930s, Rev. Theodore Turchenko (later Vesely) became the permanent pastor of the parish.[6]

The St. Mary's Mothers Club was organized in 1928. In contrast to other women's organizations within the community, this club was not a sisterhood. The aims of the club were more limited and specific: ". . . mutual work of the mothers to perform such duties as decorating, cleaning, buying of necessary ornaments for the church. . . ."[7] Informal cooperation between women to perform such tasks was breaking down, and the institution of more formal responsibility became necessary.

The community itself was growing too large to operate along informal lines. In 1923, a survey of the neighborhood showed that St. Mary's Church had an approximate membership of 2,000 people.[8] Services like the care of orphans became the responsibility of a formal orphans committee. The interests of the expanding parish, in turn, were to be protected by a building committee created in 1930.[9] The athletic activities sponsored by different organizations at various times were formally organized within the church in 1935. Basketball in competition with neighborhood groups throughout Minneapolis was the major activity.[10] Even so stable a structure as the church choir became formally organized in 1927 thanks to the efforts of its director, Father John Dzubay, who served as its president for the first five years. Each year, the choir held a banquet at which one female member and one male member were honored for their contributions to its activity.[11] The practice still continues.

The most significant development of the 1930s was the formation of the St. Mary's "R" Club, Chapter 94 of the Federated Russian Orthodox Clubs of America. The creation of the chapter in Minneapolis was supported by the younger second generation of the Russian community, born in the first and second decades of the twentieth century. The aim of this national and local club is to promote Eastern Orthodoxy through closer identification with the American way of life. The members of the club have always supported such integrating movements as introduction of the English language into religious services. The members stress the uniqueness of their religious affiliation as loyal American citizens. In all their activities and publications, little appreciation or attention is given to specifically Russian ideals.[12] Since 1927, the national headquarters of the Federated Russian Orthodox Clubs at Wilkes-Barre, Pennsylvania, has published a monthly English-language journal called *The Russian Orthodox Journal*.[13] The aims and spirit of the clubs are well illustrated by their anthem:

> Faith of our Father, Holy Orthodox,
> We will perpetuate in this land that's free
> Keep the traditions that bind us together,
> True to our heritage, and the F.R.O.C.
>
> Pray, Study, Toil, Always be Temperate
> This is our motto and proud are we!
> For it will guide us in all our endeavors,
> In all our aims and hopes for the F.R.O.C.[14]

In 1937, the Russian community celebrated the fiftieth anniversary of its parish. Those in charge of the celebrations and the church at that time included some who had organized the Platon Club in 1919 and challenged the control exercised by their European-born parents. They were the ones who successfully led the community through the readjustment period that became inevitable after the Russian Revolution and World War I.

The *Golden Jubilee Album* published at the time reveals the success of the community in its transformation. This 242-page album still remains the only major memoir of the many teachers and pastors who lived within the community at the turn of the century. It is significant for another area also—it is the only material published by the parish in both Russian and English. At a luncheon during the two days of festive celebration, the Russian community welcomed among its guests General E. Leach, Mayor of Minneapolis, an indication that the Russian community continued to increase its influence in the affairs of the majority community.

Little is known of the effects of the Great Depression on the Russian community. The 1934 social survey of 20,000 Minneapolis families gives some indication of the fate of the northeast area in the city.[15] Of 3,077 men contacted in the area, 114 were retired, 859 unemployed, and 2,104 at work. The largest number of unemployed was in the unskilled-labor category. It may be conjectured that the foreign-born Russians were one of the hardest hit groups because of their relative lack of skills. The survey utilized Sims's socio-economic scale for the classification of occupations.

Table 5—Employment Status of Men in the Northeast Area in 1934*

	EMPLOYED No.	%	UNEMPLOYED No.	%
Professional	29	1	7	1
Semi-professional and commercial service	85	4	11	1
Artisan proprietors	378	18	24	3
Skilled laborers	858	41	135	16
Unskilled laborers	745	36	369	43
C.C.C.			20	2
C.W.A.			293	34
Total	2095	100	859	100

* Source: note 15.

The predominant type of building in which the northeast families lived in 1934 was a single family or duplex frame house. There were relatively few multiple dwellings. Of the houses, 65 per cent were in good condition, 31 per cent needed repair, and 4 per cent were dilapidated.[16]

Table 6—Housing of Northeast Families in 1934

	FRAME No.	%	BRICK No.	%	STUCCO No.	%
Single houses	793	31	80	3	310	12
Duplexes	746	29	174	7	267	11
Multiple dwellings	75	3	51	2	37	2
Totals	1614	63	305	12	614	25

The survey also included a question on the national identification of families in the area. The ambivalence and lack of specific national loyalties among the various ethnic groups were revealed by the fact that some persons listed as many as three or more nationalities, although we do not know how many answered the question at all. Each nationality given to the survey worker was recorded. The following results were obtained:

Table 7—National Identification of Northeast Families in 1934*

	Number	Per Cent
Russian	68	1
Polish	1174	22
Austrian	337	6
Czech	333	6
Ukrainian	3	—
Hungarian	14	—
American (U.S.A.)	3454	64

* Source: note 15.

A more significant index of the area's cultural and communal identification was obtained by asking each family what languages were used in its home. Every language given by the family was recorded.

Table 8—Languages Spoken in Northeast Minneapolis Families in 1934*

	Number	Per Cent
Polish	1644	31
Yiddish	2	—
Russian	369	7
Slovak	259	5
Bohemian	32	1
Ukrainian	9	—
Hungarian	11	—
Austrian	7	—
English	2927	55

* Source: note 15.

During the increasing assimilation and acculturation of the immigrants and their children into the larger American community, the unity and cohesiveness of the whole northeast area in relation to the whole of Minneapolis had been primarily the work of Northeast Neighborhood House under the direction of Mr. and Mrs. Robbins Gilman. The settlement house celebrated its twenty-fifth anniversary in 1940 at ceremonies in which the multiple ethnic groups participated. The St. Mary's Russian Orthodox Church choir performed at the main event of the celebration. Many of the members of St. Mary's Church had been participating and helping in the various activities of the settlement house. Yet, in looking back, Mrs. Gilman summarized the difficulties of bringing the various ethnic groups out of their ethnocentric shells and making them co-operate for the common welfare of the whole neighborhood:

Due to the intense feeling between national groups, resulting in animosities and zealousness for the countries of origin, there has been a lack of cohesiveness in the neighborhood. Cooperative civic spirit is still unsatisfactory. The rivalries between the national groups which are characterized chiefly by a desire of one group to win an election at the expense of another, has retarded the civic development of the district.[17]

The coming of the Second World War destroyed many of the old-world loyalties and commitments in the northeast community. It forced the various ethnic groups to re-orient themselves still further toward American society. When, after the war, the northeast area received fresh immigration from Europe, the newcomers found loyalties, commitments, and ways of life so drastically different from their own as to constitute a different cultural world.[18]

THE RUSSIAN COMMUNITY TODAY

The next period in the life of the Russian community opened with World War II. More than 400 young men from the community served in the armed forces of the United States during this time.[19] Military service had given them a common basis of experience, in terms of which they attempted to reconstruct their civilian lives. As early as 1945, the veterans organized themselves into the St. Mary's Veterans' Association, which was formally incorporated. The incorporation document was filed on April 15, 1959; the service of notary public was performed by a young lawyer in the Russian community, Peter Barna.[20] The purpose of the association was "to provide for better community service, work for the good of the community and church, and to promote better relations among veterans."[21]

In 1960, the membership of the Veterans' Association consisted of sixty-five people including several honorary memberships extended to those who had not served in the war. The Association included three women who had served in the armed forces and two women honorary members. Today, the major responsibility of the Association is participation in the Memorial Day observance held annually at St. Mary's Cemetery.[22]

In 1947, some of the veterans and members of the "R" Club centered their attention on the inadequate and poorly organized Sunday school. Little effort was being made to interest children in attending the school. There were still attempts at Russian-language training, but the school's hours were considered inadequate by many. The veterans and members of the "R" Club argued that it was because of its inconvenience and the narrowness of its practices that only forty children were attending the Sunday school.[23]

During 1947–1948, they waged a campaign for the reorganization of the school, in the course of which they were put in charge. Many young people were encouraged to teach its classes, and the children were offered more "Americanized" incentives. The school adopted many features of the Protestant Sunday schools, at which the children are divided into age groups for instruction and play. The Sunday school now meets at the same time as the regular services, so that parents can attend church undisturbed while their children are being taught the history and tenets of the Eastern Orthodox Church.[24] The growing popularity of the school among both parents and children is manifested in larger attendance through the last decade.

In 1951, the Sunday school was attended by about 150 children.[25] In 1957, attendance figures rose to more than 300.[26] In 1960, the Sunday school boasted 328 pupils and was staffed by thirty-four volunteer teachers, assistants, and office personnel.[27] The Sunday-school program has also been strengthened by the construction of a new school and parish center on the grounds of the old missionary-school building. A two-story brick building, constructed at a cost of over $300,000, was dedicated on June 20, 1957. Archbishop John, head of the Russian Orthodox Diocese of Chicago and Minneapolis, officiated.[28]

In 1949, the founders of St. Mary's "R" Club undertook to

organize activities for their own children and other young people in the Russian community by forming a Junior "R" Club, the newest organization in the Russian community.[29] The activities of the members are concentrated on athletics, and the new school building is equipped with an auditorium and a basketball court. Basketball remains their favorite sport.

In 1951, Father Leonard Soroka arrived as the new pastor of St. Mary's and established a regular English-language divine liturgy. Since then, St. Mary's church has held two divine liturgies every Sunday—the English-language liturgy is performed from 8:30 to 10 a.m., while the Church Slavonic liturgy begins at 10:15 a.m.[30]

At the time St. Mary's parish and the Russian community were enjoying their greatest prosperity and fullest development, the rival community, formed in the 1920s in the Columbia Heights area and called the Sts. Peter and Paul Russian Orthodox Church, was unable to withstand the pressures of changing times. The small community was unable to support a full-time minister during the Depression. Father Turchenko-Vesely offered his services to the parish without immediate remuneration. He maintained himself by part-time farming, selling insurance, and religious services in the community. In 1952, *The Minneapolis Tribune* ran a short story on Rev. Turchenko-Vesely. The article reported that his "farm" consisted of

a cow, 22 hives of bees, 24 chickens, and a newly born calf. . . . He also has cultivated an orchard full of apples, currants, plums, and grapes.[31]

When times improved, however, Rev. Turchenko-Vesely brought a law suit against the parishioners, demanding remuneration for his services. The courts awarded him the church structure, and the parish disintegrated very rapidly. By 1950, only a handful of the parishioners remained with the church, while others had disappeared into the larger American society or returned to St. Mary's Church. The final blow to the Columbia Heights community was delivered in 1953, when Archbishop Leonty, head of the Russian Orthodox Diocese, refused recognition to Father Turchenko-Vesely for canonical reasons. Rev. Vesely remained in Minneapolis until 1956, when the church property was offered for sale, thus ending all attempts by small groups within the old Russian community to establish rival institutions in the Minneapolis area.[32]

As the Columbia Heights Russian community was undergoing gradual disintegration, another Russian community, vigorous and determined, was launched in the Minneapolis area by the arrival of the "new" Russian political refugees from the Soviet Union in the years 1949–1951. The newcomers first joined St. Mary's Church and participated in its activities. In a very short time, however, conflicts between the values of the new Russian group and those of the more acculturated group became unavoidable. The old community no longer felt close kinship with things Russian. No longer were its members eager to devote their lives to the liberation of the mother country. No longer did they demand that their children speak Russian. Some of the new Russian refugees left St. Mary's to establish their own church around which they could build their own community life.[33]

The plans did not materialize until the summer of 1956, when the new community purchased a small church in the Midway District of Minneapolis at 2210 Franklin Avenue, Southeast. At the time of its opening, a Minneapolis paper carried the following news item:

After meeting in private homes for several years, a congregation of former displaced persons will worship for the first time Sunday in its own church.[34]

Formal organization of the church took place on June 16, 1955, when the parishioners, fifty families in all, adopted the name St. Panteleimon's Russian Orthodox Church.[35]

The new parish is under the jurisdiction of the Holy Synod of Russian Orthodox Bishops Abroad. The Holy Synod is composed of immigrant anti-communist Russian bishops who represent Russian Orthodoxy to anti-communist Russian refugees throughout the world. In contrast to the Missionary church, the Holy Synod is committed to the idea of returning to its native land; its leaders conceive of their task as the preservation of Russian refugees as a distinct national entity. Consequently, the new immigrants resist assimilation of their children into American society. Much time is spent in teaching their children Russian language, history, geography, and religion. A well organized Sunday school, which meets every Saturday afternoon, is attended by practically every child in the community. Little, if any, interaction occurs with St. Mary's parish, for it is recognized that the paths and goals of the two churches are different.[36]

The number of new immigrants in St. Mary's parish has been too small to bring about major changes in the old Russian community, which has continued to adapt itself to American society. Only recently, many of the members of the old Russian community have begun to achieve real economic, political, and professional status. The first major success in the professions was that of Judge Paul J. Jaroscak of the Hennepin County District Court.

Judge Jaroscak was born in the Russian community in northeast Minneapolis in 1895. He was graduated from East High School and the University of Minnesota, from which he received the B.A. and L.L.B. degrees. Mr. Jaroscak served in the United States Army from February 26, 1918, to December 1, 1918, entering as a private and leaving as a second lieutenant. From August, 1921, to August, 1944, he was engaged in private law practice in Minneapolis. He held the position of President of the Hennepin County Bar Association from 1940 to 1941. In August, 1944, he was appointed Special Assistant Attorney General of Minnesota. From 1945 to 1951, he served as a judge in the Minneapolis Municipal Court, after which he was appointed by Governor Youngdahl to the bench of Hennepin County District Court, which office he still fills.[37]

The reputation and humane qualities of Judge Jaroscak were well described by Robbins Gilman of Northeast Neighborhood House in his letter of recommendation to Governor Youngdahl, in which he urged the appointment of Judge Jaroscak to the district bench:

Dear Governor Youngdahl:

Since the death of Judge Wright of the Hennepin County District Court and the consequent vacancy, permit me respectfully to mention to you your consideration of Municipal Judge Paul Jaroscak of Minneapolis as a proper person to be elevated to the District bench.

Judge Jaroscak has been known to me ever since the Northeast Neighborhood House was organized thirty odd years ago. He and his family lived in this district for many years. He is a highly respected member of St. Mary's Russian Eastern Orthodox Church. . . .

My desire would be to present to you his qualifications from the standpoint of his social outlook. As a social worker, I can testify to the fact that he is unusually socially minded and would, in my estimation, make a notable successor to such predecessors as Judge Waite, Judge Guilford, and Judge Wright. I have followed Judge Jaroscak's career and record closely over a period of at least 25 years. His intelligent interest and participation in social and civic affairs have always appealed to me, and I feel that he would make an understanding and excellent judge of the juvenile court.[38]

The success of Judge Jaroscak was interpreted by the Russian community as its own success. The souvenir book published on July 22, 1951, for the St. Mary's summer festival and picnic carried a full page congratulation from the community to the judge:

Congratulations on the appointment and promotion to the eminently honorable and high judicial office of Hennepin County District Court.

We are proud of you!

We pray the good Lord to bless you with good health, strength, patience, and wisdom, that you may further continue to serve the people of Hennepin County and community, wisely, justly, and fearlessly . . .
Your friends,

The Pastors,
The Board of Trustees,
The 1951 Picnic Committee, and
The members of St. Mary's R.O. Church.[39]

Another man whose success is important to the Russian community is Harold Kalina. Born in Minneapolis, the youngest of ten children, Mr. Kalina attended Edison High School and the University of Minnesota law school, from which he received B.S.L. and L.L.B degrees. He served in the United States Army from June,

1946, to December, 1947. He has been active in St. Mary's Church life and has served as its financial secretary. Early in his career, Mr. Kalina joined the Democratic-Farmer-Labor Party and became active in the Third Ward Party Club, holding the office of secretary. In 1954, he defeated a fifteen-year veteran of the state senate, Raymond J. Julkowski, in the 28th district seat. With this victory, Mr. Kalina became the youngest state senator in the Minnesota Legislature. He was active in Northeast Neighborhood House work, and, in 1955, he was named to the board of directors of the settlement house.[40]

In addition to Peter Barna who was mentioned earlier, two other prominent Minneapolis attorneys emerged from the Minneapolis Russian community. William G. Kohlan was graduated from the Minnesota Law School in 1932 at age twenty-two. He was defeated in his bid for state representative before the war but was renominated in 1942, when he was called to military service. After the war, his influence as an attorney was attested by his election as membership chairman for both the Hennepin County and Minnesota State Bar Associations.[41]

The second attorney, Andrew G. Kohlan, a graduate of the Minnesota Law School and a naval reserve lieutenant, was defeated in the state primary by U.S. Representative Roy W. Wier in 1958. Mr. Kohlan, the St. Anthony Village attorney, is active in the First Ward D.F.L. Club. As a member of St. Mary's Church, he is active in St. Mary's Veterans Association.[42]

The Russian Minneapolis community has produced one nationally known member of the professions. John E. Reshetar, Professor of Political Science at the University of Washington, Seattle, was born in Minneapolis in 1924. He received his B.A. degree at Williams College in 1945, and his M.A. and Ph.D. degrees at Harvard University in 1946 and 1950. He held an instructorship at Princeton University in 1947; he was a staff member of the Russian Research Center at Harvard University at the time the Refugee Interview Project was being conducted. He is a contributor to many professional periodicals and the author of two books, *The Ukrainian Revolution,* 1952, and *A Concise History of the Communist Party of the Soviet Union,* 1960.

The growing political influence of the Russian community in the modern period is obvious in the increased awareness of its importance among Minnesota mayors, congressmen, and senators. These men invariably appear or send their greeetings to the various church celebrations. For example, when the St. Mary's Russian Women's Society was celebrating its golden anniversary in 1954, its guests included Senator Hubert H. Humphrey and Mayor Eric Hoyer. When St. Mary's Church was dedicating its new school and parish home, the community welcomed Governor Freeman and Mayor Peterson for the celebration.[43]

In the 1951 "Souvenir Book," the following important politicians of the state printed their congratulatory messages to the parishioners: Senator Hubert H. Humphrey, Senator Edward J. Thye, and Mayor of Minneapolis Eric G. Hoyer.[44] In the 1960 "Souvenir Book," the congratulations of judges and politicians were printed: Judge of the Municipal Court Luther Sletten, Judge of the District Court Leslie L. Anderson, and Mayor of Minneapolis P. Kenneth Peterson; State Representatives Stanley J. Fudro, Edward J. Tomczyk, George Murk, and John Skeate; Park Commissioner Richard J. Kanterowicz, State Senator Donald Fraser, and Aldermen Vernon McCrady from the First Ward and Frank Welinski from the Third Ward.[45]

The Russian community has also been successful in other endeavors that have made its name known outside the Minneapolis area. In 1949, the parish printed its bilingual *Orthodox Prayer Book,* which has since been reprinted many times. In 1954, it published an English-language history and description of the Eastern Orthodox Church, written by Rev. Leonard Soroka and Stan W. Carlson. Both books were published by the Olympic Press, owned by a member of St. Mary's Church. In the middle 1950s, St. Mary's choir recorded three long-playing discs of Russian Orthodox Church songs. In 1957, the St. Mary's Mothers' Club published its popular English-language cookbook. When the Soviets advanced in technology and placed the "Sputnik" in the sky in 1957, the Russian community began to show a renewed interest in Russian-language studies. Russian classes were introduced in 1958, and in 1959 registered attendance was sixty—but by 1960 the attendance had dropped to thirty-two students.[46]

The history of the Minneapolis community is a story of struggle, hardship, and success. From an initial state of extreme poverty the former Carpathian peasants have succeeded in creating one of the most prosperous Orthodox parishes in North America. The current inventory of parish property is reported by Father Dzubay:

1. A beautiful, spacious, artistically decorated church edifice, Byzantine in style, architecture, and character.

2. A new magnificent school and parish center building of modern architecture, built at a cost of nearly $300,000.

3. A ten acre parish cemetery, on which is built a beautiful chapel, a brick edifice; there, in peaceful slumber rest over 1500 parishioners and orthodox faithful.

4. Two modern, up-to-date parish homes, built about eight years ago.

5. An old remodeled and redecorated parish home, located next to the church and presently occupied by Father Karp Pateyuk.

6. And a large six lot parking space, two blocks from the church, for which the church was offered $50,000. The entire property—cemetery, church, chapel, homes, school, and parish center building are a credit to the congregation and a great asset to the neighborhood and community in general.

The worth of the entire property is estimated at about $1,000,000. There is an encumbrance or liability balance of only $60,000, owed to individual parishioners who helped finance the building plan of the new St. Mary's School and Parish Center. This, through united effort, we hope to repay and discharge the notes within the next three or four years.[47]

CLUBS AND ORGANIZATIONS—1960

Concurrently with this study, a review was undertaken of the various organizations within the present community. A summary report of each organization is presented below. This review reveals that many formerly vigorous organizations have turned into informal social groupings—especially the several brotherhoods within the community. The active organizations at present are composed of the younger American-born generation—St. Mary's "R" Club and the Veterans Association. The number of members and the activities of these two organizations reflect their comparative vigor and strength.

St. Mary's Russian Orthodox Greek Catholic Church. The life of the Russian community is organized around St. Mary's parish. In 1960, three pastors served the parish. The oldest of the pastors, Father John Dzubay, was born and educated within the Minneapolis Russian community. He joined the church in 1918 and has been serving as pastor, teacher, and choir director ever since. Father Leonard Soroka was born in the United States and arrived in Minneapolis in 1951 to serve the church. Father Soroka introduced regular English–language services in the church. In July, 1960, he accepted a position as pastor in Clayton, Wisconsin. Since 1958, Russian-born Father Karp Pateyuk has been an associate pastor.

The board of trustees of St. Mary's Church is composed of fifteen people. Tenure of the trusteeships is for three years, with five trustees elected each year.

St. Mary's Church Choir. A formally organized association under the leadership and direction of Father Dzubay since 1927, the choir served not only as an active medium for the preservation of church singing but also as a very powerful pressure group within the community as well. With the rise of younger competing organizations within the community, the choir has been losing its political effectiveness in recent years.

The choir has seventy members—thirty-six men and thirty-four women. Every year a banquet is held at which the choir and the community honor one man and one woman who have contributed greatly to the choir. The choir meets at eight o'clock the second Wednesday of each month, and rehearsals are held every other Wednesday.

The Junior Choir. To supplement the ranks of the senior choir, the organization maintains a junior choir. The official membership is composed of seventy boys and girls between the ages of ten and sixteen. Meetings are attended by thirty or thirty-five members. The junior choir has its own president. In 1960, the president was John Dzubak, while Carol Semanko was secretary.

The Russian Orthodox Sts. Peter and Paul Church Society. This old and once active brotherhood has been transformed into an insurance association with little formal activity among its members. Males are admitted into full membership, while their wives are permitted to be insured without the right to vote. The brotherhood lists as members 154 men and 54 women. The meetings are held on the first Thursday of alternate months, starting with February. Women pay dues of thirty-five cents a month on a $200 policy. Men who have been members since the beginning of the brotherhood pay $1.40 a month, while later members are charged according to age, as is customary in the insurance field.

The St. John the Baptist Society. Another brotherhood that now functions as an insurance group is the St. John the Baptist Society. It has sixty-three members, all male, who pay seventy-five cents a month dues. Meetings are held on the first Thursday of every other month, starting with February.

The Holy Trinity Society No. 22, R.O.C. M.A.S. This brotherhood is composed of ninety members—half male and half female. Insurance is its only activity. Dues are scaled according to age, and the meetings are held on Wednesday after the third Sunday of every other month, starting with January.

The Nativity of the Blessed Virgin Mary Women's Society. This women's organization celebrated its golden anniversary in 1962. No other activity beside insurance is maintained, and dues are collected according to age from ninety-six members. Meetings are held on Wednesday after the Third Sunday of every other month, starting in January.

St. Mary's Russian Orthodox Church Women's Society. This society has 200 members. Every fall it holds a bingo party "to get the membership together." Otherwise, its only activity continues to be insurance. Meetings are held on Wednesday after the third Sunday of every other month, beginning with January. Dues are collected according to age.

The St. Mary's Mothers' Club. This club has 164 members.

The club meets the first Thursday of each month, its major aim being to assist the church in its activities. Club members help prepare food for the congregation's annual picnic. On the first Sunday in November, the traditional Christmas Fair takes place, at which the usual items, including sweets and various traditional dishes, are sold.[48]

The Russian-American Club. This social organization for men has 126 members and meets on the first Mondays of January, April, July, and October. It sponsors an annual picnic, one or two dances, an annual banquet, and a card party. Each member pays annual dues of $1.80.

The Russian Library Society. The Russian Library Society was an active educational organization in the early days of the community; today it has become an intimate social group with a membership of twenty-three men and twenty-three women. The second Thursday of each month (except June, July, and August) is their meeting night. Yearly dues are $1.20. No community activity is conducted. The group is composed of the older members of the community.

St. Mary's "R" Club, Chapter No. 94, F.R.O.C. The "R" Club (the "R" stands for Russian) is the only organization within the Russian community that takes an active part in the national organization called the Federated Russian Orthodox Clubs. It is a "youth" organization (ages 18 to 60) sponsored by the Russian Orthodox Church in America, formerly known as the Missionary Church. The headquarters of the organization are at Wilkes-Barre, Pennsylvania, where the organization publishes its monthly magazine, *The Russian Orthodox Journal,* in the English language. In January, 1960, the membership numbered 102 members—forty-five males and fifty-seven females. Eighty-eight of the members lived in the northeast area of Minneapolis, nine in the North, three in other parts of the city, and two in St. Paul.

The vitality of the club is indicated by the relatively great turnover among its officers and the willingness of its members to serve as officers. Meetings of the club are held every second Friday of the month and are quite well attended.

The club's activities are varied—parties, dances, trips, and picnics, for the benefit of the community. The club takes an active interest in the Orthodox Youth Council at the University of Minnesota, and several of its members hold positions on the Council. They participate in the Sunday-school program of the community, many serving as teachers every Sunday morning during the winter season. Some members take an active part in administering the affairs of the church and serve on the board of trustees. In fact, one way to assure one's election to the board of trustees is to serve as a president of the "R" Club.

The "R" Club insures its continued activity by the support of the Junior "R" Club. Athletic activities are the present attraction to the young members (ages 10 through 17) of the Junior "R" Club. There are about fifty junior members, of whom about 60 per cent are boys. Official meetings for the whole membership are held on the first Tuesday of every month.

The St. Mary's Veterans Association.   Another vital organization in the Russian community is made up of those who served in the armed forces of the United States. There are about sixty-five members—sixty males and five females. Eight memberships are honorary —including two women (who did not serve in the armed forces) and two pastors of the church. The meetings of the organization are held the first Monday of every month. Activities include participation in the Memorial Day program, a turkey raffle, the showing of religious films, and the sponsorship of the Russian Open Golf Tournament. The tournament is played annually in August at the Gross Golf Course, and about 150 people participate.

SUMMARY

The major events occurring in conjunction with World War I and the Russian Revolution—a sense of a common military destiny for Russia and the United States, participation in the American war effort, and the eventual cutting of traditional ties with the homeland—tended to transform the Minneapolis Russians into a financially and ideologically autonomous community. These changes coincided with a generational change, for it was about this time that the first American-born groups reached maturity.

These ideological and social facts coincided with the tides of change in the surrounding American environment—the giddy Jazz Age, the dark Depression, and, finally, the beginning of World War II. It was a time of transition, not for the Minneapolis Russian community alone, but for the world as well. It was a period of rapid creation of new social structures; it was also a period of the formation of a rival community. Finally, it was a period when the new semi-assimilated second generation took the affairs of the Russian community into its own hands.

World War II initiated the final changes in the Minneapolis Russian community and gave it its contemporary form. Assimilation to American culture is going forward at a rapid rate. Many of the old brotherhoods have lost importance, being transformed primarily into insurance associations. New groups have taken shape, reflecting the needs of the young. Meanwhile, the Columbia Heights community has melted away, and the recently arrived refugees from Soviet Communism have formed a distinct community oriented toward the homeland rather than toward an Americanized ethnic identity, as is the case with St. Mary's.

NOTES

1. "St. Mary's Honor Roll," *Golden Jubilee Album of St. Mary's Russian Orthodox Greek Catholic Church* (Minneapolis: 1937), pp. 66–7.

2. Courtesy of Mr. J. V. Masica, Keniewski-Loss Post No. 1852, Veterans of Foreign Wars of the U.S., Jan. 18, 1961.

3. "The Platon Club," *Golden Jubilee Album*, p. 111.

4. "Russian-American Club," *ibid.*, pp. 97–9.

5. Articles of Incorporation of the St. Mary's Russian Greek Catholic Church in Minneapolis, Minnesota, Book 265, page 489, Document No. 1421343.

6. Alex Simirenko, "Aspect of the Social and Ideological Adjustment of the Russian Community in Minneapolis." (Unpublished M. A. thesis, University of Minnesota, 1958), pp. 45–6.

7. "St. Mary's Mothers' Club," *Golden Jubilee Album*, p. 113.

8. "Survey of the East District of Minneapolis Prepared to Show the Sources of Constructive and Destructive Influences Affecting Youth" (1923). Gilman Papers, 1899–1952, Box 35, Manuscript Division, Minnesota Historical Society.

9. "St. Mary's Building Committee," *Golden Jubilee Album,* p. 123.

10. "St. Mary's Russian Athletic Club," *ibid.,* pp. 126–7.

11. *Golden Anniversary Souvenir Album of the St. Mary's Russian Orthodox Greek Catholic Church a capella Choir, Minneapolis, Minn.* (Minneapolis: 1941), pp. 18–9.

12. Rev. John Dzubay, ed., "20th Anniversary of St. Mary's 'R' Club, Chapter 94 (1936–1956)" (Minneapolis: 1956).

13. *1960 Year Book and Church Directory of the Russian Orthodox Greek Catholic Church of America* (New York: Metropolitan Council Publications Committee, 1960), p. 171.

14. "F.R.O.C. Anthem," words and music by Anastasia Karnow, in Dzubay, "20th Anniversary of St. Mary's 'R' Club, Chapter 94 (1936–1956)," p. 14.

15. Katherine M. Kohler and Walker A. Anderson, "A Social Survey of 20,000 Families Residing in the Ten Minneapolis Settlement House Districts." pp. 26, 30, 31. Information collected and tabulated by Civil Works Administration and Emergency Administration Workers. (Minneapolis: Adult Education Department, 1934); located with the Gilman Papers, Box 50, Manuscript Division, Minnesota Historical Society.

16. *Ibid.,* pp. 18–9.

17. Cathryn Cooke Gilman, "Neighbors United through Social Settlement Services at the Northeast Neighborhood House, Minneapolis, Minnesota, 1914–1948," 3 vols. (Unpublished manuscript, Minnesota Historical Society), pp. 739, 741, 752.

18. Alex Simirenko, "The Social Structure of the Minneapolis Russian Community," *Proceedings of the Minnesota Academy of Science for 1959,* XXVII (Minneapolis: 1960), 79–86.

19. George Michael Jalma, "The Church of St. Mary the Protectorate," *The Russian Orthodox Journal,* XXV, No. 3 (July, 1951), 6.

20. Peter Barna, attorney for the Minneapolis AFL Building Service Employees Local 26, received the attention of the Minneapolis public at his appointment by the Anoka County District Court to defend James O'Kasick in 1958. *The Minneapolis Star,* March 18, 1955; Feb. 20, 1958.

21. Articles of Incorporation of St. Mary's Veterans Association, Book 828, p. 389, Document No. 3171175, filed April 15, 1959.

22. More information on today's St. Mary's Veterans Association will be found at the end of this chapter.

23. Alex Simirenko, "Aspect of the Social and Ideological Adjustment of the Russian Community in Minneapolis," *op. cit.,* p. 37.

24. *Ibid.,* pp. 37–8.

25. Jalma, *op. cit.,* p. 6.

26. Simirenko, "Aspect of the Social and Ideological Adjustment," p. 38.

27. 1960 Financial Report, St. Mary's Russian Orthodox Greek Catholic Church (Minneapolis, 1960), p. 1.

28. Willmar Thorkelson, "Church Will Build on Site of Landmark," *The Minneapolis Star,* Dec. 13, 1956; Oct. 21, 1957.

29. Jalma, *op. cit.,* p. 6.

30. A personal interview in January, 1958, with Rev. Leonard Soroka, Minneapolis.

31. "Pastor Butchers 'Tito' and 'Stalin': Finds Peace," *The Minneapolis Tribune*, Aug. 4, 1952.

32. Simirenko, "Aspect of the Social and Ideological Adjustment," pp. 46–57.

33. Simirenko, "The Social Structure of the Minneapolis Russian Community," pp. 84–5.

34. "D.P. Group Gets Own Church," *The Minneapolis Star*, April 21, 1956; *The Minneapolis Sunday Tribune*, April 22, 1956.

35. Charles Manna, "Moses of New Land Recalls Tribulations of the Old," *The Minneapolis Morning Tribune*, June 22, 1959.

36. Alex Simirenko, "The Social Structure of the Minneapolis Russian Community," pp. 84–5.

37. Minneapolis Star and Tribune Library, "Biographical Information for Use in the 1947 Municipal Campaign of Paul J. Jaroscak"; "Jaroscak is District Judge," *The Minneapolis Star*, May 28, 1951, announcement of the appointment to the District Court bench; *The Minneapolis Star*, Sept. 3, 1951, news item on oath being taken by Hennepin County Judge Paul J. Jaroscak; "Jaroscak Wins County Bar Vote," *The Minneapolis Star*, Sept. 8, 1952; G. Aaron Youngquist, "Appraising a District Judge," *The Minneapolis Star*, October 27, 1952, and the editorial in the same issue entitled "The Judgeship Contest"; *The Minneapolis Tribune*, October 31, 1952, campaign sketch.

38. Gilman Papers, letter dated January 2, 1947.

39. "Souvenir Book of the 64th Anniversary Summer Festival and Picnic," St. Mary's Russian Orthodox Greek Catholic Church (Minneapolis: 1951), p. 26.

40. Minneapolis Star and Tribune Library, "Biographical Information on Harold Kalina"; "A.F.L. Delegates Reject Move to Ditch Julkowski," *The Minneapolis Tribune*, October 14, 1954; *The Minneapolis Star*, Nov. 11, 1954, description of new state senators; "N.E. Neighborhood House Picks Head," *The Minneapolis Star*, Feb. 16, 1955; *The Minneapolis Star*, Dec. 1, 1956, a biographical sketch of Minnesota legislators; "Legislator Praises Settlement Work," *The Minneapolis Star*, October 21, 1957; "Sen. Kalina," *The Minneapolis Star*, Dec. 11, 1958, a biographical sketch.

41. Minneapolis Star and Tribune Library, "U.S. Bar Association Names City Lawyer," *The Minneapolis Tribune*, Dec. 20, 1953; "William G. Kohlan," *The Minneapolis Star*, Jan. 18, 1954; "Air Vets Elect," *The Minneapolis Star*, Feb. 26, 1954; "Forget-Me-Not Drive to Open," *The Minneapolis Star*, Sept. 15, 1955; "Attorney Elected to State D.F.L. Committee," *The Minneapolis Tribune*, Nov. 29, 1955.

42. Minneapolis Star and Tribune Library, "Andrew G. Kohlan," *The Minneapolis Star*, July 3, 1956; "City Lawyer to Oppose Wier in D.F.L. Primary," *The Minneapolis Tribune*, July 18, 1958; "Words Fly over Renaming Attorney," *The Minneapolis Star*, Jan. 21, 1960.

43. Minneapolis Star and Tribune Library, *The Minneapolis Star*, Oct. 8, 1954; *The Minneapolis Star*, Oct. 17, 1957.

44. "Souvenir Book of the 64th Anniversary Summer Festival and Picnic," St. Mary's Russian Orthodox Greek Catholic Church (Minneapolis: 1951), pp. 33, 49.

45. "73rd Anniversary Souvenir Book, Summer Festival and Picnic," St. Mary's Russian Orthodox Greek Catholic Church (Minneapolis: 1960), pp. 3, 45, 47, 50.

46. "1959 Financial Report," St. Mary's Russian Orthodox Greek Catholic Church (Minneapolis: 1959), p. 4; "1960 Financial Report," St. Mary's Russian Orthodox Greek Catholic Church (Minneapolis: 1960), p. 1.

47. V. Rev. John Dzubay, "St. Mary's 73rd Anniversary," in "73rd Anniversary Souvenir Book," p. 5.

48. "Church Club Plans Fair—Helping Hands are Sometimes Battle-Scarred," *The Minneapolis Star,* Oct. 26, 1960.

6   Changing Occupational and Residential Status

Some difficulties in establishing the true numerical count of Russians in the Minneapolis area or, for that matter, anywhere else in the United States have been discussed in Chapter 3. The problem has been intensified in the case of the Minneapolis Russians because they were, initially, often illiterate peasants. Although the primary objective of the statistical and comparative aspects of this study was to draw samples of the generational groups for comparative analysis, it was deemed wise also to examine independently the changing occupational and residential status of Minneapolis Russians. Since there has been no particular tendency among the Minneapolis Russians to Americanize their names, the resources of the Minneapolis city directory could be drawn upon to trace the demographic and numerical development of a selected group from the earliest period to the present. This source, of course, would yield only male lines.

CRITERIA FOR SELECTION AND SAMPLE NAMES

Thirty-eight representative family names were selected from the present membership lists of St. Mary's Russian Orthodox Church. Each name was unique to the Russian community, and no other Slavic group could be identified with it. The families represented at St. Mary's by the greatest numbers were selected.

The various spellings of the original thirty-eight increased the number of names to fifty:

Barna, Bavolak, Birosch (Biros), Boris (Borris), Brinda, Dupay (Du-Pay), Dzubay, Felegy (Fellegy), Franko, Grivna, Hafich, Havrish, Homzik (Humzik), Jaroscak, Jurichko, Kalina, Kocur, Kohlan (Koch-lan), Kokosh, Kostik (Kostick), Lasho, Lazorik, Leba, Masica (Masika), Mlinar, Podany, Reshetar, Rusinak, Sarich (Sarych), Saledic, Sivanich, Slimak, Tapsak, Tarasar, Tkach, Urista, Varhol (Warhol or Warchol), Zurbay (Zurbey).

These names were traced through every ten-year period from 1880 through 1959. No representative was found for 1880. Eleven people were listed in 1890. In the first two decades, many variations in spelling were found beside those given above, and all were considered in the same category. As the community began to reach stability, the last names also were stabilized with only minor variations. To become less conspicuous, a few people have changed their names. For example, Kohlan has been transformed into Kohen; it could not be taken into account, since it might be confused with a different ethnic group.

While the results of this type of study cannot be considered completely accurate, the figures reveal an approximation of the larger trends within the Russian community. They reveal relative growth in numbers and a trend toward breaking off relations with the community. The changes in relative distribution of occupations and in places of residence are also shown. Of course, we cannot derive from these data an estimate of the population that left Minneapolis for other cities, nor can we compensate for under-representation in the city directories of population at the lower socio-economic levels.

We can, however, take into account these problems when we evaluate the figures.

Of the 930 family names in the 1959 Financial Report of St. Mary's Church, as many as 305 persons are listed under the fifty names chosen for this study. A comparison between the whole roster of members and the representatives of the fifty family names gives the following distribution:

Table 9—Representation of the Fifty Chosen Names

Units	50 FAMILY NAMES No.	%	ST. MARY'S CHURCH No.	%
Families	186	61.0	618	66.5
Lone men	62	20.3	118	12.7
Lone women	57	18.7	170	18.3
Unknown status of men			16	1.7
Unknown status of women			8	0.9
Totals	305	100.0	930	100.1*

* Due to rounding.

RESULTS OF THE STUDY

In the next two tables, the results of the study are summarized. The first shows relative shifts in the occupational profile of the Russian community, while the second illuminates changing residence patterns. These results confirm findings by Warner and his associates that in each successive decade an ethnic group tends to shift its occupational and residential profile in a more favorable direction. The Russian group arrived in Yankee City, Connecticut, in the period 1910–1920, and no such pattern could be ascertained for them when the study was conducted in 1933. The profile of the Irish group in the Yankee City from 1850 to 1933, however, has shown a constant improvement in situation.[1] Such advancement is similar to that of the Minneapolis Russians. Warner and Srole have also noted that some second-generation members of ethnic groups began to move out of the city to seek opportunities elsewhere: "The city is beginning to be too small for them."[2] A similar observation may be true for the Minneapolis Russians since 1950. The highest number of males traced in the seven decades was 381 in 1950. Up to

Analysis of Generational Changes

that time, there appeared to be a constant increase in their numbers, but in 1959, the number had been reduced to 370 men.

Table 10—Occupations of Men and Women in the City Directory Study

	1890	1900	1910	1920	1930	1940	1950	1959
Professional	—	—	1	3	6	7	17	24
Proprietors, managers, and officials:								
A. Wholesale and retail dealers	—	1	4	8	9	5	3	4
B. Others (e.g., saloon and restaurant keepers)	—	—	3	—	2	5	16	32
Clerks and kindred workers	—	1	—	35	98	141	169	134
Skilled workers and foremen	—	6	5	27	66	46	54	66
Semi-skilled	1	8	38	105	149	161	117	110
Unskilled Workers								
A. Laborers	10	41	82	39	59	76	38	20
B. Serving class	—	2	2	11	33	51	34	25
Students	—	—	2	3	2	—	20	13
No occupation reported	—	—	2	22	42	62	79	74
Totals	11	59	139	253	466	554	547	502

* Edwards's classification of occupations was used. See Alba Edwards, *Comparative Occupational Statistics for the U.S., 1870–1940* (Washington, D.C., Government Printing Office, 1943), pp. 176–82.

Table 11—Residence Areas of Men and Women in the City Directory Study

	1890	1900	1910	1920	1930	1940	1950	1959
Northeast	11	58	131	234	399	455	405	320
Columbia Heights and Fridley	—	—	—	1	7	8	5	14
North Minneapolis	—	1	1	5	11	20	45	62
Other parts of Minneapolis	—	—	3	11	45	60	77	83
Suburbs	—	—	1	—	1	8	13	23
No address	—	—	3	2	3	3	2	—
Totals	11	59	139	253	466	544	547	502

LISTINGS FOUND IN THE CITY DIRECTORY

To ascertain how complete the city directory's listings were for the Russian community, the 1959 edition was checked for known members of the community. Of the known 186 families bearing the familiar fifty last names, only 150 or 80.6 per cent were listed. Of the sixty-two men whose marital status was undetermined, only thirty-two or 51.6 per cent were listed. Of fifty-seven women, forty-six or 80.7 per cent were listed. This disparity indicates that perhaps as many as 20 per cent of the families bearing the fifty names who left the Russian community have not been reported in the city directory.

Since 1930, the Minneapolis city directory has been recording in parentheses the names of the spouses of listed individuals. It has therefore been possible to determine the marital status to some extent, although the listings of some professional men did not include the names of their wives. These data reveal certain additional information about the sample of Frontiersmen selected for this study. Since half of the cases in this group came from the city directory, it becomes clear that the sample may actually be somewhat under-represented in the professional and business occupations.

SOME COMPARISONS

The population in the city-directory study was divided into occupational groupings according to the Edwards scale and is therefore particularly appropriate for comparison with the Bureau of Census studies.

Table 12—Male Occupations in 1960

Occupational Grouping	Minneapolis City Directory	Bureau of Census for Minneapolis*
Professional	4.4%	13.3%
Managers and officials	9.4	10.1
Clerical, sales and kindred	20.9	18.8
Skilled and foremen	17.4	19.0
Semi-skilled	25.6	26.6
Unskilled	8.8	6.5
No occupation reported	13.5	5.7
Totals	100.0%	100.0%

It was found that the occupational characteristics of the sampled names were not very different from the characteristics of the general population. There is an expected lag in the professional occupations, which have been slowly increasing since 1910 but which could not be expected to rise to the level of the general population in such a short period. Since 1910, there has also been a constant decline of unskilled laborers, but it is not likely to be so low as 8.8 per cent. The city directories are known to under-represent the unskilled labor groups, and this failure undoubtedly influences the sample. Perhaps some unskilled laborers were recorded under the large category of unreported occupations.

RECAPITULATION

The study of the Minneapolis city directories by ten-year periods was undertaken to fill the gap in available statistics on the Russians in the Minneapolis area. It was important to have some rough estimates of basic information in order to undertake the larger study and to help validate the sample. Three basic estimates have been developed for these purposes:

An approximate growth in the number of Russians in Minneapolis; an approximate occupational distribution among the Russians in Minneapolis along with their increasing participation in the professional and business life of the community; and an approximate residence distribution and indication of changes in locus of residence throughout the past seventy years.

The occupational and residential mobility of individual members of the Russian community has been rising slowly with each decade. It took two decades for the community to produce its first professional man and one more to produce two additional such men. By 1959, however, the sample included twenty-four individuals of professional standing. The social improvement of Minneapolis Russians resembles the experience of the Irish group in Yankee City, as outlined by Warner and his associates.

Occupational comparison between the city-directory sample and the general male population in Minneapolis showed the expected disparities within certain categories. This result tends to confirm that the city-directory study provides an approximate representation of the occupational and other trends in the Russian community from 1890 to the present.

NOTES

1. W. Lloyd Warner and Leo Srole, *The Social Systems of American Ethnic Groups,* "Yankee City Series," Vol. III (New Haven: Yale University Press, 1945), pp. 30–75.

2. *Ibid.,* p. 66.

7   Class Changes within the
Russian Community

By DEFINITION, people with common access to wealth occupy similar class positions. This definition is a bit broader than Max Weber's definition of class standing: "The typical chance for a supply of goods, external living conditions, and personal life experiences, in so far as this chance is determined by the amount and kind of power, or lack of such, to dispose of goods or skills for the sake of income in a given economic order."[1] The source of wealth may consist of property or the possession of particular skills or values exchangeable for others. The decline of the independent entrepreneur in American society in this century has diminished the importance of property ownership as a determinant of class position, making a broader conception of class advisable.[2]

A SHORT REVIEW OF PROCEDURES AND AIMS

In the development (see Chapter 2) of a design for study of social change in an ethnic group, three distinct types representing variant degrees of adjustment to the majority community were isolated:

the Pilgrims, the Colonists, and the Frontiersmen. Two general hypotheses were formulated concerning their accommodation to the ordered community: The system of stratification in the ethnic community is gradually destroyed with the rise of later generations, and the economic and professional advancement of later generations brings about cultural assimilation with and dispersal among members of the majority community.

Six working hypotheses concerning specific changes in particular generational units may be derived from these two general hypotheses: Continuous improvement of class standing occurs in successive generations; the second generation achieves higher status in the ethnic community than the first; some members of the second generation lose ethnic group standing as they begin to seek status outside the ethnic community; the second generation has greater power in the ethnic community than the first; some members of the second generation lose power as they move outside the ethnic community; and members of successive generations show increasing acculturation until they become indistinguishable from members of the majority community.

In the absence of standardized scales to measure the distinct properties of class, status, power, and acculturation, four scales were developed expressly for this study to test these hypotheses: a class scale, a status scale, a power scale, and an acculturation scale. Since the scales were used for the first time in this study and since their reliability was tested in relation only to this study, each item in each scale is presented individually for discussion and comparison with findings of other studies. When possible, the significance of difference among the three groups was tested by chi square.[3] When numbers or percentages are reported, it is understood that unless otherwise stated the number of families in the Pilgrim group was twenty-nine; in the Colonist group, forty-two; and in the Frontiersmen group, thirty-four.

THE AGE DIFFERENCE

The age difference between the first-generation and the two groups of second-generation Minneapolis Russians may influence comparison on some of the items. The median ages of women among the Pilgrims were between fifty-five and fifty-nine, of the men in the same group between sixty and sixty-four. The Colonists' median ages were between thirty-five and thirty-nine for women and between forty and forty-four for men. The median ages for the Frontiersmen were the same as for the Colonists.

MALE OCCUPATIONS

Two studies of occupational mobility in the 1950s (one by Natalie Rogoff,[4] the other by W. Lloyd Warner and James C. Abegglen[5]) were in part concerned with comparative influences on mobility among those of foreign parentage. Unfortunately, no distinction among the various ethnic groups was drawn, limiting the possibilities for application to the present study. It was found, however, that in 1910 and in 1940 the sons of foreign-born fathers were more mobile than the sons of native-born fathers. While in 1910, it was rather difficult for sons of foreign-born fathers to advance in some occupations (for example, from clerical and sales occupations), by 1940 "in every class sons of foreign born fathers experienced as much or more ease in moving out of their fathers' class than sons of native born fathers."[6] Natalie Rogoff explained this change in her comment that by 1940 "the sons of foreign born fathers were less restricted by social and personal factors than sons of native born fathers in their mobility into the rewarding occupations."[7]

In their profile of the American business elite in 1928 and 1952, Warner and Abegglen presented data that supports Rogoff's findings. They pointed out that, while foreign-born individuals in the United States have little chance to assume the highest business positions, they occupy a disproportionately high number of the lower business positions. In 1952, when 7.5 per cent of the United States' white population was foreign born, 5 per cent of the business leaders were foreign born.[8]

The advantages for the sons of foreign-born fathers are greater than those for their fathers. In 1952, 20 per cent of all the business leaders of the United States were sons of foreign-born parents.

Furthermore, the sons of lower-status foreign-born fathers were found to be more mobile than the sons of lower-status native-born men.[9] Warner and Abegglen concluded:

In a generation, the disadvantage of foreign birth in movement to the top positions of the business hierarchy disappears—a powerful testimonial to the efficiency of the American "melting pot."[10]

The findings of the present study are similar to those of the Rogoff and Warner-Abegglen studies. The second generation has abandoned the typical jobs of its fathers. While 55.2 per cent of the Pilgrims reported unskilled jobs, only 9.5 per cent of the Colonists and 2.9 per cent of the Frontiersmen reported similiar employment. At the same time, male unskilled personnel (labor and service) in the urban Minnesota area constituted 12.5 per cent of all employed workers.[11] No managerial, professional, or semi-professional person was found in the Pilgrim group and only seven among the Colonists, while there were as many as eighteen among the Frontiersmen. For purposes of statistical comparison, the managerial and professional categories have been combined. There were more professionals among the Colonists (six) than among the Frontiersmen (only two). The Frontiersmen, however, had sixteen managerial and semi-professional occupations compared to only one in the Colonist group. Skilled occupations predominated in the Colonist group.

Table 13—Occupations of Men

Occupation	Pilgrims	Colonists	Frontiersmen
Unskilled	55.2%	9.5%	2.9%
Skilled and semi-skilled	34.5	57.1	35.3
Clerical-sales	10.3	16.7	8.8
Managerial, semi-professional, professional	—	16.7	52.9
Totals	100.0%	100.0%	99.9%
Chi square (P, C, F) =	48.9	6 d.f.	p < .001
Chi square (C, F) =	11.3	3 d.f.	p < .01

It is clear that the profile of occupational change among Minneapolis Russians compares favorably with that of the foreign born in the United States at large.

THE ANNUAL FAMILY INCOME

Family income represents an important component of class membership. Income, however, does not remain stable from year to year. Periodic work by a wife may induce a sharp fluctuation in the income of a particular family. As income distribution changes, the relative position of the family may also vary.

In general, the occupation of the head of the family is more stable than income and measures potential income with fair accuracy. The class superiority of a university professor over an experienced plumber is not based on actual annual income, for the plumber probably earns more while the professor has a greater social mobility and potential earning power.

In 1959 the median income of families in the Minneapolis-St. Paul urban areas was $6,890. The median income of families consisting of husband and wife with one earner and two children under eighteen years old was $6,917.[12] This family portrait is typical for the Colonist and Frontiersman groups of Russians in the Minneapolis area. As could be expected, the incomes of families in our samples are closely related to the occupations of the men. Significant differences were found in the joint incomes of families in the three groups. Only five families in the total sample (4.8 per cent) earned $10,000 or more a year, while in the Minneapolis-St. Paul area, 20 per cent of the families earned this sum in 1959. Two of the Russian families were in the Colonist group, while three were among the Frontiersmen—in accord with the occupational gradient predicted by the hypotheses of the study. Nine families, or 31 per cent, in the Pilgrim group earned less than $3,000 annually, while only 10 per cent of the families in the general Minneapolis-St. Paul population earned this amount.[13] Here again the economically underprivileged situation of an ethnic group was apparent. The median family earnings of Colonists and Frontiersmen were between $5,000 and $7,500.

The income of the families in our samples reflects their ethnic and peasant backgrounds. Immigrants from eastern and southern European countries usually occupy lower class positions in the United States. When Hollingshead and Redlich stratified the New Haven

Table 14—Joint Family Income

Income	Pilgrims	Colonists	Frontiersmen
Under $5,000	75.9%	29.3%	8.8%
$5,000–$7,500	17.2	34.1	58.8
$7,500 and over	6.9	36.6	32.3
Totals	100.0%	100.0%	99.9%
Chi square (P, C, F) =	34.1	4 d.f.	p < .001
Chi square (C, F) =	6.5	2 d.f.	p < .05

population into five socio-economic classes in 1950, they also discovered a differential distribution of income throughout these classes. Class I had a median income of $10,000; class II of $6,500; class III of $5,000; class IV of $3,812; and class V of $2,659. The ethnic backgrounds of the first three classes were made up largely of those with northern European backgrounds, while the fourth and fifth classes were composed of eastern and southern Europeans, including the Slavic population.[14] The incomes of the interviewed groups in the Minneapolis area are larger than the incomes of classes four and five in Hollingshead's study, since the income level of the general population has considerably increased since 1950.

In 1950, urban and rural nonfarm American families had a median income of $3,497. In 1958, median family income had risen to $5,331.[15] If adjustments are made for this increase in income, the findings of the present study correspond quite closely to those of Hollingshead and Redlich.

OWNERSHIP OF A BUSINESS, CAPITAL, AND TOOLS

Scales that seek to measure socio-economic standing do not usually include questions on income distribution, often because of the difficulty of determining respondents' incomes. Hollingshead and Redlich reported an indignant response to the question of income by an elderly gentleman from a distinguished New Haven family: "We have it."[16] The income question was initially included by Warner in the Index of Social Characteristics, but although it correlated with other factors, the information was difficult to obtain, and the factor was ultimately dropped from the Index.[17]

When discussing the limitations of income data, the United States Bureau of the Census claimed that reports are frequently based on memory and not on accurate records. Other errors occur through misunderstanding.[18] Similar problems arise when respondents are asked to report ownership of business or capital to estimate its worth. As a result, this question is usually omitted from most studies, and it is difficult to find data for comparative purposes. Warner attacked this problem indirectly in the Index of Status Characteristics by asking a question on the source of the individual's income. Respondents were stratified according to either inherited wealth or earned wealth; they lived either on profits and fees, salary, wages, private relief, or public relief and nonrespectable income.[19] It was known in advance, however, that the sources of income of the Minneapolis Russians were wages, and such a question would not distinguish among the three groups. It was therefore more important to isolate individuals possessing at least some accumulated wealth as distinguished from those who had none. Of the Frontiersmen, 26 per cent owned some kind of business or capital equipment, compared to 14 per cent of the Colonists and 10 per cent of the Pilgrims. Although the difference was in the predicted direction, it was not found to be statistically significant.[20] Of the three Pilgrim families who reported ownership of business or capital, two families valued it under $10,000, and one family valued it at $50,000 or more. Of the six Colonist families, two valued their businesses under $10,000, three families between $10,000 and $30,000, and one family at $50,000 or more. Of the Frontiersmen, five families valued their possessions under $10,000, and four families valued them between $10,000 and $30,000.

As ownership of capital affects a family's situation in the marketplace, the ownership of tools by the head of the family gives him a certain independence at his work. Of the total sample, thirty-seven men used some kind of personal tools or equipment in their trades. The Pilgrims used relatively inexpensive tools: five of them valued theirs under $100, and one valued his between $100 and $300. The value of tools among the sixteen Colonists was more varied: seven (43.8 per cent) under $100, two (12.5 per cent) between $100 and $300, two (12.5 per cent) between $300 and $500, one (6.3 per cent) between $500 and $1,000, and four (25 per cent) $1,000 and over. The fifteen Frontiersmen used somewhat more expensive tools than either the Pilgrims or the Colonists. Two of them (13.3 per cent) priced their tools under $100, five (33.3 per cent) between $100 and $300, two (13.3 per cent) between $300 and $500, one (6.7 per cent) between $500 and $1,000, and five (33.3 per cent) valued their tools at $1,000 or more.

CLASS-SCALE COMPARISON OF THE THREE GROUPS

When comparing the class positions of the three groups on the scale expressly devised for this task, significant differences were discovered. The class scale, the shortest scale of the four, contained only four items. Each item was given weight from one to five points. Individual families whose total mean scale score was closer to point one represented the least advantageous class position; families with mean scale scores over four points represented the highest class position. The mean scale scores for the whole group were established by adding all the mean scores of individual families and then dividing the total by the number of families in the particular group. The scale score results of the class scale were as follows:

Table 15—Results of the Class Scale Comparison

Group	Mean Scale Score
Pilgrims	1.7
Colonists	2.3
Frontiersmen	2.7

Table 16—Class Scale Comparison

Scale Score	Pilgrims No.	Colonists No.	Frontiersmen No.	Total No.
1	56	47	28	131
2	26	40	25	91
3	8	26	29	63
4	2	15	25	42
5	1	13	10	24
Totals	93	141	117	351
Chi square (P, C, F) =		50.7	8 d.f.	p < .01
Chi square (C, F) =		9.5	4 d.f.	p < .05

By chi square tests, significant differences were discovered among the groups. The results are shown in Table 16.

RECAPITULATION

The comparative class standing of families in each of the three groups was measured by a scale containing four items: occupations of men, annual family income, ownership of business, and ownership of tools. Significant differences among Pilgrims, Colonists, and Frontiersmen were discovered with respect to two important class variables: the occupations of men and joint family annual income. The findings of Natalie Rogoff and Warner and Abegglen for ethnic groups in general were in accord with those for Russians in the Minneapolis area. More than half the men in the Pilgrim group were found in the unskilled occupations, while more than half of those in the Colonist group performed skilled tasks. At the same time, more than half the men in the Frontiersmen group belonged in either a managerial, semi-professional, or professional category.

The Russians in the New Haven area were found to earn lower annual incomes than the general population or the ethnic groups with northern European backgrounds. The income figures for these New Haven families gathered in 1950 were considerably lower than those of Minneapolis Russians in 1960. If adjustments are made for the general national rise of incomes in the past decade, however, it becomes clear that the incomes of the Russians in the Minneapolis area are similar to those in the New Haven area. The Russians in Minneapolis were found to differ in terms of the generational unit they represented. The joint family annual incomes of a great majority of Pilgrims were below $5,000. In the Colonist group, close to 30 per cent of the families received incomes below $5,000 in comparison to less than 10 per cent of the families in the Frontiersmen group.

The class-scale comparison among Pilgrims, Colonists, and Frontiersmen yielded significant results. The Pilgrims had a mean scale score of 1.7; the Colonists 2.3; and the Frontiersmen 2.7. The chi square comparison also yielded significant results. As predicted, the Frontiersmen tended to be in a better class position than either the Pilgrims or the Colonists. On the other hand, the Colonists had greater access to wealth and its advantages than did the Pilgrims.

NOTES

1. Max Weber, *From Max Weber, Essays in Sociology*, trans. and edited by Hans H. Gerth and C. Wright Mills (New York: Oxford University Press, 1946), p. 181.

2. Hans H. Gerth and C. Wright Mills, *Character and Social Structure* (New York: Harcourt, Brace & Co., 1953), pp. 307–14; C. Wright Mills, *White Collar* (New York: Oxford University Press, 1951). Chapters 1–4; Joseph A. Kahl, *The American Class Structure* (New York: Rinehart & Co., Inc., 1957), pp. 91–121.

3. The computation of the chi square was performed with the short formula of Walker and Lev, *Statistical Inference* (New York: Henry Holt & Co., 1953), p. 99. See also Francis G. Cornell, *The Essentials of Educational Statistics* (New York: John Wiley & Sons, 1956), p. 203.

4. Natalie Rogoff, *Recent Trends in Occupational Mobility* (New York: The Free Press of Glencoe, 1953.

5. W. Lloyd Warner and James C. Abegglen, *Occupational Mobility in American Business and Industry* (Minneapolis: University of Minnesota Press, 1955).

6. Rogoff, *op. cit.*, p. 85.

7. *Ibid.*, p. 90.

8. Warner and Abegglen, *op. cit.*, pp. 27, 90.

9. *Ibid.*, pp. 27, 90, 94.

10. *Ibid.*, p. 90.

11. U.S. Bureau of the Census, *U.S. Census of Population: 1960*, Final Report PC (1) 25C (Washington, D.C.: U.S. Government Printing Office, 1961), Table 57.

12. *Ibid.*, Table 76.

13. *Ibid.* Since a number of Pilgrims were on retirement, the question was asked about their pre-retirement income, making the apparent difference between the Pilgrim families' incomes and those of the general population somewhat smaller.

14. August B. Hollingshead and Frederick C. Redlich, *Social Class and Mental Illness: A Community Study* (New York: John Wiley & Sons, Inc., 1958), pp. 70, 89, 96, 106, 116–7.

15. U.S. Bureau of the Census, *Statistical Abstract of the U.S., 1961* (Washington, D.C.: U.S. Government Printing Office, 1961), Table 434.

16. Hollingshead and Redlich, *op. cit.*, p. 71.

17. W. Lloyd Warner, Marchia Meeker, and Kenneth Eells, *Social Class in America: A Manual of Procedure for the Measurement of Social Status* (Chicago: Science Research Associates, 1949), p. 154.

18. U.S. Bureau of the Census, *U.S. Census of Population: 1960*, p. xxv.

19. Warner, Meeker, and Eells, *op. cit.*, p. 123.

20. Chi square 3.4 with two degrees of freedom, $p < .25$.

8 Status Changes within the
Russian Community

A STATUS GROUP consists of those who share equivalent honor or deference granted on the basis of valid claims. These claims may be based in turn upon many factors including "property and descent, occupation and education, income and power—in fact, almost anything that may invidiously distinguish one person from another."[1] While class and power position may influence the status of an individual, it does not exclusively determine it. Max Weber was categorical on this issue:

Quite generally, "mere economic" power, and especially "naked" money power, is by no means a recognized basis of social honor. Nor is power the only basis of social honor. Indeed, social honor, or prestige, may even be the basis of political or economic power, and very frequently has been.[2]

Warner and Lunt have presented empirical findings that demonstrate the correctness of Weber's position. Examining the status of some of the wealthiest men in town, they concluded that "great wealth did not guarantee the highest social position. Something else was necessary."[3] The inhabitants of Yankee City justified their assignment of low status to a wealthy man by the fact that "he and his family do not act right."[4]

Blumenthal presented similar evidence. He observed that it was difficult for an individual or his family in the small town of Mineville to improve his status, which tended to be established at the time of arrival. According to Blumenthal, "some families have advanced far financially and yet have been able to move but little from their original ratings in the eyes of the community."[5] At the same time, families of high status continued to receive deference "long after they . . . lost the financial positions or other sorts of eminence which had so much influence in giving them their original stations in the community."[6]

Individuals may employ various strategies to achieve their goals. Some may use the advantages they already possess to advance themselves in other respects. Some may renounce certain values for the sake of others. Max Weber illustrates this point with his examples of the typical American "boss" and the business speculator who sacrificed strivings for honor.[7] On the other hand, Blumenthal observed that certain high status families in Mineville refused to leave town and exchange status advantages for economic advantages available elsewhere.[8]

All these considerations suggest the value of measuring the changing dimensions of status among the three groups of Minneapolis Russians, apart from their class positions. Since family status is exhibited in style of life, it is possible to compare the behavior of one family with another. A status scale was developed to measure the differential use of status symbols by the Pilgrims, Colonists, and Frontiersmen.

EDUCATION

With the exception of the social position of one's ancestors, the amount and kind of education are usually accepted as the most important variable in the allocation of status. Hollingshead considered

it an important index of tastes and attitudes and included it as one
of the two basic factors for measuring the social position of individuals.[9]

At other times, education is considered simply as an important
index of class situation rather than of status, since educational advancement tends to be correlated with that of occupation.[10] The
studies of Warner and Srole, however, indicate that members of
ethnic groups view education as more than a mere stepping stone to
economic advancement. In fact, when economic advancement is the
paramount goal, they often insist that children leave school as soon
as possible and help provide for the family. One son of foreign-born
parents remarked: "Most . . . people are after the money and send
their children to work as soon as possible."[11] Other families, however, "defer class gratification" until later and encourage their children to secure the best educations possible. Some ethnic groups are
more favorably disposed toward education than others. Lipset and
Bendix report that particularly strong emphasis on education exists
among the Jews, Japanese, Scots, Armenians, and Czechs.[12]

Schools tend to train their students to appreciation of a particular style of life. Since most public schools in the United States are
typically middle class, the teachers tend to imbue their students
with attitudes and values toward the world that are characteristic of
this class.[13] This training is particularly valuable for the children
of foreign-born parents with peasant backgrounds, for they can thus
be directly acculturated into the dominant stratum of American society. The more extensive the education of members of ethnic groups,
the more adept they become at manipulating the status symbols of
American society.

The educational profile of the Minneapolis Russians is distinct
from that of the general population of the Minneapolis-St. Paul
area. The Pilgrims, who had little formal education, were handi-
capped not only by their ethnicity but also by their ages, since
universal public education was unknown in their day. The Colonists
and Frontiersmen, on the other hand, possessed greater formal education than the general population. Males over twenty-five years old
who had never gone beyond elementary school composed 31 per

cent of the men living in the Twin Cities. In comparison, 69 per cent of the Pilgrims, and only 7 and 6 per cent of the Colonists and Frontiersmen, respectively, attended only elementary school. Thirty-eight per cent of the Colonists and 50 per cent of the Frontiersmen attended college, in comparison to 26 per cent of the males in the general population. The smallest difference is shown in attendance at high schools: 43 per cent of the general population and 55 and 44 per cent of the Colonists and Frontiersmen, respectively.[14] As expected, significant differences were found between the formal schooling of the first and second generations.

Table 17—Formal Education of Men

Years of School	Pilgrims	Colonists	Frontiersmen
1–8	68.9%	7.1%	5.9%
9–12	24.1	54.7	44.1
Some college	6.9	38.1	50.0
Totals	99.9%	99.9%	100.0%
Chi square (P, C, F) =	47.5	4 d.f.	p < .001
Chi square (C, F) =	1.1	2 d.f.	n.s.

A smiliar breakdown of educational backgrounds was found among the women. In the general population of Minneapolis-St. Paul, 28 per cent of the women attended school only below high school level, 52 per cent attended high school, and 20 per cent had some college education.[15] In comparison with these figures, the Pilgrims had relatively little education, while the Colonists and Frontiersmen had a higher educational background. Four women among the Pilgrims had four years of school or less; among the Colonists and Frontiersmen, all women had more than four years of schooling. In the Pilgrim group 72.4 per cent of the women received between one and eight years of schooling, 20.7 per cent between nine and twelve years, and 6.9 per cent had some college work. In the Colonist group, 7.1 per cent completed between one and eight grades, 69 per cent completed between nine and twelve grades, and 23.8 per cent went to college. In the Frontiersmen group, 76.5 per cent attended between nine and twelve grades, and 23.5 cent attended college.[16]

It is gratifying that figures are available for comparison of educational backgrounds between the Minneapolis Russians and another ethnic group, the Jews in Detroit. The Jews are generally regarded as one of the most mobile and most educationally oriented ethnic groups in American society.[17] Nevertheless, educational profiles of the three groups of Minneapolis Russians (N = 210), with their relatively recent peasant past, compared favorably with those of the Jewish population in Detroit. None of the Russians or the Jews was without any formal education. Elementary or grammer school was attended by 23.3 per cent of the Russians and 22 per cent of the Jews. High school attendance was reported by 50.5 per cent of the Russians and 51 per cent of the Jews; and some college was attended by 26.1 per cent of the Russians and 26 per cent of the Jews.[18]

THE OCCUPATIONS OF THE FATHERS

The occupations of the fathers have two-fold importance for the changing status dimensions of the Minneapolis Russians: They reflect the preparation that the children may have received at home for a particular style of life, and they are likely to influence the educational achievements of the children. Lipset and Bendix found that children of fathers with low-status occupations tended to receive less schooling than children of fathers with high-status occupations. Even when educational attainments of children from different status groups are held constant, it is likely that the sons of nonmanual workers will start working at nonmanual jobs, while the sons of manual workers will begin work in manual occupations. The authors conclude that "if an individual comes from a working-class family, he will typically receive little education or vocational advice."[19]

Educational, as well as occupational, mobility has nevertheless been possible for sons of fathers performing low-status occupations. Among American business leaders in 1952, 15 per cent had fathers who were laborers, 8 per cent white-collar workers, and 9 per cent farmers.[20] The findings of this study clearly indicate that each generation has increased its occupational mobility, as well as its education. When the occupational backgrounds of fathers in the three groups are compared, the great majority are seen to fall into categories of skilled and unskilled labor. A small minority of Colonists and Frontiersmen come from clerical, managerial, and semi-professional backgrounds. Among the Pilgrims, 91.4 per cent had fathers who were unskilled,[21] and 8.6 per cent who were either skilled or semi-skilled (N = 58). Among the Colonists, 47.6 per cent had unskilled fathers, 38.1 per cent either skilled or semi-skilled, 2.4 per cent who performed clerical or sales work, 10.7 per cent either in the managerial or semi-professional group, and 1.2 per cent professionals (N = 84). Among the Frontiersmen, 47 per cent had fathers who were unskilled, 43.9 per cent either skilled or semi-skilled, 4.5 per cent were performing clerical or sales work, 3 per cent managers or semi-professionals, and 1.5 per cent professionals (N = 66). The relatively similar occupational profiles of the fathers of Colonists and Frontiersmen were to be expected, since both groups belonged to the same generation and shared similiar initial advantages and disadvantages.

THE OCCUPATIONS OF WOMEN

The employment of wives and mothers is a more sensitive index of a family's status in American society. The working mother (whose husband is head of the family) contributes to the improvement of her family's class position, often at the the expense of activities that might add to the family's status. A working female in the Minneapolis-St. Paul area brought home in 1959 an average of $2,500.[22] Studies of American communities reveal that the higher a family's socio-economic position, the more likely it is that the wife will remain a homemaker. In Elmtown, Hollingshead distinguished five different classes with the aid of a panel of judges. He discovered that Class I members—the elite of the community—considered "leisure, not labor, . . . dignified." Married women in Class II were mothers and homemakers, but some served as social secretaries. In Class III, 17 per cent were employed. This proportion increased to 30 per cent in Class IV and to 55 per cent in Class V.[23]

Hollingshead's next study—of New Haven, Connecticut, with more than 160,000 population in 1950—produced similar results. It was found, however, that in the larger city some wives from the two top classes in the community were also employed, but in smaller proportions than those of other classes.[24] Class I families had 8 per cent of wives working; Class II, 17 per cent; Class III, 28 per cent; Class IV, 37 per cent; and Class V, 48 per cent.[25]

If one were to stratify the three groups of Minneapolis Russians according to the distribution of working wives in the New Haven population, the Pilgrim group, with its 38 per cent of wives working, would be placed in Class IV; the Frontiersmen group with 29 per cent in Class III, and the Colonists with only 14 per cent in Class II.[26] In comparison, 32.2 per cent of the married women in the Twin Cities were in the labor force in 1960. Women with children under six years of age were less likely to be found in the labor force— only 17.7 per cent.[27] It was to be expected that second-generation Russians would be found in smaller numbers in the labor force, since many of them have families of small children. It is interesting to note, however, that the Colonist women with children under six years of age compose 45 per cent of the group, while women in this group constitute 53 per cent among the Frontiersmen. Nevertheless, more Frontiersmen's wives took jobs to improve the family's class position.

In the New Haven study women of different classes were found performing different kinds of work. In Class V, 56 per cent worked at semi-skilled factory jobs, and the rest performed a variety of unskilled jobs—as maids, cleaning women, sorters in the laundry, and so forth. In Class IV, they performed various forms of semi-skilled factory work, while some held clerical and sales jobs.[28] Russian women in the Pilgrim group were found in jobs similar to those of the New Haven women in Classes IV and V: Five held unskilled jobs, four were in semi-skilled occupations, and two were in clerical and sales positions. In New Haven, 59 per cent of Class III working women performed clerical and sales jobs, 11 per cent were technicians and elementary school teachers, while the rest helped to operate small family businesses.[29] A smiliar occupational profile was reflected in the second generation of Russian women in Minneapolis. In the Colonist group, one woman performed an unskilled job, one worked at a skilled or semi-skilled job, three women performed clerical and sales tasks, and one managed a small family store. In the Frontiersman group, five women were employed in skilled and/or semi-skilled occupations, four in clerical and sales positions, and one as a nurse. The occupations of women in Classes I and II, which include primarily professional and managerial positions, were out of reach for this Russian group.

RESPONSE TO CLASSICAL CULTURE

Writing in the days when wealth was required to partake in the pleasures of classical culture, Thorstein Veblen nevertheless distinguished between class, status, and power:

> In order to gain and to hold the esteem of men, it is not sufficient merely to possess wealth or power. The wealth or power must be put in evidence, for esteem is awarded only on evidence.[30]

To receive deference, special living standards and leisure had to be cultivated, among which the appreciation of classical culture was paramount. (Joseph Kahl calls it the art of graceful living.) The characteristic property of modern American society, however, is that the enjoyment of classical culture is no longer a prerogative of the wealthy. A person of modest means can successfully cultivate status tastes if he so wishes. In contemporary conditions, whole new categories of men have been known to distinguish themselves as connoisseurs of taste. This observation led Russell Lynes to the following conclusion:

> Good taste and bad taste, adventurous and timid taste, cannot be explained by wealth or education, by breeding or background. Each of these plays a part, but there is no longer such a thing as upper class taste and lower class taste as there was once supposed to be. In recent years a new social structure has emerged in which taste and intellectual

pretension and accomplishment plays a major role. What we see growing around us is a sort of social stratification in which the highbrows are the elite, the middlebrows are the bourgeoisie, and the lowbrows are *hoi polloi*. . . . Some lowbrows are rich . . . some . . . poor. . . . Some highbrows eat caviar with their Proust; some eat hamburger when they can afford it.[31]

According to Lynes, the modern refuge of the highbrow is a university town. Most likely he is a low-paid professional, perhaps a professor of languages, but he may be found in other places and occupations as well. A 1955 study of occupational differences in leisure activities supports Lynes's assertion that the modern day taste-maker is not an aristocrat or a wealthy patron in the old sense, but a professional person.

Studying the uses of leisure in Columbus, Ohio, Clarke discovered that the various events associated with "high culture" were attended most frequently by those who are in professional occupations. Their activities included attending plays, concerts, or special lectures, visiting museums or art galleries, reading for pleasure, and studying. Activities in which service workers, semi-skilled workers, and unskilled workers most often participated included watching television, fishing, playing poker, driving or riding in cars, attending open air auto theatres, spending time in taverns, and attending baseball games.[32]

PREFERENCE IN MUSIC

Being removed by only a generation or two from their peasant past, the Russians in Minneapolis could not be expected to show an astounding appreciation of classical culture. Yet in the past two decades the United States population has shown an increasing interest in various forms of cultural expression, and it is quite likely that at least the new generation of Russians has been influenced by this movement. Kaplan presents quantitative evidence of the recent popularity of fine music in the United States:

Expenditures in 1957 of 500 million dollars for concert tickets, 80 million dollars for classical records, 166 million dollars for hi-fi equipment and tapes, and 40 million dollars for published concert music and teaching pieces. The total of 336 million dollars compares with 240 million dollars spent in the same year for spectator sports.[33]

In our study, significant differences were discovered among all three groups in their musical preferences, for both men and women. The Pilgrims tended to favor the old-time folk music; the Colonists appreciated the semi-classical; and the Frontiersmen preferred popular music. More men than women liked folk music, the traditional music of the village, but at the same time slightly larger numbers of men also preferred jazz and/or classical music.

Women favoring the old-time music formed 65.2 per cent among the Pilgrims (N = 23), 23.8 per cent among the Colonists, and only 2.9 per cent among the Frontiersmen. Popular music was most enjoyed by 8.7 per cent of Pilgrim women, 11.9 per cent of the Colonists, and 41.2 per cent of the Frontiersmen. Semi-classical music was preferred by 21.7 per cent of the Pilgrims, 54.7 per cent of the Colonists, and 38.2 per cent of the Frontiersmen. Jazz and/or classical music was favored most by the Frontiersmen; otherwise it was the least preferred type. The Pilgrim women's group favored it with 4.3 per cent, the Colonist group with 9.5 per cent, and the Frontiersman group with 17.6 per cent.[34]

Men who preferred the old time music consisted of 79.2 per cent in the Pilgrim group, 35.7 per cent in the Colonist group, and 14.7 per cent in the Frontiersman group. Popular music was favored by 4.2 per cent of the Pilgrims, 9.5 per cent of the Colonists, and as high as 44.1 per cent of the Frontiersmen. Semi-classical music was listed by 12.5 per cent of the Pilgrims, 47.6 per cent of the Colonists, and 17.6 per cent of the Frontiersmen. Jazz and/or classical music was preferred by 4.2 per cent of the Pilgrims, 7.1 per cent of the Colonists, and 23.5 per cent of the Frontiersmen.[35] The shift in taste had already occurred in the first generation, but the most dramatic change is seen in the distinct tastes of the groups in the second generation. The Frontiersmen, who consider themselves completely Americanized, cling to the most popular music in American society.

The Colonists, on the other hand, seem to be more keenly aware of status differences among various types of music and prefer the semiclassical.

ATTENDANCE AT THE THEATRE AND SYMPHONY CONCERTS

In 1919, J. S. Cole made a study of recreational pursuits among Russian single men in Chicago. He found that their most popular form of recreation was visits to the saloon; next came attendance at movie houses; the third interest was reading; and fourth place was divided between dancing and music. Only three men out of ninety-eight respondents claimed that they visited the theatre.[36]

Similar low attendance at plays was probably also true for the first generation of the Russian community in Minneapolis. Occasional attendance has been reported by 3.4 per cent of the Pilgrims, 33.3 per cent of the Colonists, and 14.7 per cent of the Frontiersmen. The Colonists not only appreciated semi-classical music, but they also liked to go to the theatre.[37] At the same time, attendance at symphony concerts, which was mentioned by none of the ninety-eight Russian men in Chicago, also remains rare for the Russians in Minneapolis. Occasional attendance was reported by 20.7 per cent of the Pilgrims, 16.7 per cent of the Colonists, and 11.8 per cent of the Frontiersmen. Many of the concerts attended were free during the summer at Lake Harriet in Minneapolis. Proportionately, the Frontiersmen were least interested in such experiences of "high culture."[38]

VACATION ACTIVITY

During his leisure time, a man is free to turn his attention to things that make his life more worthwhile.[39] In the various leisure activities that men pursue, one can observe their intrinsic values. Recognition of this fact led Giddings to write that "a people can be judged and career can be predicted from the character of its pleasures, with more accuracy than from any other data."[40] Robert and Helen Lynd echoed Giddings: "What a people does with its leisure . . . affords a sensitive index to its values."[41] A vacation provides a family with considerable time in which to satisfy whatever aspirations it may have.

Different socio-economic classes respond in their own ways to vacation opportunities. When summer comes, Class I women and children of Elmtown move to lake cottages and are visited by their husbands and fathers during weekends. Every January or February, the family takes a vacation in California or Florida. The most popular leisure activity of Elmtown upper class society is travel, says Hollingshead.[42] In New Haven, the Class I family was expected to be absent from home between July 4 and Labor Day and to reside in its own cottage in the mountains, on the lake shore, or by the sea. In addition, for several weeks a year family members occupied either fishing or hunting lodges.[43]

No family among the Minneapolis Russians has ever had the kind of vacation enjoyed by the upper classes. All vacations by couples are generally spent together. Even the idea of separate vacations was quite strange to the persons interviewed. Five families in the total sample reported that the husbands' work has not permitted them to enjoy vacations as families.

Different vacation patterns are pursued by the two generations of Minneapolis Russians. Families in the Pilgrim group prefer either to remain at home and work around the house or else to visit relatives or friends. The Colonists and Frontiersmen, however, prefer short trips in family cars and fishing and hunting at small expense. The vacation pattern of the Pilgrims somewhat resembles that of Class V of the New Haven families; that of the Colonists and Frontiersmen resembles the vacations taken by the Class IV New Haven families. Hollingshead and Redlich portray the vacation activity of Class IV in the following way:

During the standard two-week summer vacation, the family may make an automobile trip to some point of interest, such as Niagara Falls or the White Mountains, but more often it will visit a brother, sister, or relative. These families do not own summer homes on the seashore or in the mountains, and very few rent "summer places." This behavior is out of their range of expectancy, and if it is not, they cannot afford the expense.[44]

Those who prefer to stay home during their vacations number 48.3 per cent of the Pilgrims (N = 58), 8.3 per cent of the Colonists (N = 84), and 7.4 per cent of the Frontiersmen (N = 68). Visits to relatives are preferred by 31 per cent of the Pilgrims, 15.5 per cent of the Colonists, and 14.7 per cent of the Frontiersmen. Fishing and hunting at small expense are chosen by 6.9 per cent of the Pilgrims, 25 per cent of the Colonists, and 26.5 per cent of the Frontiersmen. Leisure travel is enjoyed by 3.4 per cent of the Pilgrims, 44 per cent of the Colonists, and 32.3 per cent of the Frontiersmen. Only Colonists and Frontiersmen undertake hunting or fishing at considerable expense—3.6 per cent of the Colonists and 11.8 per cent of the Frontiersmen. Boating, the new American pastime, is preferred by 3.6 per cent of the Colonists and 5.9 per cent of the Frontiersmen. Other vacation activities were reported by 10.3 per cent of the Pilgrims and 1.5 per cent of the Frontiersmen.

Only relatively recently have the lower socio-economic classes begun to pursue leisure travel during vacations. This has been made possible by the almost universal ownership of automobiles in the last two decades. As recently as 1942, the only Elmtown families who spent vacations traveling by car were in Class II.[45] Travel by second-generation at this time does not indicate their relative affluence; more significantly, it reflects their emancipation from their peasant past and their acceptance of a new way of life.

PREFERENCE IN ALCOHOLIC BEVERAGES

The consumption of alcoholic beverages is closely related to scale of living. Some people consume liquor as often as coffee or milk; others partake only during special holidays and celebrations; still others are total abstainers. Different status groups consume liquor in different forms. In 1949, *Life* published a number of sketches illustrating different life styles among status groups, which were classified by Russell Lynes. The highbrow was said to prefer "a glass of 'adequate little' red wine," the upper middlebrow favored "a very dry martini with lemon peel," the lower middlebrow drank "bourbon and ginger ale," and the lowbrow enjoyed his beer.[46]

In 1947, Riley and Marden reported that 75 per cent of the males and 56 per cent of the females in the general American population consume alcoholic beverages.[47] Similar results were reported in 1952 for the state of Washington: 76.2 per cent of the males and 51.4 per cent of the females were at least occasional consumers of alcohol.[48] The figures of these two studies approximate closely the results obtained for the Pilgrim group of Russians in Minneapolis: 76 per cent of the males and 55 per cent of the females reported consuming alcoholic drinks. The figures for the second generation of Russians were quite distinct in comparison. Ninety-eight and 94 per cent of the males in the Colonist and Frontiersman groups, respectively, were drinkers; 90 and 94 per cent of the women in the same two groups were consumers of alcohol on occasion. Maxwell's study showed that the number of abstainers in the second and third generations tended to drop from 41.7 per cent to 34.6 per cent.[49] This drop does not explain, however, the considerable difference in consumption of alcohol between the two generations.

As in the studies of occupational mobility, Maxwell's study does not distinguish among the different ethnic groups. The Slavic peasant with his Eastern Orthodox religion has little if any tradition of abstaining from drink, especially on festive occasions. Davis was concerned with the hardships imposed on Russian immigrants with the introduction of prohibition, which made it difficult for them to obtain alcoholic beverages.[50] One would expect fewer abstainers among the Russians than among the general population. The number of abstainers among the first generation of Minneapolis Russians is explained by the old age of this group. In the state of Washington, the number of abstainers increased with the age of the population: Between 25 and 28 per cent of the abstainers were found among those between 20 and 49 years of age, 48 and 49 per cent of the abstainers among the individuals between 50 and 69 years, and

68.2 per cent of the abstainers among people who were 70 or older.[51] The findings of consistent correlation between income and drinking probably apply in lesser degree to the Russian group. In his research, Maxwell noted that more than 60 per cent of abstainers were found in families with annual incomes under $2,000, while families with annual incomes over $5,000 contained only 18.9 per cent of abstainers.[52] Nevertheless, the incomes of the families in the three groups and their consumption of alcoholic beverages follow the direction of Maxwell's data.

It is natural to expect that the new generation born in the United States will change their choice of intoxicants but will not become abstainers. Following the custom of the old country, 36.4 per cent of the men in the Pilgrim group favored the straight drink (N = 22). Change of taste in the second generation can be seen in the fact that only 17.1 per cent of the Colonists (N = 41) and 9.4 per cent of the Frontiersmen (N = 32) consume straight liquor (without a mix). Beer is a favorite with all of the men in all three groups. It was reported by 36.4 per cent of the Pilgrims, 29.3 per cent of the Colonists, and 31.2 per cent of the Frontiersmen. Mixed drinks, cocktails, or wines are enjoyed by 27.3 per cent of the Pilgrims, 53.7 per cent of the Colonists, and 59.4 per cent of the Frontiersmen. Cocktails and wines were chosen by very few men and were combined with the other category for statistical testing.[53]

The mixed drink was the first choice among women—37.5 per cent of the Pilgrims (N = 16), 63.2 per cent of the Colonists (N = 38), and 60 per cent of the Frontiersmen (N = 30). Beer was the second choice for the Pilgrim women—31.3 per cent named it—but its popularity was slight among second generation women. The Colonists included 15.8 per cent and the Frontiersmen 16.7 per cent of women who liked beer. Cocktails were favored by 6.3 per cent of the Pilgrims, 10.5 per cent of the Colonists, and 13.3 per cent of the Frontiersmen. Wine was a somewhat greater favorite with the Pilgrims, of whom 12.5 per cent reported it, while it was preferred by 7.9 per cent of the Colonists and 6.7 per cent of the Frontiersmen. Generational differences were also noted in the consumption of liquor in straight form. It was preferred by 12.5 per cent of the female Pilgrims, 2.6 per cent of the female Colonists, and 3.3 per cent of the female Frontiersmen.

CHARACTERISTICS OF BEST FRIENDS

People who share only equal class positions are not expected to form special communities of their own. Persons sharing equal honor, however, tend to develop communities as well. According to Max Weber, status communities are a product of a specific style of life, which "can be expected from all those who wish to belong to the circle. Linked with this expectation are restrictions on 'social' intercourse (that is, intercourse which is not subservient to economic or any other of business's 'functional' purposes)."[54] In such cases, for example, it may be expected that outsiders will be excluded from the *connubium* or *commensalis*. One can discover whether an individual or a family shares in a distinct status community (even if an amorphous kind) by ascertaining the characteristics of those with whom he or it maintains close social relations.

To compare the social intercourse of the three groups of Russian families, we isolated two basic characteristics of the three best family friends: place of residence and the occupation of the heads of the families. The importance of the first characteristic was noticed by Weber:

In its characteristic form, stratification by "status groups" on the basis of conventional styles of life evolves at the present time in the United States out of the traditional democracy. For example, only the resident of a certain street ("the street") is considered as belonging to "society," is qualified for social intercourse, and is visited and invited.[55]

If the three groups of Minneapolis Russians were members of distinct status communities, it would be expected that their close friends would also come from different neighborhoods. The answers to this question yielded significant differences among all three groups. The three best friends of Pilgrim families tended to come from northeast Minneapolis. Half the friends of the Colonists lived in northeast Minneapolis and half in other areas. Friends of the Frontiersmen resided predominantly in the suburbs, while some of them resided outside the Minneapolis area.

Table 18—Residence Areas of the Three Best Friends

	Pilgrims	Colonists	Frontiersmen
Northeast Minneapolis	81.8%	48.2%	18.6%
North Minneapolis	6.5	12.3	18.6
Other parts of Minneapolis	2.6	17.5	23.5
Suburbs and other cities	9.1	21.9	39.2
Totals	100.0%	99.9%	99.9%
Chi square (P, C, F) =	71.8	6 d.f.	p < .001
Chi square (C, F) =	21.3	3 d.f.	p < .001

It is likely that, if families of the three Russian groups associated themselves with different kinds of people belonging to different status communities, the characteristics of their best friends would also be dissimilar. One such additional characteristic that could be determined was the occupation of the heads of the families of the three best friends. It was discovered that members of the Pilgrim group associated primarily with persons in the unskilled occupations. The Colonists largely associated with persons with skilled and managerial or semi-professional backgrounds. The Frontiersmen tended to associate with persons in skilled, clerical, sales, managerial, or semi-professional occupations.

Table 19—Occupations of Heads of Families among the Three Best Friends

	Pilgrims	Colonists	Frontiersmen
Unskilled	62.3%	17.1%	4.9%
Skilled and semi-skilled	26.1	28.8	32.7
Clerical and sales	2.9	16.2	28.7
Managerial and semi-professional	8.7	26.1	20.8
Professional	—	11.7	12.9
Totals	100.0%	99.9%	100.0%
Chi-square (P, C, F) =	91.7	8 d.f.	p < .001
Chi-square (C, F) =	11.4	4 d.f.	p < .03

The Pilgrims are known to belong to the status community of their own ethnic group, and the results of the study confirm this fact. It is not quite certain, however, whether the Frontiersmen belong to a distinct status community, but their association with specific suburban neighborhoods and their friendships in those neighborhoods create a basis upon which eventual development of a status community can take place. The Colonists, however, find themselves torn between the ethnic and the majority community, without a firm commitment to either.

NOTES

1. Hans H. Gerth and C. Wright Mills, *Character and Social Structure* (New York: Harcourt, Brace & Co., 1953), p. 315.
2. Max Weber, *From Max Weber: Essays in Sociology* (New York: Oxford University Press, 1946), p. 180.
3. W. Lloyd Warner and Paul S. Lunt, *The Social Life of a Modern Community* ("Yankee City Series," Vol. I [New Haven: Yale University Press, 1941]), p. 82.
4. *Ibid.*
5. Albert Blumenthal, *Small-Town Stuff* (Chicago: University of Chicago Press, 1932), p. 172.
6. *Ibid.*
7. Max Weber, *From Max Weber*, p. 180.
8. Blumenthal, *op. cit.*, pp. 172–3. For further discussion of principles of social stratification, see Don Martindale, *American Social Structure* (New York: D. Van Nostrand Co., 1960), pp. 435–56.
9. August B. Hollingshead, *The Two Factor Index of Social Position* (New Haven: August B. Hollingshead, 1957), p. 9.
10. Seymour Martin Lipset and Reinhard Bendix, *Social Mobility in Industrial Society* (Berkeley: University of California Press, 1959), p. 197.
11. W. Lloyd Warner and Leo Srole, *The Social Systems of American Ethnic Groups* ("Yankee City Series," Vol. III [New Haven: Yale University Press, 1945]), p. 79.
12. Lipset and Bendix, *Social Mobility*, pp. 56, 255–6. See also Frances J. Woods, *Cultural Values of American Ethnic Groups* (New York: Harper & Bros., 1956), pp. 131–45.
13. See W. Lloyd Warner, Robert J. Havighurst, and Martin B. Loeb, *Who Shall Be Educated* (New York: Harper & Bros., 1944), p. 101.
14. See U.S. Bureau of the Census, *U.S. Census of Population: 1960*, Final Report PC (1) 25C. (Washington, D.C.: U.S. Government Printing Office, 1961), Table 73.
15. *Ibid.*
16. The difference between Colonists and Frontiersmen is not statistically significant.
17. See Marshall Sklare, ed., *The Jews: Social Patterns of an American Group* (New York: The Free Press of Glencoe, 1958); Nathan Glazer, "Social Characteristics of American Jews, 1654–1954," in Morris Fine, ed., *American Jewish Year Book, 1955* (Philadelphia: Jewish Publication Society of America, 1955).

18. Gerhard Lenski, *The Religious Factor* (Garden City, New York: Doubleday & Co., 1961), p. 236.

19. Lipset and Bendix, *Social Mobility*, p. 197.

20. W. Lloyd Warner and James C. Abegglen, *Occupational Mobility in American Business and Industry* (Minneapolis: University of Minnesota Press, 1955), p. 38.

21. Peasants on a small plot of land were classified as unskilled, while commercial farmers were classified in the skilled and semi-skilled category.

22. U.S. Bureau of the Census, *U.S. Census of Population: 1960*, Table 76.

23. August B. Hollingshead, *Elmtown's Youth: The Impact of Social Classes on Adolescence* (New York: John Wiley & Sons, Inc., 1949), pp. 92, 96, 102.

24. The stratification of the New Haven population was performed with the aid of Hollingshead's Index of Social Position, which may have influenced the results.

25. August B. Hollingshead and Frederick C. Redlich, *Social Class and Mental Illness: A Community Study* (New York: John Wiley and Sons, Inc., 1958), pp. 70, 87, 96, 106, 116.

26. The difference among all three groups is not statistically significant: chi square 5.3 with two degrees of freedom, p < .10.

27. U.S. Bureau of the Census, *U.S. Census of Population: 1960*, Table 76.

28. Hollingshead and Redlich, *op. cit.*, pp. 106, 116.

29. *Ibid.*, p. 96.

30. Thorstein Veblen, *The Theory of the Leisure Class* (New York: The Modern Library, 1931), p. 36.

31. Russell Lynes, *The Tastemakers* (Universal Library ed., New York: Grosset & Dunlap, 1954), pp. 310–11.

32. Alfred C. Clarke, "Leisure and Occupational Prestige," in Eric Larrabee and Rolf Meyersohn, eds., *Mass Leisure* (New York: The Free Press of Glencoe, 1958), pp. 205–14.

33. Max Kaplan, *Leisure in America* (New York: John Wiley & Sons, 1960), p. 206.

34. Chi square 36.8 with six degrees of freedom, p < .001.

35. Chi square 44.6 with six degrees of freedom, p < .001.

36. The unpublished study was reported in Jerome Davis, *The Russian Immigrant* (New York: The Macmillan Co., 1922), p. 84.

37. A significant statistical difference is found among the three groups: chi square 10.6 with 2 degrees of freedom, p < .005.

38. The difference among groups was not significant: p < .75.

39. For an excellent analysis of the meaning of play and the arts, see Don Martindale, *American Society* (New York: D. Van Nostrand Co., 1960), pp. 430–547.

40. Franklin Henry Giddings, *Democracy and Empire* (New York: The Macmillan Co., 1900), p. 243.

41. Robert S. and Helen Merrell Lynd, *Middletown in Transition* (New York: Harcourt, Brace & Co., 1937), p. 293.

42. Hollingshead, *Elmtown's Youth, op. cit.*, p. 87.

43. Hollingshead and Redlich, *op. cit.*, p. 80.
44. *Ibid.*, p. 113.
45. Hollingshead, *Elmtown's Youth*, p. 94.
46. *Life*, XXIX (April, 1949), 100–1.
47. Johm W. Riley, Jr., and Charles F. Marden, "Who, What, and How Often?" in Raymond G. McCarthy, ed., *Drinking and Intoxication* (New York: The Free Press of Glencoe, 1959), p. 183.
48. Milton A. Maxwell, "In One State," in McCarthy, *op. cit.*, p. 191.
49. *Ibid.*, p. 195.
50. Davis, *The Russian Immigrant*, p. 85.
51. Maxwell, *op. cit.*, p. 198.
52. *Ibid.*, p. 199.
53. Statistical results were not significant: chi square 8.3 with four degrees of freedom, $p < .10$.
54. Max Weber, *From Max Weber*, p. 187.
55. *Ibid.*, p. 188.

9 Changes in the Style of Life

MAX WEBER observed that American status communities formed on the basis of neighborhood are differentiated from other communities by "strict submission to the fashion that is dominant at a given time" in the community. With the keen discernment of a modern social psychologist, Weber noted the dominance of fashion in American life. To be treated as a gentleman it is enough to "pretend" that one is a gentleman by submitting to the requirements of fashion. By claiming a particular status and employing proper status symbols, a family or an individual qualifies as a member of a particular status group. Max Weber concludes that "the development of status is essentially a question of stratification resting upon usurpation."[1]

Fashion holds such an important place in American society that American sociologists like F. Stuart Chapin and William H. Sewell have used it to differentiate among various socio-economic groups. The Chapin scale for rating living-room articles essentially measures the degree of submission among particular families to the requirements of fashion. In American society, the style of life appropriate for a particular status community also demands an appropriate display of material items.

THE RESIDENCE AREA

Many American sociologists studying various communities have observed a relationship between the residence area of a family and its socio-economic position.[2] Initial discovery of this phenomenon was made by the social ecologists, led by Park and Burgess.[3] The concentric zones of the city discovered by the ecologists represented status communities, each with a style of life. Empirical evidence was first furnished by Warner and his associates. In the study of Yankee City, Warner distinguished among six residential areas. Each area was given from one to six points on the Residence Status Index: one point for the lowest status residence area, six points for the highest. In 1933, the ethnic groups that inhabited areas with scores between one and three points were Irish (score 2.85), Jewish (2.77), Armenian (2.57), Greek (2.54), French-Canadian (2.43), Italian (2.38), Polish (1.40), and Russian (1.32).[4]

In the study of Jonesville, where Warner developed his Index of Status Characteristics, dwelling area was included among the four characteristics. In context, the dwelling area was divided into seven different categories.[5] Hollingshead, following in Warner's footsteps, also included residence area in his Index of Social Position, which was used in *Social Class and Mental Illness*. Hollingshead claimed that "a family's mode of living is mirrored in its home."[6] The study revealed that the least desirable residence areas of New Haven were inhabited predominantly by eastern and southern Europeans.

In the study of the Minneapolis Russians, significant differences were found in the ecological distribution of families in the three groups. The Russian Church and the community are traditionally located in the northeastern area of Minneapolis, a district known as the habitation of immigrants from central and eastern Europe. The area is sometimes referred to as the Polish area, since the largest proportion of its population is Polish. In the past two decades, the new Russian generations (born in this area but undergoing rapid acculturation) have been moving to the suburbs directly adjoining the northeast area—Columbia Heights and Fridley. Some have moved farther, crossing the Mississippi river north of the city, while others have moved to the southern suburbs. Such departures are felt by the "old timers" as a loss—as a betrayal of the community. Many of the interviews revealed that the most face-saving and psychologically least distressing way of tearing oneself from the community was to move to the suburbs and then to claim distance as the reason for decreasing interaction. For the purpose of statistical testing three different types of residence area were distinguished.

Table 20—Ecological Distribution of the Three Groups

	Pilgrims	Colonists	Frontiersmen
Northeast Minneapolis	86.2%	57.1%	20.6%
Columbia Heights, Fridley, and the North	—	26.2	23.5
Other Minneapolis areas and suburbs	13.8	16.7	55.9
Totals	100.0%	100.0%	100.0%
Chi square =	33.3	4 d.f.	p < .001

THE PREFERENCE OF RESIDENCE AREA

During the interviews, the nucleus of a new community not formally recognized by the Minneoplis Russians was discovered. In an area covering fifteen city blocks and bordering on Columbia Heights and Minneapolis, a group of fifteen families from the Colonist group have established residence. They maintain constant communication and friendship with the original community. The new community is, however, sufficiently crystallized to be conscious of its own uniqueness, for its members call it "Little Moscow," and they join together in celebration of various Russian holidays. On Easter Sunday, especially, the members go from house to house in the middle of the night, waking those who are asleep, to celebrate together. The community is located within an area bounded by University Avenue on the East, Central Avenue on the West, 38th Avenue on the North, and Columbia Park on the South.

The interviews revealed general satisfaction among families in all three groups with the neighborhoods in which they live. Two of the Colonists wished they could live closer to the church in the northeast area, while one family of Frontiersmen wanted to move away from the northeast area. More than half Colonists preferred the Northeast, while more than half Frontiersmen preferred the suburban areas. The preferences coincide with the actual ecological distribution of these groups.[7]

Rossi observed that horizontal mobility of families is often an affirmation of vertical mobility. Some families who were extremely unhappy about the social characteristics of their neighborhoods, "where expressing the way in which their home no longer fitted in with their social aspirations."[8] The general satisfaction of the three groups of Russians with the social environments of the neighborhoods in which they lived suggests that they are happy with their situations.

HOME OWNERSHIP AND VALUE OF THE HOUSE

Ownership of a house is often a prerequisite for membership in a particular status community. The Russian community in Minneapolis respects the man who buys or builds his own home. Most of the families in the first generation built their homes themselves with the aid of their friends, as they built their first church. In the early period, little housing was available to the new arrivals in Minneapolis. They had no alternative but to build their homes on the free land in the northeastern part of Minneapolis. At present, a large majority of the families express a strong drive toward home ownership. Only five families out of the 105 studied rented their dwellings.

In New Haven, only Class I families lived in their own homes. Class II families aspired to home ownership, but only 55 per cent had reached their goal at the time of the interviews. With each successive lower class, the proportion of families owning homes diminished. In Class IV, 46 per cent of the families held title to their homes, while the families in Class V usually rented low-cost apartments.[9] The widespread ownership of homes among the Minneapolis Russians stands in sharp contrast to the New Haven pattern.

The housing census in 1960 reported 52.7 per cent of housing units in Minneapolis occupied by their owners.[10] A recent study of the Minneapolis Jewish community revealed home ownership by the majority of upper- and lower-class Jews. The difference, however, is revealed in the prices of homes owned by different classes: upper-class Jewish homes were priced at an average of $33,593, and lower-class homes at an average of $13,833.[11]

Different status communities not only establish their own requirements for home ownership, but they also create standards for particular kinds of homes, prices and sizes. The styles of life of different status communities often require different types of houses. Families who keep servants need rooms in which to house them. The same families are likely to entertain week-end guests, necessitating additional space. This need for space affects the prices of the houses. The Class I family in New Haven owned a home that was priced in 1950 between $30,000 and $50,000 and contained an average of ten to fifteen rooms.[12]

The sizes of the houses inhabited by the Minneapolis Russians in all three groups do not differ significantly from group to group.[13] The modal number of rooms (exclusive of bath) in the homes of the Pilgrims and Frontiersmen was five, while the modal number for the Colonists was six rooms. In New Haven, Class III families averaged houses with five and six rooms.[14] The Pilgrims in Minneapolis continue to live in the homes that they themselves built and in which they raised their children. Since they are not eager to move out of their church community, many are now living in houses that are larger than they need. The numbers of rooms occupied by the Pilgrims approximates those of other residents in northeast Minneapolis. In 1960, the average number of rooms for each unit in this area was 5.6.[15] The Frontiersmen tend to live in smaller homes than the Colonists, primarily because more of them live in new suburban two-bedroom housing developments. The smallest number of rooms inhabited by any of the 105 families was three. In the Pilgrim group, only 17.2 per cent lived in three- or four-room houses, in the Colonist group 19.9 per cent, and in the Frontiersman group 8.8 per cent.

Unlike many large American cities settled by many ethnic groups, the Minneapolis area occupied by the central and eastern European immigrants is not made up of large apartment buildings in poor condition. Instead, it is a well kept neighborhood composed of single or double family houses. The unpopularity of the neighborhood in the eyes of the larger community is primarily social in character and is not based upon the condition of the neighborhood. The average value of homes in the area inhabited by the Pilgrims is $11,250. Of available housing units in this area, 54 per cent are occupied by their owners.[16] The interviews with Pilgrims revealed that 67.9 per cent of them live in homes valued under $15,000, 25 per cent in homes valued between $15,000 and $20,000, and 7.1 per cent live in homes valued at $20,000 and over (N = 28). Among the Colonists, 48.7 per cent valued their homes below $15,000, 30.8 per cent at between $15,000 and $20,000, and 20.5 per cent at $20,000 and over (N = 39). Among the Frontiersmen, a similar distribution prevailed: Forty-five and five tenths per cent valued their homes below $15,000, 36.4 per cent between $15,000 and $20,000, and 18.2 per cent at $20,000 and over (N = 33). Only five homes in the total sample were valued at over $30,000—one each among the Pilgrims and Colonists and three among the Frontiersmen. The modal price for the homes in all three groups was between $10,000 and $15,000.[17]

The five families renting their homes pay less than $100 a month. The one Pilgrim family pays between $70 and $85 a month rent, the three Colonist families under $70 a month, and the one Frontiersman family between $85 and $100 a month rent.

LIVING-ROOM ITEMS

Measurement of status with the aid of a living-room scale was pioneered by Chapin.[18] The requirements of fashion apply not only to the location and type of a house but also to the things inside it. Such items as telephones, television sets, musical instruments, and other material equipment all form an integral part of a particular style of life. Among the Minneapolis Russians, the Pilgrims and non-Pilgrims can be differentiated by some of these items. Little difference, however, was found between the Colonists and Frontiersmen.

TELEPHONE

In 1960, of all occupied housing units in the city of Minneapolis only 9.5 per cent did not have a telephone.[19] In our sample, only one Pilgrim family in 105 did not have a telephone, and only 10.3 per cent had private telephone lines. Among the Colonists, 42.9 per cent subscribed to party lines and 33.3 per cent to private lines; 21.4 per cent had telephones with one extension, and one familiy (2.4 per cent) had more than one line. Comparable distribution was found among the Frontiersmen, of whom 38.2 per cent had party lines, 38.2 per cent had private lines, 20.6 per cent had telephones with extensions, and one family (2.9 per cent) had more than one line. It is quite evident that, nowadays, rapid communication by telephone is a requirement for all urban dwellers. When Louis Guttman gave new weights to Chapin's Social Status Scale in 1942, he underscored the importance of the telephone by assigning to it weight number 24.4 instead of 8.[20]

TELEVISION, RADIO, AND PHONOGRAPH

In 1952, only 50.5 per cent of the New Haven Class I families had television sets, all found in the homes of the *nouveaux riches*. All the other classes in New Haven, however, considered television viewing as part of their lives. Seventy-three per cent of the Class III families owned television sets; in Class IV, television owners totaled 89 per cent, and in Class V, 76 per cent of the families had sets.[21] The importance of television in contemporary American life is further attested by census reports. In Minneapolis, 77.8 per cent of all occupied units had one television set, 9.9 per cent of the units contained two sets, and 12.3 per cent were without television sets.[22]

Every Russian family interviewed possessed a television set. None of the Pilgrims had more than one black and white set, while nineteen of the non-Pilgrims had two. In the Colonist group, 78.6 per cent and in the Frontiersmen group 67.6 per cent of the families had only one television set.[23] The second sets had usually been purchased by the families for their children. One family (Frontiersman) in the total sample had a color television set.

The great majority of the families interviewed possessed small A.M. radio sets. Phonographs, however, were much less popular than either radio or television sets. Seven homes had neither a radio nor a phonograph. Each successive generational unit had somewhat greater access to mass communication by means of the radio. Among families who reported neither radios nor phonographs, 13.8 per cent were Pilgrims, and 7.1 per cent were Colonists; there were no Frontiersmen. Among those reporting possession of A.M. radios, 48.3 per cent were Pilgrims, 31 per cent were Colonists, and 58.8 per cent were Frontiersmen.

Possession of radio-phonograph combination sets were reported by 37.9 per cent of the Pilgrims, 45.2 per cent of the Colonists, and 23.5 per cent of the Frontiersmen. None of the Pilgrim families owned either an F.M. radio or a hi-fi set or both, but 16.6 per cent of the Colonists and 17.6 per cent of the Frontiersmen reported ownership of these items. Radio ownership by these groups of Minneapolis Russians followed a pattern similar to the whole city of Minneapolis, in which only 6.2 per cent of all housing units had no radios.

MUSICAL INSTRUMENTS

Of the $11,716,000 spent on various leisure activities by Americans in 1952, as many as $2,324,000 or 19.8 per cent was spent on radios, television, phonograph records, and musical instruments. This sum represents a considerably larger expenditure than that spent on all spectator amusements in the same year, which totaled only 13.5 per cent of all expenditures.[24]

The members of higher socio-economic classes are prepared from childhood to enjoy and appreciate a variety of leisure activities, including learning to play musical instruments. Musical instruments, however, may be kept in the house even though no one in the family plays them. They may be placed at the disposal of guests or even paid musicians who are occasionally asked to entertain. Some instruments—especially the piano—are often used for accompaniment and may be kept for this purpose. Whatever the purpose of the musical instruments, their possession reflects the sensitivity of the owners to status symbols of the higher circles. It was to measure this sensitivity that Chapin included a question about a piano bench in his living-room scale.

Among the Minneapolis Russians, the second generation showed greater interest in possessing musical instruments than did the first generation.[25] Families who had no musical instruments in their homes included 75.9 per cent of the Pilgrims, 42.9 per cent of the Colonists, and 41.2 per cent of the Frontiersmen. Seventeen and two-tenths per cent of the Pilgrim families, 26.2 per cent of the Colonists, and 20.6 per cent of the Frontiersmen had smaller instruments like the guitar or violin. The piano, the darling of the old northern European middle classes,[26] was the most popular single instrument possessed by the Minneapolis Russians. There were twenty-three owners of pianos and five owners of small electric organs. Families who owned either a piano or an organ composed 6.9 per cent of the Pilgrims, 31 per cent of the Colonists, and 38.2 per cent of the Frontiersmen.

READING MATERIAL

Reading material available in a home also reflects the sensitivity of family members toward the requirements of their respective status communities. Chapin's Social Status Scale includes an item on "bookcases with books." The same scale assigns credit for each newspaper and periodical to which the family subscribes.

In their empirical study, Hollingshead and Redlich categorically stated that Class V members "read nothing except an occasional local or ethnic newspaper."[27] Members of each successive class, however, tended to purchase more reading material. The reading patterns of the Minneapolis Russians resemble the habits of New Haven's Class IV and Class III members, who almost always subscribed to the local paper and read an occasional article in a popular magazine.[28] All the Russians read either *The Minneapolis Morning Tribune, The Minneapolis Star,* or *The Minneapolis Sunday Tribune.* Some read both morning and evening papers. No statistically significant differences were found in the purchase of papers by the members of the three groups.[29] Proportionately, however, the Frontiersmen were more interested in the daily news than the other two groups. Two daily papers were purchased by 26.5 per cent of the Frontiersmen, 14.8 per cent of the Pilgrims, and 16.7 per cent of the Colonists. A daily paper and a Sunday paper were taken by 66.7 per cent of the Pilgrims, 73.8 per cent of the Colonists, and 61.8 per cent of the Frontiersmen. Only one daily paper was read by 18.5 per cent of the Pilgrims, 9.5 per cent of the Colonists, and 11.8 per cent of the Frontiersmen.

Chapin's Social Status Scale does not differentiate among the different kinds of books that may be owned by the interviewed families. Differentiation was attempted in the present study without obtaining statistically significant results.[30] The families possessing no books or only westerns and mysteries were divided as follows: Thirty-one per cent were Pilgrims, 16.7 per cent were Colonists, and 26.5 per cent were Frontiersmen. Professional or classical books were displayed by 20.7 per cent of the Pilgrims, 23.8 per cent of the Colonists, and 26.5 per cent of the Frontiersmen. Families who possessed other kinds of books, including quality paperback editions, totaled 48.3 per cent of the Pilgrims, 59.5 per cent of the Colonists, and 47.1 per cent of the Frontiersmen.

The Colonists showed a proportionately higher number of persons interested in books. They tended to buy somewhat more magazines than the other two groups. No magazines were purchased by 44.8 per cent of the Pilgrims, 16.7 per cent of the Colonists, and 26.5 per cent of the Frontiersmen. From one to three magazines were being purchased by 41.4 per cent of the Pilgrims, 42.9 per cent of the Colonists, and 35.3 per cent of the Frontiersmen. Four or more magazines were regularly purchased by 13.8 per cent of the Pilgrims, 40.4 per cent of the Colonists, and 38.2 per cent of the Frontiersmen. The first generation purchased fewer magazines than the second generation.[31] In part, this difference may be explained by the presence among the families of the second generation of growing children, for whom these magazines were often purchased. The Colonists, however, tended to show a somewhat greater appreciation of books and magazines.

Ownership of Automobiles

In 1925, Robert and Helen Lynd noted the revolutionary influence of the automobile on the American style of life:

But if the automobile touches the rest of Middletown's living at many points, it has revolutionized its leisure; more, perhaps, than the movies or any other intrusion new to Middletown since the nineties, it is making leisure-time enjoyment a regularly expected part of every day and week rather than an occasional event. The readily available leisure-time options of even the working class have been multiplied many-fold.[32]

Of 123 working class families whom the Lynds interviewed, sixty had cars. Some reported that they would rather go without clothes or food than without cars.[33] Studying Yankee City in the 1930s, Warner and his associates discovered that the socio-economic classes ranked the automobile differently. Taking the money spent on different items as an index of preference, Warner found that among the lower upper-class families the car is given second place in the budget after the cost of maintaining the home; among the two middle classes, the automobile was fifth on the budget; among the upper lower classes it was sixth; and among the lower lower classes it had ninth place on the budget. The upper upper classes spent comparatively little of their budget on automobiles, placing them in seventh place after such items as shelter, food, clothing, education, and taxes. There is no doubt that the automobile was considered less of a necessity by the upper upper classes if compared to the lower upper classes. The incomes of these two classes did not differ greatly—in both categories the average yearly income was slightly over $6,000. Yet a family in the upper upper class spent only an average of $363 on a car, while a family in the lower upper class spent as much as $914.[34]

The upper upper-class families were secure in their social position and were allocating their money on the proper style of life for their class. On the other hand, a car for a lower upper- or middle-class family served as an item of display and emphasized its affluence or rise in the social scale. It also gave it an opportunity to imitate some of the life styles of the traditional upper classes—such as leisure travel. Despite the widespread ownership of cars in American society in 1960, there were still many families who for one reason or another did not own automobiles. The 1960 housing census reported 27.1 per cent of all occupied units in the Minneapolis area without an available automobile.[35]

In the study of Minneapolis Russians, generational differences in car ownership were revealed. More than 40 per cent of the Pilgrims did not own a car. Some felt they were too old to drive, while some had never learned to drive. For the most part, they preferred to stay at home and, when necessary, depended on their grown children to take them places. On the other hand, every family in the Colonist and Frontiersman samples owned one or more automobiles.[36] Families owning two or more cars made up 3.4 per cent of the Pilgrims, 16.7 per cent of the Colonists, and 23.5 per cent of the Frontiersmen. The proportion of families with two or more cars in the Colonist group corresponded to the 16.2 per cent of Minneapolis occupied dwelling units to which two or more cars were available.[37] The families in the Frontiersman group with two or more cars represented a somewhat higher proportion than the general population.

The estimated cost of the newest car owned among these three groups of families was higher for the Colonists. It was only in the highest cost category of $3,000 and over that the Pilgrims and Frontiersmen represented a larger proportion than the Colonists. The following table shows the 1960 prices of automobiles owned by the Minneapolis Russians.

The differential costs of automobiles were also reflected in the ages of the cars driven by the three groups of families. The Colonists drove cars with a median age of two or three years, while the cars of Pilgrims and Frontiersmen had a median age of four or five years. The distribution of the new and one-year old cars was the same throughout the samples: 25 per cent for the Pilgrims and 26 per cent for the Colonists and Frontiersmen.[38]

Table 21—Cost of the Newest Automobile*

	Pilgrims	Colonists	Frontiersmen
	(N = 16)	(N = 42)	(N = 34)
Under $500	31.3%	14.3%	26.5%
$500–$1,000	25.0	19.0	26.5
$1,000–$2,000	18.8	35.7	20.6
$2,000–$3,000	12.5	28.6	17.6
$3,000 and over	12.5	2.4	8.8
Totals	100.1%	100.0%	100.0%

* The statistical test between the Colonists and Frontiersmen, after combining the two highest categories, was not significant: chi square 3.5 with 3 degrees of freedom, $p < .50$.

While the Colonists drove newer and somewhat more expensive cars than the other two groups, the Frontiersmen were more aware of status distinctions among the different models. The most popular makes of cars for the Pilgrim group were in the following order (including only those models making up more than 10 per cent of the total): Chevrolet, Ford, and Pontiac. Similar preferences were expressed by the Colonists: Chevrolet, Ford, Pontiac, and Plymouth. The families of the Frontiersmen, however, drove the following most popular models: Chevrolet, Buick, Plymouth, Ford, and Oldsmobile. None of the families in the Pilgrim and Colonist groups drove an Oldsmobile, and Buick was one of the less popular makes.

In comparison with these preferences, Class I families in New Haven favored either a Cadillac, Chrysler, Oldsmobile, or Buick.[39] Members of the Frontiersman group already operating within the majority community also claimed deference by displaying automobiles popular among the upper classes of the wider American community.

THE OWNERSHIP OF BOATS

The new leisure activity of the middle classes—boating—has increased in popularity so rapidly that *Life,* in its 1959 issue on leisure, called it a "national aquamania." It reported 8,000,000 leisure boats in use, a volume that had tripled since 1951.[40] It has been estimated that in 1955 alone the number of people using boats for leisure increased from 20,000,000 to 30,000,000.[41] There is no doubt that boating for pleasure is not likely to contribute to the improvement of class position, but it represents a status symbol with which deference may be claimed. Kahl's statement is particularly useful in explaining this phenomenon:

True, most [families] would like more money, but that does not mean that they are willing to organize their lives (or feel that they have a realistic chance to organize them) in a way that will maximize their chances of substantially improving their incomes.[42]

The Russians in Minneapolis have also been influenced by this new leisure pattern, each successive generational unit more so than the one preceding it. Boats were owned by 3.4 per cent of the Pilgrims, 9.5 per cent of the Colonists, and 14.7 per cent of the Frontiersmen.[43]

CHARGE ACCOUNTS

It was Veblen who said that "by virtue of its descent from a patriarchal past, our social system makes it the woman's function in an especial degree to put in evidence her household's ability to pay."[44] In contemporary American society, undeniable public evidence of ability to pay rests on the possession of one or more charge accounts in the major stores of a city. The percentage of interviewed families reporting charge accounts in downtown stores consisted of 37.9 per cent of the Pilgrims, 85.7 per cent of the Colonists, and 85.3 per cent of the Frontiersmen. A statistically significant difference was revealed between the two generations.[45] The first (foreign born) generation still prefers to pay cash for its purchases and distrusts financial manipulations involving no visible currency.

MEDICAL CHECK-UPS

In studying the budgets of the six socio-economic classes, Warner and his associates discovered that the families in each class spent different sums for medical care. The families of the two lower classes spent an annual average of $44 for medical care; lower middle-class families spent $63; upper middle-class families spent $92; lower upper-class families spent $158; and upper upper-class families spent $313.[46] There is a tendency for families in the lower socio-economic classes to defer attending to their medical needs until it becomes absolutely necessary. Davis tells the story of a Russian woman in New York who could not afford an appendicitis operation and was cared for by a kind neighbor.[47] At the same time, a study sponsored by the New York Academy of Medicine in 1919 revealed that very few ailing Slavs made use of available institutional care: Only 2.2 per cent went to dispensaries, 2.3 per cent to general hospitals, and none at all to maternity hospitals. The Slavs, however, more than any other ethnic group with the exception of the Italians, turned to private physicians in case of need—58.2 per cent of them.[48]

While no statistically significant difference was found in the frequency of medical check-ups among the three groups, the significant difference between Colonists and Frontiersmen is very revealing.[49] Families who turned to physicians only when sick made up 37.9 per cent of the Pilgrims, 28.6 per cent of the Colonists, and 44.1 per cent of the Frontiersmen. Check-ups every two or three years were reported by 20.7 per cent of the Pilgrims, 9.5 per cent of the Colonists, and 20.6 per cent of the Frontiersmen. Yearly check-ups were reported by 41.4 per cent of the Pilgrims, 61.9 per cent of the Colonists, and 35.3 per cent of the Frontiersmen. The frequency of check-ups among the Pilgrims is probably due to the advanced age of the interviewees. The differences between the Colonists and the Frontiersmen, however, may indicate differences in their life styles. It is of signal interest that the families who devoted the least attention to their health are Frontiersmen—suggesting that they value their class situation more than their health situation.[50]

THE STATUS SCALE COMPARISON OF THE THREE GROUPS

The status scale represented the longest scale of the four with thirty-seven items in it. Each item, as in the preceding class scale, was given five different weights. The mean scale scores on the status scale differentiated well between the first and second generations, but only a small mean difference was registered between the Colonists and the Frontiersmen. The status scale results were as follows:

Table 22—Results of the Status Scale Comparison

Group	Mean Scale Score
Pilgrims	2.0
Colonists	2.8
Frontiersmen	2.9

Tests of significance among the three and between the two groups were performed with the aid of the chi square. In all cases, significant results were obtained. As measured by the scale devised for this study, the three groups differ in status. The results of the test of significance point in an opposite direction from that suggested by the third hypothesis. It was predicted that the Frontiersmen, as they entered the majority community, would lose ethnic-group standing and would receive lower status-scale scores than the Colonists. It is likely, however, that the status scale measured the relative standing of the groups in their relation to the majority community and did not succeed in isolating status variables within the ethnic group itself. Warner's method of "evaluated participation" would have probably isolated status variables within the ethnic community more successfully but would not have permitted us comparison with the group outside the community.

Table 23—Status Scale Comparison

Scale Score	Pilgrims	Colonists	Frontiersmen
1	511	434	280
2	188	235	220
3	129	361	304
4	59	222	167
5	101	269	278
Totals	988	1521	1249
Chi square (P, C, F) =	291.7	8 d.f.	$p < .001$
Chi square (C, F) =	20.1	4 d.f.	$p < .01$

A SOCIO-ECONOMIC COMPARISON OF THE THREE GROUPS

Since class and status are closely related variables, some students speak of socio-economic standing. A socio-economic scale was formed by combining the status scale with the class scale. Statistical tests could then be performed among all three groups. The two following tables show results obtained from the scale-score comparison and from a statistical test.

Table 24—Results of the Socio-Economic Scale Comparison

Group	Mean Scale Score
Pilgrims	2.0
Colonists	2.7
Frontiersmen	2.9

RECAPITULATION

The presentation of interview material on the style of life of the Pilgrims, Colonists, and Frontiersmen was divided for convenience into two parts: behavioral items and the display items. Chapter 8 on behavioral items reviewed basic information on educational backgrounds of family members, occupations of the fathers, occupations of the women, participation of families in cultural events, their preferences in music, their vacation activities, their use of alcoholic beverages, and the characteristics of their best friends. Significant

Table 25—Socio-Economic Scale Comparison

Scale Score	Pilgrims	Colonists	Frontiersmen
1	567	481	308
2	214	275	245
3	137	387	333
4	61	237	192
5	102	282	288
Totals	1081	1662	1366
Chi square (P, C, F) =	228.2	8 d.f.	p < .001
Chi square (C, F) =	19.8	4 d.f.	p < .01

differences between the first and second generations were discovered in educational backgrounds, occupations of fathers, preferences of music, attendance at the theatre, visits to museums and galleries, vacation activity, and backgrounds of their best friends. Significant differences between Colonists and Frontiersmen were found in their preferences in music and the characteristics of their best friends. If the behavior of the Minneapolis Russians is compared with the general American population, it roughly approximates that of the respectable lower middle class—or classess III and IV of Hollingshead's classification.

Chapter 9 reviewed material-display items—ecological distribution of the three groups, their mobility aspirations, ownership of homes, major living-room items, ownership of cars and boats, charge accounts, and the frequency of medical check-ups. Significant generational differences were discovered in residence areas, musical instruments, purchase of magazines, possession of cars, and the use of charge accounts. A significant difference between the Colonists and Frontiersmen was found in the residences of the two groups, their preferences of residence areas and frequency of medical check-ups. On some items of material display, many families in the second generation resembled the Class II families of New Haven; in general, however, they approximated more closely to the Class III pattern of life. The first generation families tended to resemble more closely the Class IV families of New Haven.

The status scale comparison between the Pilgrims, Colonists, and Frontiersmen gave significant results. The Pilgrims had a mean scale score of 2.0, the Colonists 2.8, and the Frontiersmen 2.9. As predicted in our second hypothesis, the Colonists tended to be located in a higher status situation than did the Pilgrims. The prediction made by our third hypothesis, however, did not materialize. Instead of placing the Frontiersmen below the Colonists, the status-scale results placed them above. The combined socio-economic comparison among the three groups yielded significant results. The results indicate that each successive generational unit experiences a rise in general socio-economic well being.

NOTES

1. Max Weber, *From Max Weber: Essays in Sociology*, Hans H. Gerth and C. Wright Mills, trans. and eds. (New York: Oxford University Press, 1946), p. 188.

2. To cite some recent studies: Judith R. Kramer and Seymour Leventman, *Children of the Gilded Ghetto* (New Haven: Yale University Press, 1961); Oscar Handlin, *The Newcomers* (Cambridge: Harvard University Press, 1959), Chapter 4; Arthur J. Vidich and Joseph Bensman, *The Small Town in Mass Society* (Princeton University Press, 1958), Chapter 3; and Herman R. Lantz, *The People of Coal Town* (New York: Columbia University Press, 1958), p. 232.

3. See Robert E. Park, Ernest W. Burgess, and Roderick D. McKenzie, *The City* (Chicago: University of Chicago Press, 1925). For an analysis of these ideas, see Don Martindale, "Prefatory Remarks: The Theory of the City," in Max Weber, *The City* (New York: The Free Press of Glencoe, 1958), pp. 9–62.

4. W. Lloyd Warner and Paul S. Lunt, *The Social Life of a Modern Community* ("Yankee City Series," Vol. I [New Haven: Yale University Press, 1941]), pp. 39–43.

5. W. Lloyd Warner, Marchia Meeker, and Kenneth Eells, *Social Class in America: A Manual of Procedure for the Measurement of Social Status* (Chicago: Science Research Associates, Inc., 1949), pp. 151–154.

6. August B. Hollingshead and Frederick C. Redlich, *Social Class and Mental Illness: A Community Study* (New York: John Wiley & Sons, Inc., 1958), pp. 389–390.

7. Chi square 31.8 with four degrees of freedom, $p < .001$.

8. Peter H. Rossi, *Why Families Move* (New York: The Free Press of Glencoe, 1955), p. 179.

9. Hollingshead and Redlich, *op. cit.*, pp. 79–80, 87, 106, 118–20.

10. U.S. Bureau of the Census, *U.S. Census of Housing: 1960*, Series HC (3)–224 (Washington, D.C.: U.S. Government Printing Office, 1961), Table 1.

11. Kramer and Leventman, *op. cit.*, p. 73.

12. Hollingshead and Redlich, *op. cit.*, pp. 79–80.

13. Chi square 11.2 with 6 degrees of freedom, $p < .10$.

14. Hollingshead and Redlich, *op. cit.*, p. 99.

15. U.S. Bureau of the Census, *op. cit.*, Census Tracts 11, 17, 18, 19, 24, and 25 in Table 2.
16. *Ibid.*
17. Statistical results were not significant: chi square 4.3 with 4 degrees of freedom, $p < .50$.
18. See Louis Guttman, "A Review of Chapin's Social Status Scale," *American Sociological Review*, VIII (June, 1942), 362–9.
19. U.S. Bureau of the Census, *U.S. Census of Housing: 1960*, HC (1) No. 25 (Washington, D.C.: U.S. Government Printing Office, 1961), Table 16.
20. Guttman, *op. cit.*, p. 366.
21. Hollingshead and Redlich, *op. cit.*, pp. 83, 93, 103, 111, 128.
22. U.S. Bureau of the Census, HC (1) No. 25, Table 16.
23. Chi square 10.7 with 2 degrees of freedom, $p < .005$.
24. Max Kaplan, *Leisure in America* (New York: John Wiley & Sons, Inc., 1960), p. 6.
25. Statistical tests among all three groups were significant: chi square 11.6 with 4 degrees of freedom, $p < .03$. There was no difference between the Colonists and Frontiersmen.
26. For an excellent discussion of the social significance of selected musical instruments, see Max Weber, *The Rational and Social Foundations of Music*, Don Martindale, Johannes Riedel, and Gertrude Neuwirth, trans. and eds. (Carbondale, Illinois: Southern Illinois University Press, 1958).
27. Hollingshead and Redlich, *op. cit.*, p. 127.
28. *Ibid.*, pp. 111–3, 102–3.
29. Chi square 3.0 with 4 degrees of freedom, $p < .75$.
30. Chi square 2.5 with 4 degrees of freedom, $p < .75$.
31. The difference among the three groups was statistically significant: chi square 9.6 with 4 degrees of freedom, $p < .05$. The difference between the Colonists and Frontiersmen was not significant.
32. Robert S. and Helen Merrell Lynd, *Middletown* (New York: Harcourt, Brace & Co., 1929), p. 260.
33. *Ibid.*, pp. 154–6.
34. Warner and Lunt, *op. cit.*, pp. 290–6.
35. U.S. Bureau of the Census, *Housing: 1960*, HC (1) No. 25, Table 16.
36. The difference between the one-car and two-car families of Colonists and Frontiersmen was not statistically significant: chi square .06 with 1 degree of freedom. There were, however, differences in the proportions between the two groups.
37. U.S. Bureau of the Census, *Housing: 1960*, HC (1) No. 25, Table 16.
38. The statistical test between the Colonists and Frontiersmen was not significant: chi square 2.0 with 3 degrees of freedom, $p < .75$.
39. Hollingshead and Redlich, *op. cit.*, p. 81.
40. See Kaplan, *op. cit.*, p. 5.
41. *Ibid.*, p. 198.
42. Joseph A. Kahl, *The American Class Structure* (New York: Rinehart & Co., Inc., 1957), p. 121.

43. The statistical test among all three groups was not significant: chi square 2.4 with 2 degrees of freedom, p < .50.

44. Thorstein Veblen, *The Theory of the Leisure Class* (New York: The Modern Library, 1931), p. 180.

45. Chi square 23.9 with 2 degrees of freedom, p < .001.

46. Warner and Lunt, op. cit., p. 296.

47. Jerome Davis, *The Russian Immigrant* (New York: The Macmillan Co., 1922), p. 71.

48. *Ibid.*, pp. 68–9.

49. Chi square 6.4 with 4 degrees of freedom, p < .25; chi square for Colonists and Frontiersmen 15.6 with 2 degrees of freedom, p < .01.

50. Harold D. Lasswell and Abraham Kaplan, who have gone beyond Max Weber, identify eight instead of only three major values, including "well being" or the health and safety of the organism. See Lasswell and Kaplan, *Power and Society* (New Haven: Yale University Press, 1950), p. 55.

10   Power Dimensions

MAX WEBER DEFINED POWER as "the chance of a man or of a number of men to realize their own will in a communal action even against the resistance of others who are participating in the action."[1] He argued that men participate in parties to attain their political ends which may often be those of a particular class or status community and sometimes purely political. The means by which power is attained may be equally varied—including naked violence, social influence, or the use of money.[2] In classical capitalistic society, for example, political power is usually exercised to serve class interests, as was correctly noted by Karl Marx. Weber emphasized that "the existence of a capitalistic enterprise presupposes that a very specific communal action exists and that it is specifically structured to protect the possession of goods *per se*, and especially the power of individuals to dispose, in principle freely, over the means of production."[3]

In the United States today, however, such communal action is no longer a reality. In place of communal action based primarily upon class situation, other communal actions have emerged, which represent other interests. This revolutionary change was well described by Daniel Bell:

Two "silent" revolutions in the relations between power and class position in modern society seem to be in process. One is a change in the *mode of access* to power insofar as inheritance alone is no longer all-determining; the other is a change in the *nature of power-holding itself* insofar as technical skill rather than property, and political position rather than wealth, have become the basis on which power is wielded.[4]

As Daniel Bell, C. Wright Mills, Don Martindale, and others have noted, some of the most important aggregations of power in the modern world are exercised by men who control institutional bureaucracies or similar organized groups. In the words of Vidich and Bensman, "power in local political affairs . . . tends to be based on accessibility to sources of decision in larger institutions."[5]

It is significant that empirical study of power *per se* by American sociologists is a quite recent development. Most community studies before 1950 treated community power structure as a dependent variable of the socio-economic structure.[6] Those in favorable socio-economic positions were found also to be the decision-makers of the community. In the 1950s, sociologists began to focus their attention upon the community power structure as an independent phenomenon. Nevertheless, these studies continued to show considerable overlap between the power position of an individual and his status and class position.[7] These observations reinforce the idea that there exists a proportionally small intimate group or elite that comprises the decision-makers and influential leaders in the community. It has further been assumed that members of the elite are agreed on the ends and means of power.

At the turn of the 1960s, however, there emerged a vigorous new opposition to sociological interpretations of power on the basis of status and particularly of class position. The opposition is mainly among political scientists like Robert A. Dahl and his associates who identify themselves as "pluralists" in contrast to the elitists.[8] They argue persuasively that, instead of single power centers, many American communities revolve around many varied centers that share no agreement on either ends or means. Shifting alliances and coalitions, of either temporary or permanent nature, are formed to influence the outcome of particular issues. Concentrating their attention on specific communal issues, the pluralists note that some influential people or groups participate in some decisions, while at other times they abstain. They insist, furthermore, that influential people or groups may or may not be highly ranked in class or status.[9] Each must be observed in action before a definite statement can be made about his relative influence.

Dahl found that those with high incomes, high status, higher educations, and higher occupations tend to participate in local community decisions more often than those with low status. He points out, however, that these relationships are only statistical and do not positively indicate that a particular person in a low position will not participate in the decision-making process. For example, among interviewees in New Haven, 4 per cent of the politically active earned less than $2,000 a year, 17 per cent between $2,000 and $5,000, and 20 per cent from $5,000 to $8,000.[10] These and other of Dahl's findings indicate a society in which power can be exercised regardless of status or class values. It is no longer a theoretical possibility, as it was in the days of Max Weber, but an empirical fact.

Polsby, another leading pluralist, advises students of power politics never to enter a community with the assumption that some group or clique dominates it. Instead, one should assume that no one man or no one group controls the affairs of the town.[11]

In the present study it was assumed that those with high status and class characteristics were not necessarily the most influential members of the community. It was accepted, furthermore, that each citizen was able to exercise some degree of power. The assessment of the relative power positions of the interviewed groups was chiefly conducted in terms of their social participation in various voluntary and involuntary associations and of their shares in the decision-making processes of these associations.

VOTING BEHAVIOR

Lasswell and Kaplan note that "a *vote* is a unit of expression of support or opposition to a proposed decision. . . . The vote is an essential process regardless of the provisions made for it in the regime."[12] The vote is thus the most elementary exercise of influence by an individual and can be used as a measure of influence. Today's members of the Russian community in Minneapolis, like the first settlers, are jealous of this prerogative, and 90 per cent of them participate in national elections. Only seven of a sample of 210 people did not vote in the national elections. Three of the seven were among the Pilgrims, and there were two each in the groups of Colonists and Frontiersmen. Those who seldom or never voted in national elections were grouped as follows: 8.6 per cent of the Pilgrims ($N = 58$), 9.5 per cent of the Colonists ($N = 84$), and 8.8 per cent of the Frontiersmen ($N = 68$).

A different picture emerges in comparison of the voting behavior of the three groups in local elections. Only ten people of 210 did not vote in the local elections: Six Pilgrims and two each of the Colonists and Frontiersmen. The Frontiersmen in general tended to vote less regularly in local elections, however, and were less concerned about them. Only 69 per cent of them always voted in local elections, compared to 84 per cent of the Pilgrims and 83 per cent of the Colonists. The differences among the groups were statistically significant.

Table 26—Voting Behavior in Local Elections

Response	Pilgrims	Colonists	Frontiersmen
Never or sometimes	5%	16.7%	30.9%
Always	84.5	83.3	69.1
Totals	100.0%	100.0%	100.0%
Chi square (P, C, F) =	6.2	2 d.f.	$p < .05$
Chi square (C, F) =	4.2	1 d.f.	$p < .05$

The differences in voting behavior in local elections may perhaps be explained on two counts. First, our historical survey of the Russian community demonstrated the importance to its members of local political affairs. The Russian community is proud of its politicians and feels that these men owe their elections in some degree to communal support of their campaigns. When they vote in local elections, the members of the community see their politicians as symbols of their own success and quite naturally want them to win. On the other hand, those who have left the community identify themselves psychologically with the larger American society, and their interests are more closely tied to events in Washington than in Minneapolis. From this focus flows a decreasing interest in local elections.

THE SUPPORT OF POLITICAL PARTIES

Dahl has distinguished among three main stages of the "political assimilation" of an ethnic group. In the first stage, the ethnic community—made up of those who share similar characteristics of class, status, and power, fused with their ethnicity—tends to exhibit homogeneous political attitudes and preferences. At first it tends to follow the political leadership of a previously assimilated ethnic group, in return for which its members are rewarded with minor political jobs that permit them to develop their own ethnic leadership. In the second stage, the ethnic group begins to differentiate within itself politically as well as socially. Although many of its members perform white-collar jobs their ethnicity will tend to bind them to the rest of the community, provided the candidates and politicians are skillful in avoiding the issues of socio-economic significance upon which this group is already differentiated. In the third stage, many members of the ethnic group have already been acculturated or drawn into the wider American society, and those who still remain within the the community are already highly heterogeneous with respect to class and status variables. Ethnic appeal in political campaigns tends to reach the ears only of the members of the lower socio-economic group. It fails utterly among the upper strata who are more interested in the socio-economic attitudes of the candidates. Politically, the ethnic group will also be highly heterogeneous.[13]

Table 27—Party Support

Response	Pilgrims	Colonists	Frontiersmen
None	34.5%	23.8%	35.3%
Democratic	65.5	69.0	47.1
Republican	—	7.1	17.6
Totals	100.0%	99.9%	100.0%

Using assorted evidence on voting patterns, residence areas and occupational distribution among the various ethnic groups in New Haven, Dahl was able to assign dates for the corresponding stages in the political assimilation of each ethnic group. The first stage for the New Haven Russian group fell between 1880 and 1920, the second between 1920 and 1940, and the third since 1940.[14]

The three generational units in Minneapolis may also be viewed as representatives of the three stages of political assimilation described by Dahl. The previous chapters have already demonstrated differences in class and status variables. There is also evidence that they differ among themselves in political attitudes as well. Traditionally, the Russian community has supported the Democratic party, and the majority of them still do. Political differentiations were visible in the second generation, however, and some members began to support the Republican party. Seven per cent of the Colonists and 17 per cent of the Frontiersmen reported supporting the Republican party. This difference between the Colonists and Frontiersmen is statistically significant.[15]

Although many individuals from all three groups support specific parties with their votes, few participate in party activities. Only nine out of 210 were members of a party organization. Four were women. There were six Colonists and three Frontiersmen. All six of the Colonists were members of the Democratic-Farmer-Labor party; one Frontiersman was a Democrat, and two were Republicans—further testament to the political assimilation of the Frontiersmen group.

Direct political activity by Minneapolis Russians themselves was slight. Twelve people—six Colonists and six Frontiersmen—participated in political campaigns, distributing leaflets, working as secretaries, addressing campaign letters, and so forth. None of the 105 women held a public office, but two of their husbands did—one a Colonist and one a Frontiersman.

ASSOCIATION WITH THE INFLUENTIALS

While some persons may not be in strategic positions for the exercise of direct power, they exercise it indirectly through friends who hold strategic positions. Association with politicians may also bring direct and indirect patronage. According to Dahl, "politicians who play the game of ethnic politics confer individual benefits like jobs, nominations, bribes, gratuities, and assistance of all sorts on individuals more or less according to ethnic criteria."[16] In the present study, no significant difference in power was discovered between families who had close friends among elected officials of the Minneapolis area and those who had not. Families who reported no such friends represented 86.2 per cent of the Pilgrims, 66.7 per cent of the Colonists, and 73.5 per cent of the Frontiersmen.[17] Proportionally, the Colonists associated in greater numbers with elected politicians than did the Frontiersmen.

Differentiation among the three groups becomes more pronounced on the question of close friends who are active in politics. The largest number of political friends was reported by the Colonists. It is the second generation of Minneapolis Russians that remains politically active, and its members' close friends also come from the second generation. Fewer families among the Frontiersmen reported close friends active in politics. The difference between the groups is statistically significant.

Table 28—Families Reporting Close Friends Active in Politics

No. of Friends in Politics	Pilgrims	Colonists	Frontiersmen
None	86.2%	47.6%	64.7%
One	6.9	28.6	5.9
Two or more	6.9	23.8	29.4
Totals	100.0%	100.0%	100.0%
Chi square (P, C, F) =	16.4	4 d.f.	p < .005
Chi square (C, F) =	6.4	2 d.f.	p < .05

Beside those active in party politics, who exercise considerable power by virtue of their position, one other profession in the United States is located equally strategically: the lawyers. According to Vidich and Bensman, "the lawyer gains his paramountcy through knowledge and personalized non-party contacts up the political hierarchy with other lawyers. He is the mediator between the local party and the party hierarchy, and transforms his personalized contacts into political indispensability in the local community."[18] Close friendships with lawyers of the community may therefore also be used as an index of the relative influence of a particular family. No difference in influence was discovered between the groups of families that reported close friends among lawyers and the groups that had no such influential friends. Families reporting no lawyers among their close friends made up 75.9 per cent of the Pilgrims, 59.5 per cent of the Colonists, and 64.7 per cent of the Frontiersmen.[19] The Colonist group did tend, however, to have more contacts with lawyers.

LABOR-UNION ACTIVITY

There is little disagreement among scholars that the labor union is an important instrument of political power. There remains to determine the degree of union power. When Mills was enthusiastic about the future of the labor movement in the United States, he wrote:

The union is a human institution established to accumulate power and to exert it. The leader of the union is not of the elite of money or of prestige, but he is a member of the elite of power.[20]

Eight years later, Mills wrote that, because of their great dependence upon the federal government, the labor unions "suffered rapid decline in power and now have little part in major national decisions."[21] He criticized labor leaders for their constant striving for recognition. At the same time, he admitted that labor unions still possessed considerable power, that their leaders' "claim for status and power rests on their already increased power—not on property, income, or birth."[22]

A worker who has no interest in his union's activities and who is a passive participant in its decisions is certainly no more influential than a nonunion member. Membership in the union, however, opens to the individual the possibility of exercising influence. In his study of labor union members in St. Louis, Arnold Rose discovered that those laborers who were most satisfied with their unions also approved of their unions' engagement in political action. He concluded that "it seems clear that there is some association between an enthusiasm for the union management and a willingness to have the union grow and engage in political action."[23] Rose did not choose to explain his findings, but it is probable that workers who are enthusiastic about their unions also like to participate in the exercise of union power.

In the total sample of 105 women, thirteen were members of labor unions—four Pilgrims, three Colonists, and six Frontiersmen. None of them participated actively in union activities. (Other studies of American communities have noted, also, that women union members tend to participate less actively than men in union affairs.)[24] On the other hand, the men not only belonged to the unions in greater numbers but also participated more actively in union affairs. There is a significant generational difference among the three groups. Seventy-two and four tenths per cent of the Pilgrims belonged to unions, but they participated only infrequently in union activities— only 10.3 per cent were active. Fewer Colonists belonged to unions, but they were more apt to participate actively in union affairs if they were members. Of the Colonists, 31 per cent were active union members, 28.6 were members but not active, and 40.5 per cent did not belong to unions. Fewer Frontiersmen belonged to unions, and those who did participated less actively. Fifty-five and nine tenths per cent of the Frontiersmen did not belong to unions, 29.4 per cent were inactive members, and only 14.7 per cent participated actively in union activities.[25] While no statistically significant difference was found between the Colonists and Frontiersmen, their replies indicated small interest in union activities among the Frontiersmen and greater influence in union affairs among the Colonists. The Frontiersmen were less likely to be union members because many had become white collar workers.

PARTICIPATION IN THE MAJORITY COMMUNITY

Chapin's Social Participation Scale was intended to isolate community leaders and to measure the relative influence of individuals. It scaled individual memberships in various formal organizations, distinguished degrees of commitment to these organizations, and inquired into their influence in each organization. Those of higher occupational standing also received a higher social participation rating, on the assumption that they tend to participate more often in various organizations and exhibit greater leadership qualities.[26] While it still remains a question whether or not leadership necessarily correlates with class standing, community studies confirm the relationship between socio-economic standing and participation in various clubs and organzations. In his study of New Haven, Hollingshead discovered that 97 per cent of adult members of Class I families held at least one membership in private clubs; 93 per cent of adult members in Class II families belonged to one or more organizations; among Class III families, 84.5 per cent of the adult members belonged to one organization; among Class IV families, only 9 per cent of all adult members participated in one organization; and members of Class V families usually were not active in organized activities. Participation included membership in church organizations, primarily in Class III and, to a lesser extent in Class II.[27]

The participation of the Minneapolis Russians in majority community activities differed for the two generations. Only 10 per cent of the Pilgrim women belonged to a majority community club or organization, but 52 per cent of the women Colonists and 50 per cent of the women Frontiersmen, belonged to at least one organization.[28] Of the three women in the Pilgrim group who reported such participation, one belonged to a Lutheran women's group, one to a card club, and one to a sewing circle. These clubs have little, if any, political influence. Nine Colonist women were members of the Parent-Teachers Association, two belonged to Masonic lodges, two were members of the Veterans of Foreign Wars, and one belonged to the American Legion Auxiliary. One woman was the national chairwoman of a sorority, one participated in the City of Lakes Figure Skating Club, and one belonged to a bowling league. A number of Colonists belonged to card clubs, sewing circles, and other minor associations. In the Frontiersmen group, only two women were members of the Parent-Teachers Association, and two belonged to the O.E.S. Masonic Lodge. Four concerned themselves with the Girl Scouts and Boy Scouts, while one woman was a Camp Fire leader.

A few others belonged to dancing clubs, study clubs, and bowling leagues. It seems that a particular degree of acculturation must be attained before women start participating as leaders in the majority community's boys' and girls' clubs. It should be noted, however, that the Parent-Teachers Association to which the Colonists tended to belong is an organization designed for political action, while the boys' and girls' clubs are social in character.

Similar generational differences appeared in the membership of men in majority community organizations. Only 10.3 per cent of the Pilgrims belonged to such organizations, compared to 47.6 per cent of the Colonists and 52.9 per cent of the Frontiersmen.[29] Of three Pilgrims, two were Masons and one a member of the Eagles. In the Colonist group, four men were Masons, four were members of the Parent-Teachers Association, and five belonged to either the Veterans of Foreign Wars or the American Legion. Some belonged to professional organizations like the Minnesota Coaches Association, Postal Workers Association, or the Editorial Association. A number belonged to other organizations like the Lions Club, the D.F.L. Club, and the Boy Scouts, in which one was a scoutmaster. The Frontiersmen belonged to somewhat similar organizations. Proportionally many more, however, belonged to the professional associations. Five were members of Masonic lodges, three of the Knights of Columbus, and four of the American Legion. The only man belonging to a country club was a Frontiersman. It should be noted that many men and women did not belong to any majority community organization. The following was a typical comment by a good percentage of those belonging to no organization: "I think if a fellow minds his own business and leads his own life, he will have the best reputation."

The Pilgrims held no offices in any of the organizations to which they belonged. A greater number of Colonists held office in their organizations than did the Frontiersmen. The Frontiersmen, however, showed a greater proportion of families whose close friends held positions in majority community organizations. Of the forty-two women who were members of the majority community organizations, nine were officers—six (27 per cent) among the Colonists and three (17 per cent) among the Frontiersmen. Of the forty-one men eleven held offices—eight (40 per cent) Colonists and three (16 per cent) Frontiersmen. Significant generational differences were shown in the reports of close friends who held positions in these majority community organizations. At least one such close friend was reported by 6.9 per cent of the Pilgrims. 33.3 per cent of the Colonists, and 41.2 per cent of the Frontiersmen.[30]

INFLUENCE IN CHURCH AFFAIRS

In the Russian community, women traditionally allow men to govern church affairs. As late as 1955, there were no women on the fifteen-member board of trustees of St. Mary's Church. Two women were elected in 1956, and two women were members of the board in 1960, continuing to serve in 1961. In our samples of Pilgrims and Colonists, no woman held a position on the board of trustees. From among the Frontiersmen, twenty-nine of whom belonged to various churches, four women held positions in their respective churches. Four men among the Frontiersmen also served on church boards. Among the Pilgrims, two men held positions on the board in 1960, and there was one man from the Colonist group.

The Pilgrims and Colonists were compared as to participation in church organizations and their relative influence on the affairs of the church. Since they had left the community, the Frontiersmen were excluded from this comparison. The attempt to isolate relative influence in church affairs by close friendships with those on the board of trustees showed no significant difference. No close friends on the board of trustees were reported by 55.2 per cent of the Pilgrims and 50 per cent of the Colonists. One such friend was reported by 17.2 per cent of the Pilgrim families and 26.2 per cent of the Colonist families. Two or more friends were reported by 27.6 per cent of the Pilgrims and 23.8 per cent of the Colonists.

PARTICIPATION IN CHURCH ORGANIZATIONS

During its long history, the Minneapolis Russian community has established as many as sixteen major clubs, brotherhoods, and other organizations. In the old days, each member participated in one or more of these clubs. Brotherhoods were especially noted for their appeal among the immigrants, since they were more or less consciously regarded as substitutes for the extended family left behind in Europe. After 1936—when St. Mary's "R" Club, Chapter 94, was organized—only one major organization was established. This was the Veterans Association, established shortly after the end of World War II. Besides these two organizations, which have remained relatively strong until the present, the other associations have been losing influence in the community.

With the end of World War II, there was a gradual shift away from many of these old-time associations. Awareness of the shift was revealed in 1951 in the booklet published during the celebration of the church's sixty-fourth anniversary. After a list of clubs, organizations, brotherhoods, and committees, there appeared the following statement:

Every Orthodox Christian should be a member of at least one of the listed organizations. Which one are you connected with?[31]

When a comparison is made between the participation of the first and second generations, significant changes in the activities of the men are obvious, but there seems little or no significant change in the activities of the women. The women traditionally have belonged to the Mothers Club or to one or both of the two women's societies —St. Mary's Russian Orthodox Church Women's Society and the Nativity of the Blessed Virgin Mary Women's Society. The second-generation women have continued membership in the Mothers Club, and a small number have joined either the "R" Club or the Russian Orthodox Church Women's Society.

Of the Pilgrim women, 31 per cent belonged to no community organization, in comparison to 47.6 per cent of the Colonists. Membership in one organization was reported by 41.4 per cent of the Pilgrims and 35.7 per cent of the Colonists. Membership in two or three organizations was maintained by 27.6 per cent of the Pilgrims and 16.7 per cent of the Colonists.[32] Only two women, out of forty-two in both groups who belonged to church organizations, held positions in these organizations. Both were from the Colonist group.

In contrast to the women, the second-generation men have greatly reduced their participation in church organizations. Men who belonged to no community organization numbered 34.5 per cent of the Pilgrims and 64.3 per cent of the Colonists. Membership in one organization was reported by 24.1 per cent of the Pilgrims and 21.4 per cent of the Colonists. Memberships in from one to five organizations were reported by 41.4 per cent of the Pilgrims and only 14.3 per cent of the Colonists.[33] Of the nineteen Pilgrim men who belonged to church societies, two held positions in them. Of the fifteen Colonists two held offices in the organization to which they belonged.

In their study of the Jewish community, Judith Kramer and Seymour Leventman also found that women tended to cling more strongly than men to the traditional patterns of association. In the Jewish community, however, fewer women participated in the organizations of the majority community.[34]

A POWER SCALE COMPARISON OF THREE GROUPS

To measure the relative influence and power of the three groups of Minneapolis Russians, a special power scale was developed. It contained thirty items, six of which applied only to the Pilgrims and Colonists. With the aid of this scale, a significant difference was discovered between the two generations. There were no differences, however, between the Colonists and Frontiersmen. The following results were obtained from the scale-score comparison:

Table 29—Results of the Power Scale Comparison

Group	Mean Scale Score
Pilgrims	2.1
Colonists	2.4
Frontiersmen	2.4

The chi-square test of significance among the three groups on the power scale showed significant differences between the Pilgrims on the one hand and the Colonists and Frontiersmen on the other. No significant results were obtained when the Colonists and Frontiersmen were compared. Most of the responses were found concentrated at scale scores 1, 3, and 5. The few responses for scale score 2 were fused with scale score 3, and the responses on score 4 were fused with number 5.

Table 30—Power Scale Comparison

Scale Score	Pilgrims	Colonists	Frontiersmen
1	549	710	470
3	74	131	68
5	176	340	235
Totals	799	1181	773
Chi square (P, C, F) =	21.0	4 d.f.	p < .001
Chi square (C, F) =	2.9	2 d.f.	n.s.

The Frontiersmen tended to share the same power position as their generational compatriots in the Russian community. They did not increase their power by leaving the community, and in some respects they were less interested in exercising influence in local affairs. One should actually expect a loss of power among the Frontiersmen, compared to the Colonists, and although significant differences do not appear, a number of signs point to such a loss of comparative power.

RECAPITULATION

In comparing the relative influence and power of the three groups, differences between the first and second generations were uncovered. The second generation participated more completely in the majority-community organizations, and its members were associated with people of greater influence. A decline in interest in the ethnic community was revealed by the fact that church organizations and clubs held less interest for the men from the Colonist group as compared with the men from the Pilgrim group. While little significant difference was discovered between the Colonists and the Frontiersmen, the location of power for the Colonists is more ethnic.

More families in the Colonist group reported having close friends active in political parties, and they also participated with greater zeal in the local elections than did the Frontiersmen. A greater number of Colonists had also held office in unions and majority-community organizations. Those who had left the Russian community also tended to change their political attitudes. A significantly greater number of Frontiersmen than Colonists supported the Republican party. Since they had transferred their support to the Republican party only recently, the Frontiersmen were not likely to have acquired as much influence in its affairs as the Colonists held in Democratic party circles.

The comparison of the three groups on the power scale yielded a mean score of 2.1 for the Pilgrims and 2.4 for both the Colonists and the Frontiersmen. The chi-square test produced significant results when all three groups were compared but no significant results when only the Colonists and the Frontiersmen were compared.

NOTES

1. Max Weber, *From Max Weber: Essays in Sociology* (New York: Oxford University Press, 1946), p. 180.
2. *Ibid.*, pp. 194–5. Weber's analysis is understood more clearly in the light of Lasswell and Kaplan's isolation of five additional values in the name of which and with the use of which political power may be attained: well-being, skill, enlightenment, rectitude, and affection. See Harold D. Lasswell and Abraham Kaplan, *Power and Society* (New Haven: Yale University Press, 1950), pp. 55–6.
3. *Ibid.*, p. 185.
4. Daniel Bell, *The End of Ideology* (New York: The Free Press of Glencoe, 1960), p. 42.
5. Arthur J. Vidich and Joseph Bensman, *The Small Town in Mass Society* (Princeton: Princeton University Press, 1958), p. 100. See also chapters on social control in Don Martindale, *American Society* (New York: D. Van Nostrand Co., 1960), pp. 357–427; C. Wright Mills, *The New Men of Power* (New York: Harcourt, Brace & Co., 1948), and C. Wright Mills, *The Power Elite* (New York: Oxford University Press, 1956).
6. See, for example, Robert S. and Helen Merrell Lynd, *Middletown* (New York: Harcourt, Brace & Co., 1929); and *Middletown in Transition* (New York: Harcourt, Brace & Co., 1937); Albert Blumenthal, *Small-Town Stuff* (Chicago: University of Chicago Press, 1932); W. Lloyd Warner and Associates, *Democracy in Jonesville* (New York: Harper & Bros., 1949); and August B. Hollingshead, *Elmtown's Youth: The Impact of Social Classes on Adolescence* (New York: John Wiley & Sons, Inc., 1949).

7. Some of these studies have used different methods of investigation but observed the same basic process at work. See Floyd Hunter, *The Community Power Structure* (Chapel Hill: University of North Carolina Press, 1953); C. Wright Mills, *The Power Elite*; Robert O. Schulze, "Economic Dominants and Community Power Structure," *American Sociological Review*, XXIII (February, 1958), 3–9; Delbert C. Miller, "Industry and Community Power Structure," *American Sociological Review*, XXIII (February, 1958), 9–15; and Vidich and Bensman, *op. cit.*, which at the same time notes new political forces at work.

8. See Robert A. Dahl, *Who Governs?* (New Haven: Yale University Press, 1961), and "A Critique of the Ruling Elite Model," *American Political Science Review*, LII (June, 1958), 463–9.

9. See the arguments advanced by Nelson W. Polsby, "How to Study Community Power: the Pluralist Alternative," *The Journal of Politics*, XXII (August, 1960), 474–84. For the latest review of community power studies, see David Rogers, "Community Political Systems: A Framework and Hypothesis for Comparative Studies," *Current Trends in Comparative Community Studies*, Bert E. Swanson, ed. (Kansas City, Mo.: Community Studies, Inc., 1962), pp. 31–48.

10. Robert A. Dahl, *Who Governs?* pp. 282–3.

11. Polsby, *op. cit.*, p. 476.

12. Lasswell and Kaplan, *op. cit.*, pp. 167–8.

13. Dahl, *Who Governs*, pp. 34–6.

14. *Ibid.*, p. 36.

15. Chi square 6.7 with 1 degree of freedom, $p < .01$.

16. Dahl, *Who Governs?* p. 53.

17. Chi square 3.4 with 2 degrees of freedom, $p < .25$.

18. Vidich and Bensman, *op. cit.*, p. 100.

19. Chi square 1.9 with 2 degrees of freedom, $p < .50$.

20. C. Wright Mills, *The New Men of Power*, p. 7.

21. C. Wright Mills, *The Power Elite*, p. 262.

22. *Ibid.*, p. 263.

23. Arnold M. Rose, *Union Solidarity* (Minneapolis: University of Minnesota Press, 1952), p. 148.

24. See August B. Hollingshead and Frederick C. Redlich, *Social Class and Mental Illness: A Community Study* (New York: John Wiley & Sons, Inc., 1958), p. 129.

25. Chi square of the three groups 13.6 with 4 degrees of freedom, $p < .01$; chi square for Colonists and Frontiersmen 3.1 with 2 degrees of freedom, $p < .25$.

26. See F. Stuart Chapin, *Social Participation Scale* (Minneapolis: University of Minnesota Press, 1952).

27. Hollingshead and Redlich, *op. cit.*, pp. 82, 92–3, 103, 112, 128.

28. Chi square 14.8 with 2 degrees of freedom, $p < .001$. No significant results were obtained in the comparison between the participation of Colonists and Frontiersmen.

29. Chi square 14.1 with 2 degrees of freedom, $p < .001$. There was no statistically significant difference between the Colonists and Frontiersmen.

30. Chi square 9.8 with 2 degrees of freedom, p. < .01. The statistical comparison of the Colonists and Frontiersmen showed no significant difference.

31. "Souvenir Book of the 64th Anniversary Summer Festival and Picnic," St. Mary's Russian Orthodox Greek Catholic Church (Minneapolis: 1951), p. 46.

32. Chi square 2.4 with 2 degrees of freedom, p < .50.

33. Chi square 7.8 with 2 degrees of freedom, p < .02.

34. Judith R. Kramer and Seymour Leventman, *Children of the Gilded Ghetto* (New Haven; Yale University Press, 1961), p. 187.

11   Acculturation

In ORDER TO UNDERSTAND the concept of acculturation, the nature
of the ethnic community must be clearly comprehended. Martindale
has effectively defined it as a complete way of life and the system
of institutions that makes it possible. Like any community, it is
a product of the forces always operative in human social affairs toward stability, consistency, and completeness. In the case of the alien
living as a guest within the framework of a majority community, two
new principles of community formation were evolved: selective receptivity and partial closure. In response to these forces in the wider
community, the ethnic community responds with a combination of
yielding and defense. Specifically, one precondition of an ethnic
community is the capacity of the alien to offer his services to the
majority community and have them accepted sufficiently to permit
him to earn a living. On the other hand, the alien is usually barred
from full social acceptance by the majority, and, for his own part,
he is not always willing to abandon all those cultural forms that
formerly gave meaning to his life. Under these circumstances, the
alien is inclined to find in his traditional culture a new point of
synthesis for his way of life in a foreign land. Thus the ethnic community is born.[1]

From the first formation of an ethnic community, the preservation of its ethnicity takes on a unique value of its own, apart from the values of class, status, or power. Under special conditions, however, some members of ethnic communities may be willing to abandon their ethnic values. The process by which the goals and values of one community are adopted by the members of another is called acculturation.[2] In the case of the Russian community in Minneapolis, acculturation involves acceptance of the general American value system and the relocation of loyalties. S. N. Eisenstadt has described it as a process of "continuous limitation of the sphere of purely ethnic activities and symbols, and their transformation into alternative, secondary spheres of activities."[3]

The transformation of loyalties by members of an ethnic community is usually gradual. The change occurs in stages: It is initiated by increasing participation in the affairs of the majority community; it progresses through development of interests and friendships in the outside community; and it is completed with rejection by the children of their parents' ethnic way of life. To isolate this process of transformation and to measure the relative acculturation of the Pilgrims, Colonists, and Frontiersmen—apart from their class, status, or power positions—an acculturation scale was developed.[4]

PLACES OF BIRTH

By definition, the first-generation families were units in which either the wife or the husband or both were born in Europe. If only one person in the family was born in Europe, he had to be forty years of age or older for the family to be classified in the first generation; otherwise the family would be classified in the second generation. The second-generation families were classified as those in which at least one member of the family was born in the United States to a family of the first generation. It would be possible to have American-born individual members of the first generation and, at the same time, European-born individual members of the second generation. It could be expected, however, that the majority of the Colonists and Frontiersmen were born in the United States, while the majority of the Pilgrims were born in Europe. In the sample of twenty-nine Pilgrim families, twenty-three men and nineteen women were born in Europe. Among forty-two Colonist couples, one woman and one man were born in Europe, while the rest were born in the United States. All men and women in the Frontiersman group were born in the United States.

INTERMARRIAGE

The preservation of an ethnic community is possible only under conditions of strict segregation from the wider community and *vice versa*. The prejudice from without and the insistence on tradition within promote the continuity of the ethnic community with minimal influence of acculturation. Wirth noted that "in countries where the contact between Jew and non-Jew has been continued for a few generations, and where no new immigration from other countries in which the Jews retained their old status has taken place, the ghetto has, to a large extent, disintegrated."[5] Wirth went on to conclude that the most significant external factor in the disintegration of the Jewish community was intermarriage between Jews and Gentiles:

The falling away of the children of mixed marriages and the increased rate of intermarriage among the children and grandchildren of Jewish immigrants are factors of especial significance in the changing character of the Jewish group.[6]

The findings of the present study support Wirth's observation. The Frontiersmen, who left the Russian community, included only one family that was Slavic and Eastern Orthodox on both sides. By contrast, the Colonist group included seventeen such families and the Pilgrim group twenty-six. It should be noted, however, that many families continued to belong to the church even though one member was an "outsider." Other factors beside intermarriage affected the decision to remain in the community. Names like Carlson, Nelson, Anderson, and others were found in the church register. The admission of members from the wider community into the ethnic community also tended to foster further acculturation of the Russians.

When the origins of husbands and wives were compared, significant differences appeared among all three groups. The wives with Slavic backgrounds composed 93.1 per cent of the Pilgrim group, 71.4 per cent of the Colonist group, and 47.1 per cent of the Frontiersman group.[7] Husbands with Slavic origins composed 96.6 per cent of the Pilgrim group, 69 per cent of the Colonist group, and 55.9 per cent of the Frontiersman group.[8] The families with more than one member of Slavic origin tended to sever their connections with the ethnic community less often than families in which only one member had ties in the ethnic community.

The members of ethnic communities are well aware of the dangers of intermarriage and utilize various sanctions to bring about conformity. M. K. Argus has described the attitudes of the Russian community toward him after his marriage to an American:

When my Russian friends discovered that the situation was beyond remedy, they changed their attitude, and open hostility was replaced by a mixture of chagrin and pity. It was, after all, possible that I was merely the victim of a plot, a willing one, perhaps, but nevertheless a victim. . . . There was some excuse for marrying a foreign, that is an American, girl if she had plenty of money. But a Russian who marries a poor American girl is definitely a psychopathic case, and my friends never hesitated to tell me exactly how they felt about my mental state.[9]

LANGUAGE

Once the members of an ethnic community accept the inevitability of the marriage of one of their members to an outsider, they attempt to acculturate this outsider to their ethnic ways. The foreigner's appreciation of a particular ethnic group is largely dependent on his or her knowledge of the language of the group. Argus has wittily observed the pressures put upon his wife by his Russian friends to learn Russian:

"You really don't understand any Russian at all?"

"No."

"What a pity. It is a beautiful language. You really must learn it."

"I guess I should."

"Oh, yes! It is the language of Pushkin, Lermontov, and Chekhov." (Pushkin, Lermontov, and Chekhov have by now become my wife's pet hates.) "You must learn it."

"I surely must."

"A cousin of mine married an American girl, too. Right after marriage she began to study the Russian language. Now she speaks Russian like a native *Moskvichka*, I mean a real Moscow-born girl."

"How nice."

"Very nice. But then, of course, my cousin's wife is very much in love with her husband."[10]

The language of an ethnic group is clearly of tremendous importance for the preservation of the community. Nevertheless, the second and consecutive generations of the ethnic community are more comfortable with the language of the wider community and tend to abandon the Russian language, to the sorrow of their parents. In their study of Yankee City, Warner and Srole quoted the complaint of a first-generation Russian father about his second-generation son:

He doesn't understand half of what I say to him in Russian. Sometimes I will be talking for a long time and he will break in (speaking Russian) with "I can't understand half you're saying. Why can't we talk English?" It makes me sore.[11]

Warner and Srole observed that frequently the parents would speak their native language, while the children would perist in using English. They could understand each other but would remain emotionally disquieted. Warner concluded that "this language difference is an undisguised source of conflict and antagonism between parent and child, and symbolizes the fundamental difference in the orientation and pattern of their personality systems."[12]

Of the Minneapolis Russians, the parents of the 96.6 of the Pilgrim women conversed in their native tongue at home when the children were growing up. Of the parents of the Colonist women, 66.7 per cent conversed in their native tongue, while the rest mixed the languages. Only 41.2 per cent of the parents of the Frontiersman women talked to them in their native language.[13] This difference was no doubt related to the ethnic backgrounds of the women themselves, for the majority of the Frontiersmen came from non-Slavic families. Currently, all families in the Colonist and Frontiersman groups use English as the only conversational medium in the home. Among the Pilgrims, 27 per cent use their native language, 10 per cent use both English and their native tongue, and 62 per cent use English primarily in their daily lives.

CHILDREN

The discarding of their parents' language by the American-born generations of ethnic communities is true not only for Caucasians, who can more easily pass into the wider American society, but also for such groups as the Chinese and Japanese. In her study of the Chinese in American society, Rose Hum Lee states that the "Chinese language loses its effectiveness when the families become more established."[14] The language tends to be used somewhat longer by those living in or near the Chinese ghettos, but as soon as families move away from Chinatown and the distance between the homes and language-schools widens, Chinese children have fewer opportunities to learn and speak the language. By the third generation, Chinese is often as much of a foreign language to Americans of Chinese ancestry as it is to other Americans.[15]

The importance of their native language for the American Japanese was underscored in the study by LaViolette:

An older informant gave it as his opinion that the American-born children to the "nth" generation must learn Japanese. When asked why, he answered that there was no other way by which "we may keep our connections with Japan."[16]

LaViolette found that even many of the second-generation Japanese reported their intentions to teach their children the Japanese language.[17]

Emphasis on the Russian language among the Minneapolis Russians was not found to be very strong—in part, as a result of the peculiar situation of these people. Politically and religiously, they have identified themselves with the Russians, while linguistically and ethnically they have nothing in common with the true Russian background. In the church school, however, their children were taught the Russian language, which the parents themselves did not understand and so could not aid their children in understanding. The English language thus became an acceptable common basis for both parents and children.

Among the sample of Pilgrims, only 62 per cent made an attempt to teach their children their native language. Of the Colonists and Frontiersmen, only 15 per cent indicated that they either taught or intended to teach their children the native language of their parents.[18] Close to 80 per cent of the children in the Pilgrim group attended St. Mary's Sunday school. Of the Colonist families, 61 per cent sent their children to St. Mary's Sunday school or intended to do so when the children became old enough. Despite the fact that the children are no longer instructed in the Russian tongue, interest in the Sunday school has declined among the second generation.

The average number of children in the Pilgrim families was 3.4; in the families of Colonists, 2.4; and in the families of Frontiersmen, 2.8. The families in the two latter groups were still young enough to increase in size to the same average as their parents' families.

READING RUSSIAN LITERATURE

The peasant and Austro-Hungarian background of the families in the Pilgrim group manifested itself in their reading of Russian books, magazines, and newspapers. Thirty-two per cent read some kind of Russian literature, but it was very limited in scope. They read their brotherhood newspapers, *Svet* and *Vistnik,* and the annual Russian calendars, which are almanac-type publications. The most-read book was the Bible. The Colonists (8.3 per cent) and the Frontiersmen (1.5 per cent) reported occasional reading of some Russian literature. The tastes of these few persons in the second generation were similar to those of their parents.[19]

ACTUAL MEMBERSHIP IN ST. MARY'S CHURCH

According to Eisenstadt, "the adherence of the younger generation to the 'ethnic' school, church, newspaper, etc., weakens. Even if in practice the social world of the younger immigrant generations is to some extent confined to their own kind, it lacks a specific 'ethnic' content."[20]

The weakening of ties with the Russian school and newspaper among second-generation Russians has already been illustrated. Ties with the Russian church have been broken by the Frontiersmen, while the Colonists have transformed the church to suit the new conditions of life. The Minneapolis Russian community is proud of the fact that many intermarriages with outsiders bring converts to the Orthodox faith. Our study revealed, however, that the number of actual conversions is smaller than the church roster indicates. To be sure, although one member of the family remains in the church and pays family dues ($16 rather than $11 for a single person), the spouse does not necessarily regard himself as a member of the church. This kind of nominal participation is revealed in analysis of the second-generation families. Of the forty-two families interviewed, there were twenty-five (59.5 per cent) in which either the wife or the husband was non-Orthodox—ten wives and six husbands. Nineteen per cent of the Colonists thus do not consider themselves members of the Russian Orthodox Church (N = 84), in comparison with only 1.7 per cent in the Pilgrim group (N = 58).[21]

TYPE OF SERVICE ATTENDED

Those attending St. Mary's Church have a choice of the early English-language services or the longer Slavonic services on Sunday morning. The English-language services are popular among the Pilgrims, as well as among the Colonists. The English services are usually attended by 34.5 per cent of the Pilgrims and 83.3 per cent of the Colonists. Many Pilgrims still prefer the Slavonic services, and 44.8 per cent attend them regularly in comparison with only 14.3 per cent of the Colonists. Both services are attended by 20.7 per cent of the Pilgrims and 2.4 per cent of the Colonists. Long Slavonic services are traditional for this ethnic group, but the second generation, with the aid of some members of the first, has instituted English-language services lasting one hour. The services "lack a specific 'ethnic' content," as indicated above.

The yearly envelope contributions of the Pilgrims and Colonists were somewhat similar. Thirty-four and five tenths per cent of the Pilgrims and 45 per cent of the Colonists donated less than $25 a year. Between $25 and $49 was donated by 41.4 per cent of the Pilgrims and 25 per cent of the Colonists. Fifty dollars or more was contributed by 24.1 per cent of the Pilgrims and 30 per cent of the Colonists.[22]

RELIGIOUS AFFILIATION OF THE FRONTIERSMEN

Of great interest are the present religious loyalities of those who have terminated their ties with the Orthodox church. Twenty-three (67.6 per cent) are members of Protestant denominations, six (17.6 per cent) are Roman Catholics, and five (14.7 per cent) belong to no church. Of the twenty-three Protestant families, fourteen are affiliated with various Lutheran denominations. This fact is explained by the preponderance of Scandinavian Lutherans in the Twin Cities. Those who become acculturated to the wider community tend to assume the characteristic traits of the particular region in which they live.

FAVORED ASSOCIATIONS

A recent study of the Minneapolis Jewish community shows that even third-generation Jews tend to pursue intimate associations

primarily with other Jews and that "continued intimacy with childhood friends suggests some reluctance to forfeit social ties in the
interest of mobility."[23] The third generation of Jews is, however, no
longer as segregated from the wider community as were its parents.
Many of them cultivate Gentile friendships and "cite occupation and
college as the two social settings in which such friendships are
formed."[24]

The second generation of Minneapolis Russians has also formed
some of its friendships through business associations—4.8 per cent of
the Colonists and 17.6 per cent of the Frontiersmen reported the
majority of their close friends among their business associates.
Proportionally larger numbers of Frontiersmen associate with business
friends, but the statistical difference is not significant.[25] The majority
of families in all three groups associate most often with relatives and
neighbors rather than with their business co-workers. None of the
Pilgrims associates with his business companions. As far as the
Minneapolis Russians are concerned, buiness association represents
only one of the minor settings for forming friendships with members
of the wider community.

The Pilgrims who reported no friendships with their business
associates made up 24.1 per cent of the families whose close associations were conducted primarily with persons outside the Russian
community. In the group of Colonists, 66.7 per cent reported as-
sociating more often with persons outside the Russian community. As
expected, 91.2 per cent of the Frontiersmen reported that the
majority of their friends were not members of the Russian community.[26] The Colonists are potentially able to sever connections
with their ethnic community, but they are not as yet willing to
give up the advantages it offers them.

More specific quantitative information was obtained about the
best friends of the interviewed families when a question was asked
about the church memberships of the three best friends of each
family. The families who had left St. Mary's parish also tended to
dispense with closer ties among those who remained in the church,
or perhaps they had never formed close ties. The Colonists shared
friendships both inside and outside the ethnic community.

Table 31—The Number of Best Friends Who Are Members of St. Mary's Church

No. of Friends	Pilgrims	Colonists	Frontiersmen
All 3	51.7%	16.7%	—
2 out of 3	17.2	26.2	5.9%
1 out of 3	20.7	23.8	17.6
None	10.3	33.3	76.5
Totals	99.9%	100.0%	100.0%
Chi square (P, C, F) =	38.7	6 d.f.	p < .001
Chi square (C, F) =	17.2	3 d.f.	p < .001

AN ACCULTURATION-SCALE COMPARISON

To measure the relative acculturation of the three groups, a special acculturation scale was developed, which contained twenty-three items, four of which applied only to the Colonists and Pilgrims. With the aid of the scale, significant differences were found among all three generational units. The following results were obtained from the scale-score comparison:

Table 32—Results of the Acculturation Scale Comparison

Group	Mean Scale Score
Pilgrims	2.6
Colonists	3.5
Frontiersmen	4.2

The chi-square test applied to all three groups on the acculturation scale showed a significant difference among the Pilgrims, Colonists, and Frontiersmen. As predicted, the Colonists revealed greater acculturation to American society than did the Pilgrims, and, in turn, the Frontiersmen achieved a higher acculturation score than did either the Pilgrims or the Colonists. The Frontiersmen had lost their ethnic values but gained in terms of the values of class and membership in a distinct status community. The Colonists, however, were trying to extend their class and status positions but not at the expense of losing their ethnicity.

Table 33—Acculturation Scale Comparison

Scale Score	Pilgrims	Colonists	Frontiersmen
1	361	298	134
3	63	89	56
5	232	559	527
Totals	656	946	717
Chi square (P, C, F) =	226.3	4 d.f.	p < .001
Chi square (C, F) =	40	2 d.f.	p < .001

RECAPITULATION

Significant differences were found among all three groups on many acculturation items. The Pilgrims intermarried least with outsiders, and made greater use of the native language in their homes. They also attempted to teach their native language to their children. They read a limited number of Russian language publications and attended the Slavonic church services. Pilgrim families associated with their close kin and their neighbors, most of whom were also members of St. Mary's Church and the Russian community.

The families of the Colonists and Frontiersmen associated more frequently with non-Russian friends and preferred the English language. The Colonists intermarried with majority-community members more than did the Pilgrims, while the Frontiersmen intermarried to a greater degree than did the Colonists. In general, the Frontiersmen were almost indistinguishable from the majority community.

The acculturation-scale comparison confirmed the observation that the Frontiersmen were more acculturated into the general American society than either the Pilgrim group or the Colonist group. These data confirmed the hypotheses that cultural transformation of the ethnic community occurs gradually with each successive wave of new generations. Those who had become acculturated into the American society and so lost their ethnicity tended, however, to gain in class and special kind of status advantages but were not able to improve themselves sufficiently to exercise greater power and influence.

NOTES

1. Don Martindale, *American Social Structure* (New York: Appleton-Century-Crofts, Inc., 1960), pp. 377–432.

2. For a thorough historical and theoretical review of the concept of acculturation, see Ralph Beals, "Acculturation," in *Anthropology Today*, A. L. Kroeber, ed. (Chicago: University of Chicago Press, 1953), pp. 621–41; and Bernard J. Siegel, Evon Z. Vogt, James B. Watson, and Leonard Broom, "Acculturation: An Exploratory Formulation," *American Anthropologist*, LVI (Dec., 1954), 973–1002.

3. S. N. Eisenstadt, *The Absorption of Immigrants* (London: Routledge & Kegan Paul Ltd., 1954), p. 247.

4. For earlier studies that used quantitative procedures for measuring acculturation, see George C. Spindler and Walter Goldschmidt, "Symposium on Acculturation," *American Anthropologist*, XLIII (1941), 1–61; and "Experimental Design in the Study of Culture Change," *Southwestern Journal of Anthropology*, VIII (1952), 68–83. See also Paul J. Campisi, "A Scale for the Measurement of Acculturation" (Unpublished Ph.D. Dissertation, University of Chicago, 1947).

5. Louis Wirth, *The Ghetto* (Chicago: University of Chicago Press, 1928), p. 125.

6. *Ibid.*, p. 126.

7. Chi square 13.9 with 2 degrees of freedom, $p < .001$.

8. Chi square 13.3 with 2 degrees of freedom, $p < .005$.

9. M. K. Argus, *Moscow-on-the-Hudson* (New York: Harper & Bros., 1948), pp. 103–4.

10. *Ibid.*, pp. 106–7.

11. W. Lloyd Warner and Leo Srole, *The Social System of American Ethnic Groups* ("Yankee City Series," Vol. III [New Haven: Yale University Press, 1945]), p. 138.

12. *Ibid.*

13. Significant differences were found among all three groups: chi square 21.7 with 2 degrees of freedom, $p < .001$; chi square for Colonists and Frontiersmen 4.9 with 1 degree of freedom, $p < .05$.

14. Rose Hum Lee, *The Chinese in the United States of America* (Hong Kong: Hong Kong University Press, 1960), p. 248.

15. *Ibid.*

16. Forrest E. LaViolette, *Americans of Japanese Ancestry* (Toronto: Canadian Institute of International Affairs, 1946), p. 55.

17. *Ibid.*

18. Chi square between the three groups was 29 with 2 degrees of freedom, $p < .001$.

19. Chi square for the three groups was 29.5 with 2 degrees of freedom, $p < .001$; no significant difference exists between the Colonists and Frontiersmen in Russian reading habits.

20. Eisenstadt, *op. cit.*, pp. 251–2.

21. Chi square 9.6 with 1 degree of freedom, $p < .005$.

22. Comparison between the two groups is not statistically significant: chi square 2.2 with 2 degrees of freedom, $p < .50$.

23. Judith R. Kramer and Seymour Leventman, *Children of the Gilded Ghetto* (New Haven: Yale University Press, 1961), p. 178.

24. *Ibid.*

25. Chi square for Colonists and Frontiersmen 2.5 with 1 degree of freedom, $p < .25$.

26. Statistically significant results were obtained: chi square 30.4 with 2 degrees of freedom, $p < .001$; chi square for Colonists and Frontiersmen, 6.5 with 1 degree of freedom, $p < .02$.

12 The Russian Community in Transition

THIS STUDY has attempted to isolate some of the major processes by which an ethnic community is undergoing transformation and is preserved. Among the theorists who have studied these processes, Max Weber, Hans Gerth, C. Wright Mills, and Don Martindale have been particularly helpful for our purposes. All argue that the preservation of the ethnic community rests upon the internal and external closure of that community and upon the advantages and privileges accruing from such closure to members of both ethnic and majority communities.

Theoretically, the preservation of the ethnic community is possible only as long as this partial closure is maintained. As soon as outside opportunities are opened for members of an ethnic community, some members find it more advantageous to leave the community and seek their fortunes in the larger world. Access to majority-community advantages accrues to those who acquire the knowledge of majority-community symbols and values and of the required skills. In an ethnic community like that of Minneapolis Russians, with its background of foreign peasant experience, such knowledge is only realistically possible to second and later generations. By utilizing symbols of the majority community and acquiring its skills, some second-generation members have won significant socio-economic positions within the greater metropolitan area.

GENERAL WORKING HYPOTHESES

The concept of the ethnic community as a partially closed minority community serves as foundation for the two general hypotheses developed for this study:

1. The system of stratification in the ethnic community is gradually destroyed with the rise of the second and later generations.
2. The economic and professional advancement of later generations brings about cultural assimilation with, and dispersal among, the members of the majority community.

The notion of generation employed follows the ideas outlined by Karl Mannheim, who has devoted serious attention to this problem. Mannheim's usage avoids purely mechanical division among age groups, relying instead upon the new concept of "generation units," characterized by the members' shared "common destiny." Three distinct generational units can be isolated in the Minneapolis Russian community. The first is composed of the founders of the Russian community, who have been termed Pilgrims. The second is composed of the conservative segment of the sons and daughters of the Pilgrims, the Colonists. The third is also composed of sons and daughters of the Pilgrims—the radicals who have left the Russian community to seek individual fortunes in the majority community. We have called this group the Frontiersmen.

For testing purposes, the two general hypotheses were broken down into a number of specific working hypotheses, which were then tested by means of four scales developed expressly for this study. The first three scales measured the socio-economic and power dimensions of the generational units: They are the class scale, the status scale, and the power scale. The fourth scale measured the relative acculturation of the three groups. The total comparison should have shown a gradual displacement of the values of the ethnic community by those of the majority community. The first general hypothesis predicts displacement of the stratification of the ethnic community by that of the majority community; the second predicts displacement of the values of the ethnic community by those of the majority community.

The specific working hypotheses thus involve three generational units and four dimensions of change. The working hypotheses:

A. A general improvement in class situation is discernible, as one moves from the Pilgrims through the Colonists to the Frontiersmen.
B. An imporvement of status within the ethnic community is discernible, as one moves from the Pilgrims to the Colonists.
C. The basis of status is transformed, as one moves from the Colonists to the Frontiersmen, that is Pilgrims and Colonists find status within the ethnic community; Frontiersmen increasingly find it outside the ethnic community.
D. As one moves from the Pilgrims to the Colonists, an improvement in power situation is discernible.
E. As one moves from Colonists to Frontiersmen, the basis for power is shifted, and a drop in comparative power is discernible.
F. As one moves from Pilgrims through the Colonists to the Frontiersmen, a general increase in acculturation to the American community is discernible.

The Method of Study

Study of the Russian community required solution of two major types of methodological problem: technical and procedural. The technical problems were solved by the development of instruments for the quantification of the major stratification variables. In fashioning such instruments, various classical studies by American students of stratification were consulted. They included those of F. Stuart Chapin, W. Lloyd Warner, William H. Sewell, and August B. Hollingshead. With the aid of these studies, our own scales were developed. The major difference between these scales and those used in earlier studies is that they isolate, rather than combine, the three distinct dimensions of stratification: class, status, and power. The resulting scales were then applied to the task of determining the comparative standings of the three groups of Russians in the Minneapolis area. The technical and procedural aspects of the study were thus integrated.

The procedural problems were solved by the empirical design of the study in two steps: Location of the Russian community in the Minneapolis area was undertaken, and the history and structure of it were described; a study design was formulated in terms of the theory of ethnic-community change plus a number of practical considerations. The sampling of former members of the Russian community (the Frontiersmen) proved to be the most difficult task. A study was made of city-directory data in order to locate former members of the Russian community in the Minneapolis area. The other two samples were selected by random procedures from church-roll data. As a further check on former members, the families interviewed in all three groups were asked for the names of former community members. Ultimately, 150 families were selected for interviewing, and 105 interviews were obtained: twenty-nine Pilgrim families, forty-two Colonist families, and thirty-four Frontiersman families.

FINDINGS

The findings on the six working hypotheses are summarized in the table below.

Table 34—Results of Scale Comparisons Recorded by Mean Scale Scores

Scale	Pilgrims	Colonists	Frontiersmen
Class	1.7	2.3	2.7
Status	2.0	2.8	2.9
Power	2.1	2.4	2.4
Combined socio-economic scale	2.0	2.7	2.9
Acculturation	2.6	3.5	4.2

The findings as measured by the short class scale confirm hypothesis A. As one moves from Pilgrims through Colonists to Frontiersmen, the scale score changes from 1.7 to 2.7. Joint family income and occupation of men improve as one moves through the successive generational units. The highest class position is enjoyed by the Frontiersmen who have left the Russian community to make their way in the metropolitan wilderness. The least wealth and poorest occupations are found among the Pilgrims, while the Colonists are located in the intermediate position between the Pilgrims and the Frontiersmen.

Hypothesis B was also confirmed. The status index shows an improvement from 2.0 to 2.8. Significant differences were discernible in items of material display and general leisure time activity, as one moves from the Pilgrims to the Frontiersmen.

The findings on hypothesis C are not so positive. Frontiersmen seek status through the symbols of the majority community and in the world outside the ethnic community. The Pilgrims and Colonists operate within the ethnic community and with the symbols of that community. Our findings of the study do not register this transformation. There is still another difficulty, for the anticipated drop in status after a move from the Colonists to the Frontiersmen is also not confirmed by the data. The Colonists enjoy status within the ethnic community, while the Frontiersmen must struggle for status in the majority community, and it would be reasonable to expect that a person ranking high among the circles of his kind might sacrifice rank in moving into the wider society. On this particular point, the findings reverse theoretical expectation, for while the status score of the Colonists is 2.8, the status score of the Frontiersmen is 2.9. The difference is not great, to be sure, but it is not in the expected direction.

There are two possible interpretations of these findings. Either the hypothesis itself is false, or the instruments for measuring it are imprecise. In this particular case, the second alternative appears to be more plausible. The scale did not isolate the social context within which status was sought but only the various tangible evidence (styles of life and leisure-time pursuits) of status achieved. Before rejecting hypothesis C, it is necessary to develop more delicate instruments for determination of status. Meanwhile, however, it must be noted that the existing evidence, far from confirming hypothesis C, actually contradicts theoretical expectations.

The findings do confirm hypothesis D, however. The Colonists participate with greater frequency in the political life of the local community. They also participate in greater numbers in various local organizations and possess greater influence over the decision-making processes of the community. The power-scale score of the Pilgrims was 2.1; that of the Colonists was 2.4.

The problem with hypothesis E is similar to that of hypothesis C, actually contradicts theoretical expectations.
ethnic community, while the Frontiersmen abandon community opportunities in favor of joining the majority community. Hypothesis E is, however, unfortunately also not confirmed by the findings. The evidence is a bit more positive than for hypothesis C—the Frontiersmen do not register a gain in power over the Colonists, and both score 2.4 on the power scale. The considerations that apply to hypothesis C are also relevant here. There is, however, minor evidence that greater precision of the scale for measuring power would reveal both changed foundations of power striving and a loss of power, after a move from the Colonists to the Frontiersmen. For one thing, the voting pattern changes radically from one group to the next. The Colonists vote Democratic; the Frontiersmen begin to vote Republican. Interest in local elections declines radically among those who join the Frontiersmen, suggesting a shift in interest from the local to the national scene.

The findings also confirm hypothesis F. The acculturation score rises from 2.6 to 3.5 to 4.2. The Frontiersmen operate in the outside world with the values and symbols of the majority community, and the Pilgrims cling to the values of the ethnic community—while the Colonists operate with symbols and values of both communities, exhibiting the classical features of the marginal man.

The suggested distinctions among the different dimensions of stratification receive full empirical justification in all these findings. Had the study been content to follow the path of previous work in social stratification, which lumps the different dimensions of stratification into one, such findings would not have been achieved.

VALIDATION OF THE STUDY

A check of the findings on socio-economic distribution of the three groups, using Hollingshead's "Two Factor Index of Social Position," yields very similar results. In Table 35, the scores of the two-factor index computation are given.

Table 35—Results of Comparison among the Three Groups, Using Hollingshead's Two-Factor Index

Social Class	Range of Computed Scores	Score of Pilgrims	Score of Colonists	Score of Frontiersmen
I (highest)	11–17			
II	18–27			
III	28–43			39.2
IV	44–60		45.5	
V (lowest)	61–77	64.2		

As with the socio-economic scale, distinction between the two generations is much greater than that between the Frontiersmen and the Colonists. Yet, Hollingshead's two-factor index places each group in the distinct socio-economic class anticipated in our hypotheses. The two types of procedure thus confirm one another.

SUMMARY AND CONCLUSION

The ethnic community is formed within the majority community by persons of foreign origin who carry on a semi-autonomous way of life. The conditions conducive to formation of the ethnic community involve a combination of receptivity and resistance. The attitudes of permissiveness and prejudice on the part of the majority community lead to construction of partially closed ghetto-like minority systems that have little influence on the majority and are in turn left alone to pursue their ways of life in a new land.

It is difficult to maintain the ethnic community when attitudes of hostility and prejudice among the majority community begin to diminish. The task becomes even more arduous when members of the ethnic community themselves begin to borrow their way of life from the majority community. The time comes when the children and grandchildren of the former newcomers speak the language of the majority community, dress in the attire of the largest department store in town, and move out of the stigma-ridden original location of the ethnic community. Gradually members of a once underprivileged minority obtain respectable jobs within the majority community and prove their loyalty to their new country by public service, perhaps even risking their lives in its military causes. In the course of all these activities, they come to accept the goals and values of the majority community.

When this process occurs, the truly integrated ethnic community begins to crumble. The process of disintegration is, however, not sudden. It is a gradual process in which some members of the second generation remain attached to the values of their parents long after others have already terminated their ties with the community.

The concept of the ethnic community served as foundation for our two general hypotheses, which in turn provide the basis for six working hypotheses concerning specific changes in particular generational units.

In order to trace the dynamics of social change by which the Russian community of Minneapolis first took shape and later began to change and eventually to decay under the influence of the wider social environment, the community was divided into generational units following the criteria of Karl Mannheim. A comparison of the scale scores of the respective generational units permitted testing of the six hypotheses. All but two hypotheses were verified by the findings, while some evidence could be interpreted as confirmation for hypotheses C and E; these require further study.

A final problem involves the application of our findings to other communities in the United States. Generalization must be cautious and limited to those minority communities that display traits similar to those found among the Minneapolis Russians. These traits include peasant backgrounds, limited educational opportunities in the old country, ethnic backgrounds other than northern European, and high homogeneity. It is quite possible, for example, that, if the first generation of the Russian Tzarist refugees of the 1920s were compared with their second-generation offspring, the results would be different from those in the present study.

It should be emphasized, however, that the majority of Russian immigrants in the United States share ethnic backgrounds similar to those of the members of the Minneapolis community, for they also came from the Austro-Hungarian Empire before World War I. We may tentatively conclude that the Russian community of Minneapolis is fairly typical of Russian communmunities everywhere in the United States.

APPENDIX — Questionnaire and Description
of the Scales

Questionnaire for a Russian Community Study

1. Code Number
2. Wife's age
   - 20–24 ( )
   - 25–29 ( )
   - 30–34 ( )
   - 35–39 ( )
   - 40–44 ( )
   - 45–49 ( )
   - 50–54 ( )
   - 55–59 ( )
   - 60–64 ( )
   - 65 and over ( )
3. Husband's age
   - 20–24 ( )
   - 25–29 ( )
   - 30–34 ( )
   - 35–39 ( )
   - 40–44 ( )
   - 45–49 ( )
   - 50–54 ( )
   - 55–59 ( )
   - 60–64 ( )
   - 65 and over ( )
4. Wife's birthplace
   - Europe ( ) 1
   - United States ( ) 5

5. Husband's birthplace
   Europe   ( ) 1
   United States   ( ) 5
6. Wife of Slavic origin?
   No   ( ) 1
   Partly   ( ) 3
   Yes   ( ) 5
7. Husband of Slavic origin?
   No   ( ) 1
   Partly   ( ) 3
   Yes   ( ) 5
8. Wife's ethnic generation
   Born in Europe, first generation   ( )
   Father born in Europe, second   ( )
   Grandfather born in Europe, third   ( )
   Fourth or older generation   ( )
9. Husband's ethnic generation
   Born in Europe   ( )
   Father born in Europe   ( )
   Grandfather born in Europe   ( )
   Fourth or older generation   ( )
10. If born in Europe, when arrived in U.S.A.?
    Before 1900   ( )
    1900–1919   ( )
    1920–1945   ( )
    After 1946   ( )
11. If born in Europe, at what age arrived in U.S.A.?
    14 or younger   ( )
    15–19   ( )
    20–24   ( )
    25–29   ( )
    30 or older   ( )
12. If wife born in Europe, when did she receive her citizenship?
    Never   ( )
    Before 1919   ( )
    1919–1945   ( )
    After 1945 (year?)   ( )
13. If husband born in Europe, when did he receive his citizenship?
    Never   ( )
    Before 1919   ( )
    1919–1945   ( )
    After 1945 (year?)   ( )
14. If husband born in Europe, his occupation there
    Farmer   ( )

Skilled craftsman ( )
Other———— ( )

15. If husband born in Europe, his first job in America
Unskilled ( )
Skilled ( )
Other———— ( )

16. Language currently spoken in family
Native ( ) 1
English ( ) 5
Both ( ) 3

17. Parents' language
Native ( ) 1
English ( ) 5
Both ( ) 3

18. Ages of children presently alive: a. ————, b. ————, c. ————,
d. ————, e. ————, f. ————

19. If children under 20, what are their general occupational aims?
Unskilled ( )
Skilled ( )
Clerical ( )
Managerial or semi-professional ( )
Professional ( )

20. Total number of children who lived one year or longer
( ) 0   ( ) 5
( ) 1   ( ) 6
( ) 2   ( ) 7
( ) 3   ( ) 8
( ) 4   ( ) 9 or
                                          more

21. Did your children attend, or will they attend St. Mary's Sunday
School?
Yes ( ) 1
No ( ) 5

22. Did you teach or will you teach your children the native language of
your parents?
Yes ( ) 1
No ( ) 5

23. Neighborhood
Northeast Minneapolis ( ) 1
Columbia Heights or Fridley ( ) 2
North Minneapolis ( ) 3
Other parts of Minneapolis ( ) 4
Suburbs (except Columbia Heights and Fridley)
( ) ( ) 5

24. Last previous residence
    Northeast Minneapolis ( )
    Columbia Heights or Fridley ( )
    North Minneapolis ( )
    Other parts of Minneapolis ( )
    Other suburbs (except Columbia Heights and
        Fridley) ( ) ( )
25. Wife's formal education
    1–4 years ( ) 1
    5–8 years ( ) 2
    9–12 years ( ) 4
    13–16 years ( ) 3
    Graduate school ( ) 5
26. Husband's formal education
    1–4 years ( ) 1
    5–8 years ( ) 2
    9–12 years ( ) 3
    13–16 years ( ) 4
    Graduate school ( ) 5
27. Occupation of wife's father
    Unskilled ( ) 1
    Skilled ( ) 1
    Clerical ( ) 3
    Managerial or semi-professional ( ) 4
    Professional ( ) 5
28. Occupation of husband's father
    Skilled ( ) 2
    Unskilled ( ) 1
    Clerical ( ) 3
    Managerial or semi-professional ( ) 4
    Professional ( ) 5
29. Wife's occupation
    Unskilled ( ) 1
    Skilled ( ) 2
    Clerical ( ) 3
    Managerial or semi-professional ( ) 4
    Professional ( ) 5
    Housewife ( ) 5
    Type of work performed: _____
30. Husband's occupation ( ) 1
    Unskilled ( ) 1
    Skilled ( ) 2
    Clerical ( ) 3
    Managerial or semi-professional ( ) 4

Professional ( ) 5
Type of work performed: _____
Where? _____

31. Joint income
    Under $3,000 ( ) 1
    $3,000–$5,000 ( ) 2
    $5,000–$7,500 ( ) 3
    $7,500–$10,000 ( ) 4
    $10,000 and over ( ) 5
32. Ownership of business and other capital investment—approximate value
    None ( ) 1
    Under $10,000 ( ) 2
    $10,000–$30,000 ( ) 3
    $30,000–$50,000 ( ) 4
    $50,000 and over ( ) 5
33. Ownership of tools or equipment used in trade—approximate value
    Under $100 ( ) 1
    $100–$300 ( ) 2
    $200–$500 ( ) 3
    $500–$1,000 ( ) 4
    $1,000 and over ( ) 5
34. If house owned, approximate present value
    Under $10,000 ( ) 1
    $10,000–$15,000 ( ) 2
    $15,000–$20,000 ( ) 3
    $20,000–$30,000 ( ) 4
    $30,000 and over ( ) 5
    Taxes paid on property last May: ( )
35. If housing rented, what is the monthly payment? (If furnished, one point less up to 1)
    Under $70 ( ) 1
    $70–$85 ( ) 2
    $85–$100 ( ) 3
    $100–$125 ( ) 4
    $125 and over ( ) ( ) 5
36. Type of living quarters
    Apartment (rented) ( ) 1
    Duplex (rented) ( ) 2
    Fourplex (rented) ( ) 3
    Home (rented) ( ) 4
    Home (owned) ( ) 5
37. Number of rooms excluding bathroom
    2 ( ) 1

　　　　3 and 4　　　　　　　　　　　　　　　( ) 2
　　　　5　　　　　　　　　　　　　　　　　( ) 3
　　　　6　　　　　　　　　　　　　　　　　( ) 4
　　　　7 or more ( )　　　　　　　　　　　( ) 5
38. Living room floors
　　　　Plain　　　　　　　　　　　　　　　( )
　　　　Linoleum　　　　　　　　　　　　　( )
　　　　Small rugs　　　　　　　　　　　　( )
　　　　Asphalt, rubber, tile, cork　　　　　　( )
　　　　Wall-to-wall carpeting or parquet　　( )
39. Window decoration in the living room
　　　　None　　　　　　　　　　　　　　　( )
　　　　Shades　　　　　　　　　　　　　　( )
　　　　Venetian blinds　　　　　　　　　　( )
　　　　Curtains　　　　　　　　　　　　　( )
　　　　Draperies　　　　　　　　　　　　　( )
40. Telephone
　　　　None　　　　　　　　　　　　　　　( ) 1
　　　　1-party line　　　　　　　　　　　　( ) 2
　　　　1 private telephone　　　　　　　　( ) 3
　　　　1 telephone & extension　　　　　　( ) 4
　　　　More than 1 line　　　　　　　　　　( ) 5
41. Television
　　　　None　　　　　　　　　　　　　　　( ) 1
　　　　1 black & white　　　　　　　　　　( ) 2
　　　　2 black & white　　　　　　　　　　( ) 3
　　　　Color television　　　　　　　　　　( ) 4
　　　　1 black & white, 1 Color　　　　　　( ) 5
42. Radio or phonograph
　　　　None　　　　　　　　　　　　　　　( ) 1
　　　　A.M. radios only　　　　　　　　　　( ) 2
　　　　Radio-phonograph　　　　　　　　　( ) 3
　　　　A.M. radio and hi-fi　　　　　　　　( ) 4
　　　　F.M. radio and phonograph　　　　　( ) 4
　　　　F.M. radio and hi-fi　　　　　　　　( ) 5
43. Musical instruments
　　　　None　　　　　　　　　　　　　　　( ) 1
　　　　Guitar, accordion, or similar　　　　( ) 2
　　　　Violin, viola, flute
　　　　Recorders, or similar　　　　　　　　( ) 3
　　　　Piano　　　　　　　　　　　　　　　( ) 4
　　　　Organ　　　　　　　　　　　　　　　( ) 5
44. Number of magazines taken regularly
　　　　None　　　　　　　　　　　　　　　( ) 1

1	( )	2
2	( )	3
3	( )	4
4 or more ( )	( )	5

45. Daily newspaper
    None — ( ) 1
    1 paper purchased — ( ) 2
    1 paper delivered — ( ) 3
    Sunday paper and daily — ( ) 4
    2 daily papers — ( ) 5
46. Books
    Less than 10 — ( ) 1
    Westerns, mysteries, etc. — ( ) 2
    Miscellaneous (or paperbacks) — ( ) 3
    Professional — ( ) 4
    Classical — ( ) 5
47. Does wife read any Russian books or magazines?
    Yes ( ) — ( ) 1
    No — ( ) 5
48. Does husband read any Russian books or magazines?
    Yes ( ) — ( ) 1
    No — ( ) 5
49. Does wife read any Russian newspapers?
    Yes ( ) — ( ) 1
    No — ( ) 5
50. Does husband read any Russian newspapers?
    Yes ( ) — ( ) 1
    No — ( ) 5
51. Pictures in the living room
    Photographs — ( )
    Reproductions — ( )
    Originals — ( )
    Other _____ — ( )
52. Cleanliness of the house
    Stained or spotted — ( )
    Dusty — ( )
    Dustless or spotless — ( )
53. Orderliness of the house
    Articles in disorder — ( )
    Articles in usable order — ( )
54. Condition of house articles
    Torn, scratched, ripped, or broken — ( )
    Patched up — ( )
    In good repair & well kept — ( )

55. Age and style of articles
      Old and out of style   ( )
      Old, but well preserved & still in style   ( )
      New or almost new   ( )
56. How many cars owned
      None   ( ) 1
      1   ( ) 3
      2 or more   ( ) 5
57. Cost of newest car
      Under $500   ( ) 1
      $500–$1,000   ( ) 2
      $1,000–$2,000   ( ) 3
      $2,000–$3,000   ( ) 4
      $3,000 or more (   )   ( ) 5
58. Age of newest car
      8 years or older   ( )
      6–7 years   ( )
      4–5 years   ( )
      2–3 years   ( )
      1 year old or newer (   )   ( )
59. Does the family own a boat?
      No   ( ) 1
      Yes   ( ) 5
60. Down town charge account?
      No   ( ) 1
      Yes   ( ) 5
61. Where do you do most grocery shopping?
      Large supermarket   ( )
      Local grocer   ( )
      Both   ( )
62. How often do you have medical check-ups?
      Only when sick   ( ) 1
      Every 2 or 3 years   ( ) 3
      Every year   ( ) 5
63. Who is your physician?
      No one special   ( )
      Member of St. Mary's   ( )
      Not a member of St. Mary's   ( )
64. How often do you have dental check-ups?
      Only when feel pain   ( )
      Every 2–3 years   ( )
      Once or twice a year   ( )
65. Who is your dentist?
      No one special   ( )

Member of St. Mary's   ( )
Not a member of St. Mary's   ( )
66. Do you have your own lawyer?
    No   ( )
    Member of St. Mary's   ( )
    Not a member of St. Mary's   ( )
67. Are there lawyers among your close friends?
    No   ( ) 1
    Yes   ( ) 5
68. Do you eat out?
    Almost never   ( )
    At nearby restaurants   ( )
    At expensive places in town   ( )
69. Wife's favorite music
    Old-time music   ( ) 1
    "Pop" music   ( ) 2
    Semi-classical   ( ) 3
    Jazz   ( ) 4
    Classical   ( ) 5
70. Husband's favorite music
    Old-time music   ( ) 1
    "Pop" music   ( ) 2
    Semi-classical   ( ) 3
    Jazz   ( ) 4
    Classical   ( ) 5

71. Wife's favorite movies

Western	( )	Comedy	( )	
Adventure	( )	Drama	( )	
Mystery & thriller	( )	Musical	( )	
Science fiction	( )	Foreign	( )	
Horror	( )	Does not attend movies	( )	

72. Husband's favorite movies

Western	( )	Comedy	( )	
Adventure	( )	Drama	( )	
Mystery & thriller	( )	Musical	( )	
Science fiction	( )	Foreign	( )	
Horror	( )	Does not attend movies	( )	

73. Attendance at symphony concerts
    Never   ( ) 1
    Occasionally (free) ( ) 2
    Occasionally (paid)
    3–11 a year   ( ) 4
    Regularly (paid)

        12 or more a year   ( ) 5
74. Membership in the Art Institute or Walker Art Center
        No   ( ) 1
        Yes   ( ) 5
75. Attendance at museums and art galleries
        Never   ( ) 1
        Occasionally (1 or 2 times a year)   ( ) 3
        Regularly (3 or more times a year)   ( ) 5
76. Attendance at plays
        Never   ( ) 1
        Occasionally (free)   ( ) 2
        Occasionally (paid)
        3 to 5 plays a year   ( ) 4
        Regularly (paid)
        6 or more a year   ( ) 5
77. Wife's favorite participation sports
        Billiards or pool   ( )
        Bowling   ( )
        Skiing   ( )
        Tennis   ( )
        Golf   ( )
78. Husband's favorite participation sports
        Billiards or pool   ( )
        Bowling   ( )
        Skiing   ( )
        Tennis   ( )
        Golf   ( )
79. Wife's favorite spectator sports
        Wrestling   ( )
        Basketball   ( )
        Boxing   ( )
        Baseball   ( )
        Football   ( )
80. Husband's favorite spectator sports
        Wrestling   ( )
        Basketball   ( )
        Boxing   ( )
        Baseball   ( )
        Footbal   ( )
81. Wife's favorite nonalcoholic beverages
        Soda   ( )
        Fruit juice   ( )
        Milk   ( )
        Tea   ( )

Coffee ( )
Other _____
82. Husband's favorite nonalcoholic beverages
    Soda ( )
    Fruit juice ( )
    Milk ( )
    Tea ( )
    Coffee ( )
    Other _____ ( )
83. Wife's alcoholic-beverage preference
    Straight drinks ( ) 1
    Beer ( ) 2
    Mixed drinks ( ) 3
    Cocktails ( ) 4
    Wine ( ) 5
84. Husband's alcoholic-beverage preference
    Straight drinks ( ) 1
    Beer ( ) 2
    Mixed drinks ( ) 3
    Cocktails ( ) 4
    Wine ( ) 5
85. Vacations
    Always together ( )
    Sometimes without husband ( )
    Always without husband ( )
86. Wife's vacation activity
    Stay home ( )
    Visit relatives ( )
    Fish or hunt with husband at small expense ( )
    Leisure travel ( )
    Accompany husband on expensive fishing or hunting trips in re-
        sort or out-of way place ( )
    Boating ( )
    Other ( )
87. Husband's vacation activity
    Stay home ( )
    Visit relatives ( )
    Fish or hunt at small expense ( )
    Leisure travel ( )
    Fish or hunt at considerable expense ( )
    Boating ( )
    Other ( )
88. Wife votes in national elections
    No ( ) 1

Sometimes ( ) 3
Always ( ) 5

89. Husband votes in national elections
No ( ) 1
Sometimes ( ) 3
Always ( ) 5

90. Wife votes in local elections
No ( ) 1
Sometimes ( ) 3
Always ( ) 5

91. Husband votes in local elections
No ( ) 1
Sometimes ( ) 3
Always ( ) 5

92. Is wife active in politics?
No ( ) 1
Yes ( ) 5

93. Is husband active in politics?
No ( ) 1
Yes ( ) 5

94. What political party does wife vote for?
None ( ) 1
Democratic ( ) 5
Republican ( ) 5

95. What political party does husband vote for?
None ( ) 1
Democratic ( ) 5
Republican ( ) 5

96. Of what political party is wife a member?
None ( ) 1
Democratic ( ) 5
Republican ( ) 5

97. Of what political party is husband a member?
None ( ) 1
Democratic ( ) 5
Republican ( ) 5

98. Do you have close friends active in either the Democratic or the Republican party?
None ( ) 1
One ( ) 3
2 or more ( ) 5

99. Has wife ever held public office?
No ( ) 1
Yes ( ) 5

100. Has husband ever held public office?
    No   ( ) 1
    Yes   ( ) 5
101. Do you have a close friend who is an elected official of Minneapolis area?
    No   ( ) 1
    Yes   ( ) 5
102. Who did you vote for in the last presidential election?
    Eisenhower   ( )
    Stevenson   ( )
    Other   ( )
    Did not vote   ( )
    Refused to answer   ( )
103. Who did you vote for in the last senatorial election?
    Edward Thye   ( )
    Eugene McCarthy   ( )
    Other   ( )
    Did not vote   ( )
    Refused to answer   ( )
104. Who did you vote for in the last congressional election?
    George L. Mikan   ( )
    Roy W. Wier   ( )
    Other   ( )
    Did not vote   ( )
    Refused to answer   ( )
105. Wife's labor-union activity
    Does not belong   ( ) 1
    Belongs but not active   ( ) 3
    Belongs and is active   ( ) 5
106. Husband's labor-union activity
    Does not belong   ( ) 1
    Belongs but not active   ( ) 3
    Belongs and is active   ( ) 5
107. Does wife belong to St. Mary's Church?
    No   ( ) 1
    Yes   ( ) 5
108. Does husband belong to St. Mary's Church?
    No   ( ) 1
    Yes   ( ) 5
109. What church service do you attend?
    Slavonic   ( ) 1
    English   ( ) 5
110. Contributions to the church—envelope offerings
    0–$9.99   ( ) 1

$10–$24   ( ) 2
$25–$49   ( ) 3
$50–$99   ( ) 4
$100 or more   ( ) 5

111. Does wife hold a position in the church?
No   ( ) 1
Yes   ( ) 5

112. Does husband hold a position in the church?
No   ( ) 1
Yes   ( ) 5

113. Do you have close friends who hold positions in St. Mary's?
No   ( ) 1
1   ( ) 3
2 or more   ( ) 5

114. Are you and your husband good friends of one of the pastors of your church?
No   ( )
Yes   ( )

115. How many St. Mary's clubs and organizations does wife belong and pay dues to?
None   ( ) 1
1   ( ) 2
2   ( ) 3
3   ( ) 4
4 or more   ( ) 5

116. How many St. Mary's clubs and organizations does husband belong and pay dues to?
None   ( ) 1
1   ( ) 2
2 or 3   ( ) 3
4 or 5   ( ) 4
6 or more   ( ) 5

117. In how many of these clubs and organizations does wife hold office?
None   ( ) 1
1 or 2   ( ) 3
3 or more   ( ) 5

118. In how many of these clubs and organizations does husband hold office?
None   ( ) 1
1 or 2   ( ) 3
3 or more   ( ) 5

119. Do you have close friends who have offices in these St. Mary's clubs?

None	( )	1
1 or 2	( )	3
3 or more	( )	5

120. Does wife belong to any American clubs outside St. Mary's?

None	( )	1
1 or 2	( )	3
3 or more	( )	5

121. Does husband belong to any American clubs and organizations outside St. Mary's?

None	( )	1
1 or 2	( )	3
3 or more	( )	5

122. Does wife hold any position in these American clubs or organizations?

No	( )	1
Yes	( )	5

123. Does husband hold any position in these American clubs or organizations?

No	( )	1
Yes	( )	5

124. Do you have close friends who hold offices in these American clubs?

None	( )	1
1	( )	3
2 or more	( )	5

125. You and your family associate most of the time with

Kinfolk and neighbors	( )	1
Business associates	( )	5
Both	( )	3

126. How many good friends do you have who are not of Slavic origin and are not members of St. Mary's?

None	( )
1	( )
2 or 3	( )
4 or 5	( )
6 or more	( )

127. Are most of your close friends members of St. Mary's?

Yes	( )	1
No	( )	5
Both equally	( )	3

128. Do you send Christmas cards to your relatives and friends?

No	( )
Yes	( )

129. Do you exchange Christmas gifts with your relatives and friends?

No	( )

Yes ( )

130. What is most important for a good reputation in the community?
    To lead an honest and good life ( )
    To have dependable friends ( )
    To belong to good clubs & organizations ( )
    To have a good education ( )
    To have money ( )
    Other ( )

131. What do you like least about the neighborhood where you now live?
    Many friends have moved out ( )
    It is getting run down ( )
    Not knowing anybody in the neighborhood well ( )
    Other _____ ( )

132. What do you like best about the neighborhood in which you now live?
    Friends live here ( )
    It has a better class of people ( )
    It has better schools and facilities for the family ( )
    Other _____ ( )

133. If you were to move in the near future, where would you prefer to live?
    Northeast Minneapolis ( ) 1
    Columbia Heights and Fridley ( ) 2
    North Minneapolis ( ) 3
    Other parts of Minneapolis ( ) 4
    Other suburbs (except Columbia
        Heights and Fridley) ( ) 5

134. (For those of Slavic origin only) If you have brothers and sisters living in Minneapolis who are not members of St. Mary's Church, please give the following information:
    Name   Address   Marital Status   Occupation   Education
    A.
    B.
    C.

135. If you have children 20 or older, please give the following data:
    Name   Address   Marital Status
    Occupation   Education   Church Membership
    A.
    B.
    C.
    D.

136–150. Please give the following information about your
        3 best friends:

Approximate address
A. B. C.
Occupation of husband
A. B. C.
Length of Friendship
A. B. C.
Where you first met (St. Mary's, neighborhood, school clubs, job, etc.)
A. B. C.
Do they belong to St. Mary's Church?
A. B. C.

151. Please give me the name (and addresses, if possible) of people you know who no longer attend St. Mary's Church or other similar church and who live in the Minneapolis area:
    A.
    B.
    C.
    D.

152. Organizational participation
Wife

St Mary's organizations	Organizations outside St. Mary's
Brotherhoods	Professional and business
Civic and Service	Civic and Service
Recreational	Social and recreational
Social	Other

  (Please indicate if office is held in any of these organizations)

153. Organizational participation
Husband

St. Mary's Organizations	Organizations outside St. Mary's
Brotherhoods	Professional and business
Civic and Service	Civic and Service
Recreational	Social and recreational
Social	Other

  (Please indicate if office is held in any of these organizations)

CODING INSTRUCTIONS FOR QUESTIONS 136–150

Questions 136, 137, 138: Approximate addresses of best friends

Northeast Minneapolis	( ) 1
Columbia Heights and Fridley	( ) 2
North Minneapolis	( ) 3
Other parts of Minneapolis	( ) 4
Other suburbs and places outside Minneapolis	( ) 5

Questions 139, 140, 141: Occupation of husbands
    Unskilled   ( ) 1
    Skilled   ( ) 2
    Clerical   ( ) 3
    Managerial and semi-professional   ( ) 4
    Professional   ( ) 5
Questions 142, 143, 144: Lengths of friendships
    2 years or less   ( )
    3–5 years   ( )
    6–9 years   ( )
    10–19 years   ( )
    20–29 years   ( )
    30 years or more   ( )
Questions 145, 146, 147: Places of first meetings
    St. Mary's church   ( )
    Neighborhood   ( )
    School   ( )
    American clubs and organizations   ( )
    Job   ( )
    Other places (friends' homes, for example)   ( )
Questions 148, 149, 150: Memberships in St. Mary's church
    Yes   ( ) 1
    No   ( ) 5

A Description of the Four Scales

THE FOUR SCALES measuring class, status, power and acculturation of individual families in the community have been integrated into the preceding questionnaire. Each question was weighted on a 5-point scale, and the weights are indicated in the questionnaire. Only those questions for which weights are indicated were included in the four scales. In reporting the questions that went into each scale, we will indicate the numbers and titles of the questions.

CLASS SCALE

30. Husband's occupation
31. Joint income
32. Ownership of business or other capital investment
33. Ownership of tools or equipment used in trade

(4 items)

STATUS SCALE

23. Neighborhood
25. Wife's formal education
26. Husband's formal education
27. Occupation of wife's father
28. Occupation of husband's father
29. Wife's occupation
34. Approximate value of owned house
35. Monthly rent payments, if housing is rented

36. Type of living quarters
37. Number of rooms in the house
40. Telephone
41. Television
42. Radio or phonograph
43. Musical instruments
44. Number of magazines
45. Daily newspaper
46. Books
56. Number of cars owned
57. Cost of newest car
59. Boat owned
60. Downtown charge account
62. Medical check-ups
69. Wife's favorite music
70. Husband's favorite music
73. Attendance at symphony concerts
74. Membership in the Art Institute or the Walker Art Center
75. Attendance at museums and art galleries
76. Attendance at plays
83. Wife's alcoholic-beverage preference
84. Husband's alcoholic-beverage preference
133. Preference of future residence area
136. Residence area of best friends
137. Residence area of second best friends
138. Residence area of third best friends
139. Husband's occupation of the best friends
140. Husband's occupation of the second best friends
141. Husband's occupation of the third best friends

(37 items)

POWER SCALE

67. Lawyers among close friends
88. Voting behavior of wife in national elections
89. Voting behavior of husband in national elections
90. Voting behavior of wife in local elections
91. Voting behavior of husband in local elections
92. Political activity of wife
93. Political activity of husband
94. Specific party voted for by wife
95. Specific party voted for by husband
96. Wife's membership in a specific party

97. Husband's membership in a specific party
98. Close friends active in either Democratic or Republican party
99. Public office ever held by wife
100. Public office ever held by husband
101. Elected officials among close friends
105. Wife's labor-union activity
106. Husband's labor-union activity
111. Position held in church by wife
112. Position held in church by husband
113. Positions held in St. Mary's Church by close friends
115. Wife's membership in St. Mary's organizations
116. Husband's membership in St. Mary's organizations
117. Positions held in St. Mary's organizations by wife
118. Positions held in St. Mary's organizations by husband
119. Close friends holding positions in St. Mary's organizations
120. Wife's membership in majority-community organizations
121. Husband's membership in majority-community organizations
122. Positions held in majority-community organizations by the wife
123. Positions held in majority-community organizations by the husband
124. Close friends holding positions in majority-community organizations

> (30 items. Items numbered 113, 115, 116, 117, 118, 119 apply only to the groups of Pilgrims and Colonists)

ACCULTURATION SCALE

4. Wife's birthplace
5. Husband's birthplace
6. Wife's origins
7. Husband's origins
16. Language currently spoken in family
17. Parents' language
21. St. Mary's Sunday school attendance of children
22. Children taught the native language of parents
47. Russian books and magazines read by wife
48. Russian books and magazines read by husband
49. Russian newspapers read by wife
50. Russian newspapers read by husband
94. Specific party voted for by wife
95. Specific party voted for by husband
107. Membership of wife in St. Mary's Church
108. Membership of husband in St. Mary's Church

109. Church service attended at St. Mary's
110. Contributions to St. Mary's Church
125. Favorite family associations
127. Church membership of the majority of close friends
148. Church membership of best friends
149. Church membership of second best friends
150. Church membership of third best friends

* Items 94 and 95 have been given different weights from those stated in the questionnaire. Preference for the Democratic Party was given the weight of 3, and preference for the Republican Party was given the weight of 5.

(23 items. Items 107, 108, 109, 110 apply only to Pilgrims and Colonists)

Computation of the Scale Score

The mean scale score for each respondent is computed by adding all the weighted numbers of his responses on a particular scale and dividing the total score by the number of questions answered on that scale. This method permits the computation of a mean scale score for any respondent who was unable or who refused to answer some questions on a scale. It is possible to receive a mean score between one and five on each scale.

Bibliography

GENERAL

Argus, M. K. *Moscow-on-the-Hudson*. New York: Harper & Bros., 1948.

Baltzell, E. Digby. *Philadelphia Gentlemen*. New York: The Free Press of Glencoe, 1958.

Batchinsky, Julian. *Ukrainian Immigration in the United States of America*. Lwiw: 1914.

Beals, Ralph. "Acculturation," *Anthropology Today*, A. L. Kroeber, ed. Chicago: University of Chicago Press, 1953.

Belcher, John C., and Emit Sharp. "A Short Scale for Measuring Farm Family Level of Living: A Modification of Sewell's Socio-Economic Scale," (Technical Bulletin No. T-46). Stillwater: Oklahoma Agricultural Experiment Station, September, 1952.

Bell, Daniel. *The End of Ideology*. New York: The Free Press of Glencoe, 1960.

Bendix, Reinhard, and Seymour Martin Lipset, eds. *Class, Status, and Power: A Reader in Social Stratification*. New York: The Free Press of Glencoe, 1953.

Blumenthal, Albert. *Small-Town Stuff*. Chicago: University of Chicago Press, 1932.

Bogardus, Emory S. *Immigration and Race Attitudes*. New York: D. C. Heath & Co., 1928.

Campisi, Paul J. "A Scale for the Measurement of Acculturation." Unpublished Ph.D. dissertation, University of Chicago, 1947.

Centers, Richard. *The Psychology of Social Classes: A Study of Class Consciousness*. Princeton: Princeton Press, 1949.

Chapin, F. Stuart. *Contemporary American Institutions*. New York: Harper & Bros., 1935.

——. *Experimental Designs in Sociological Research.* New York: Harper & Bros., 1947.

——. "The Measurement of Sociability and Socio-Economic Status," *Sociology and Social Research,* XII (January-February, 1928), 208–17.

——. *The Measurement of Status by the Use of the Social Status Scale.* Minneapolis: University of Minnesota Press, 1933.

——. "A Quantitative Scale for Rating the Home and Social Environment of Middle Class Families in an Urban Community," *Journal of Educational Psychology,* XIX (October, 1928), 99–111.

——. *Scale for Rating Living Room Equipment.* (Institute of Child Welfare Circular No. 3). Minneapolis: University of Minnesota, January, 1930.

——. *Social Participation Scale.* Minneapolis: University of Minnesota Press, 1938.

——. *Social Participation Scale.* 1952 ed. Minneapolis: University of Minnesota, 1952.

——. *The Social Status Scale.* Minneapolis: University of Minnesota Press, 1933; revised in 1936.

——. "Socio-Economic Status: Some Preliminary Results of Measurement," *American Journal of Sociology,* XXXVII (January, 1932), 581–7.

Chapman, Dennis. *The Home and Social Status.* London: Routledge and Kegan Paul Ltd., 1955.

Clarke, Alfred C. "Leisure and Occupational Prestige," *Mass Leisure,* Eric Larrabee and Rolf Meyersohn, eds. New York: The Free Press of Glencoe, 1958.

Cornell, Francis G. *The Essentials of Educational Statistics.* New York: John Wiley & Sons, 1956.

Dahl, Robert A. *Who Governs.* New Haven: Yale University Press, 1961.

Davis, James Allan. "Living Rooms as Symbols of Status: A Study in Social Judgment," Unpublished Ph.D. dissertation, Harvard University, January, 1955.

Davis, Jerome. *The Russian Immigrant.* New York: Macmillan Co., 1922.

——. *The Russians and Ruthenians in America.* New York: George H. Doran Co., 1922.

Day, George Martin. *The Russians in Hollywood.* Los Angeles: University of Southern California Press, 1934.

Eisenstadt, S. N. *The Absorption of Immigrants.* London: Routledge & Kegan Paul Ltd., 1954.

————. *From Generation to Generation*. New York: The Free Press of Glencoe, 1956.

Gerth, Hans H., and C. Wright Mills. *Character and Social Structure*. New York: Harcourt, Brace and Co., 1953.

Giddings, Franklin Henry. *Democracy and Empire*. New York: The Macmillan Co., 1900.

Glazer, Nathan. "Social Characteristics of American Jews, 1654–1954," *American Jewish Year Book, 1955*, Morris Fine, ed. Philadelphia: Jewish Publication Society of America, 1955.

Guilford, J. P. "Racial Preferences of a Thousand American University Students," *Journal of Social Psychology*, II (May, 1931), 179–202.

Guttman, Louis. "A Review of Chapin's Social Status Scale," *American Sociological Review*, VIII (June, 1943), 362–9.

Halich, Wasyl. *Ukrainians in the United States*. Chicago: University of Chicago Press, 1937.

Handlin, Oscar. *The Newcomers*. Cambridge: Harvard University Press, 1959.

Hollingshead, August B. *Elmtown's Youth: The Impact of Social Classes on Adolescence*. New York: John Wiley & Sons, Inc., 1949.

————. *The Two Factor Index of Social Position*. New Haven: August B. Hollingshead, 1957.

Hollingshead, August B., and Frederick C. Redlich. *Social Class and Mental Illness: A Community Study*. New York: John Wiley & Sons, Inc., 1958.

————. "Social Stratification and Psychiatric Disorders," *American Sociological Review*, XVIII (April, 1953), 163–70.

Hughes, Everett Cherrington. "Principles and Rationalization in Race Relations," *Where Peoples Meet*, Everett Cherrington Hughes and Helen MacGill Hughes. New York: The Free Press of Glencoe, 1952.

Hunter, Floyd. *The Community Power Structure*. Chapel Hill: University of North Carolina Press, 1953.

Kahl, Joseph A. *The American Class Structure*. New York: Rinehart & Co., Inc., 1957.

Kaplan, Max. *Leisure in America*. New York: John Wiley & Sons, Inc., 1960.

Katz, David, and Kenneth Braly. "Racial Stereotypes of One Hundred College Students," *Journal of Abnormal and Social Psychology*, XXVIII (October, 1933), 280–90.

Kornhauser, Ruth Rosner. "The Warner Approach to Social Stratification," *Class, Status, and Power: A Reader in Social Stratification*, Reinhard Bendix and Seymour Martin Lipset, eds. New York: The Free Press of Glencoe, 1953.

Kramer, Judith R., and Seymour Leventman. *Children of the Gilded Ghetto.* New Haven: Yale University Press, 1961.

Lantz, Herman R. *The People of Coal Town.* New York: Columbia University Press, 1958.

Lasswell, Harold D., and Abraham Kaplan. *Power and Society.* New Haven: Yale University Press, 1950.

LaViolette, Forrest E. *Americans of Japanese Ancestry.* Toronto: Canadian Institute of International Affairs, 1946.

Lee, Rose Hum. *The Chinese in the United States of America.* Hong Kong: Hong Kong University Press, 1960.

Lenski, Gerhard. *The Religious Factor.* Garden City: Doubleday & Co., 1961.

Lipset, Seymour Martin, and Reinhard Bendix. *Social Mobility in Industrial Society.* Berkeley: University of California Press, 1959.

Lynd, Robert S., and Helen Merrell Lynd. *Middletown.* New York: Harcourt, Brace and Co., 1929.

————. *Middletown in Transition.* New York: Harcourt, Brace and Co., 1937.

Lynes, Russell. *The Tastemakers.* Universal Library ed., New York: Grosset & Dunlap, 1954.

MacIver, Robert M. *Society.* New York: Farrar & Rinehart, Inc., 1937.

Mandel, Nathan G. "Mandel Social Adjustment Scale Manual." Minneapolis: Department of Psychiatry Research, University of Minnesota, 1959.

Mannheim, Karl. *Essays on the Sociology of Knowledge.* London: Routledge and Kegan Paul, Ltd., 1952.

Martindale, Don. American Social Structure. New York: Appleton-Century-Crofts, Inc., 1960.

————. *American Society.* New York: D. Van Nostrand Co., 1960.

————. "Prefatory Remarks: The Theory of the City," *The City*, Max Weber. New York: The Free Press of Glencoe, 1958.

Maxwell, Milton A. "In One State," *Drinking and Intoxication*, Raymond G. McCarthy, ed. New York: The Free Press of Glencoe, 1959.

Merton, Robert K. *Social Theory and Social Structure.* New York: The Free Press of Glencoe, 1957.

Miller, Delbert C. "Industry and Community Power Structure," *American Sociological Review*, XXIII (February, 1958), 9–15.

Mills, C. Wright. *The New Man of Power.* New York: Harcourt, Brace and Co., 1948.

———. *White Collar.* New York: Oxford University Press, 1951.

———. *The Power Elite.* New York: Oxford University Press, 1956.

Park, Robert E., and H. A. Miller. *Old World Traits Transplanted.* New York: Harper & Bros., 1921.

Park, Robert E., Ernest W. Burgess, and Roderick D. McKenzie. *The City.* Chicago: University of Chicago Press, 1925.

Parsons, Talcott. *The Social System.* New York: The Free Press of Glencoe, 1951.

Parten, Mildred. *Surveys, Polls and Samples: Practical Procedures.* New York: Harper & Bros., 1950.

Polsby, Nelson W. "How to Study Community Power: the Pluralist Alternative," *The Journal of Politics,* XXII (August, 1960), 474–84.

Riley, John W., Jr., and Charles F. Marden. "Who, What, and How Often?" *Drinking and Intoxication,* Raymond G. McCarthy, ed. New York: The Free Press of Glencoe, 1959.

Rogers, David. "Community Political Systems: A Framework and Hypothesis for Comparative Studies," *Current Trends in Comparative Community Studies,* Bert E. Swanson, ed. Kansas City: Community Studies, Inc., 1962.

Rogoff, Natalie. *Recent Trends in Occupational Mobility.* New York: The Free Press of Glencoe, 1953.

Rose, Arnold M. *Union Solidarity.* Minneapolis: University of Minnesota Press, 1952.

Rossi, Peter H. *Why Families Move.* New York: The Free Press of Glencoe, 1955.

Schermerhorn, R. A. *These Our People: Minorities in American Culture.* Boston: D.C. Heath, 1949.

Schulze, Robert O. "Economic Dominants and Community Power Structure," *American Sociological Review,* XXIII (February, 1958), 3–9.

Sewell, William H. *The Construction and Standardization of a Scale for the Measurement of the Socio-Economic Status of Oklahoma Farm Families.* (Technical Bulletin, No. 9) Stillwater: Oklahoma Agricultural Experiment Station, 1940.

———. "A Short Form of the Farm Family Socio-Economic Status Scale," *Rural Sociology,* VIII, No. 2 (June, 1943), 161–70.

Shriver, William P. *Immigrant Forces.* New York: Missionary Education Movement of the United States and Canada, 1913.

Siegel, Bernard J., and Evon Z. Vogt, James B. Watson, and Leonard Broom. "Acculturation: An Exploratory Formulation," *American Anthropologist*, LVI (December, 1954), 973–1002.

Simpson, George E., and J. Milton Yinger. *Racial and Cultural Minorities*. New York: Harper and Bros., 1958.

Sklare, Marshall, ed. *The Jews: Social Patterns of an American Group*. New York: The Free Press of Glencoe, 1958.

Sokoloff, Lillian. *The Russians in Los Angeles*. Los Angeles: University of Southern California Press, 1918.

Spindler, George C., and Walter Goldschmidt. "Experimental Design in the Study of Culture Change," *Southwestern Journal of Anthropology*, VIII (1952), 68–83.

———. "Symposium on Acculturation," *American Anthropologist*, XLIII (1941), 1–61.

Stonequist, Everett V. *The Marginal Man*. New York: Charles Scribner's Sons, 1937.

Thomas, William I., and Florian Znaniecki. *The Polish Peasant in Europe and America*. 4 vols. Boston: Gorham Press, 1920.

Veblen, Thorstein. *The Theory of the Leisure Class*. New York: The Modern Library, 1931.

Vidich, Arthur J., and Joseph Bensman. *The Small Town in Mass Society*. Princeton: Princeton University Press, 1958.

Warner, W. Lloyd, and James C. Abegglen. *Occupational Mobility in American Business and Industry*. Minneapolis: University of Minnesota Press, 1955.

Warner, W. Lloyd, and Associates. *Democracy in Jonesville*. New York: Harper & Bros., 1949.

Warner, W. Lloyd, Robert J. Havighurst, and Martin B. Loeb. *Who Shall Be Educated*. New York: Harper & Bros., 1944.

Warner, W. Lloyd, and Paul S. Lunt. *The Social Life of a Modern Community*. ("Yankee City Series," Vol. 1.) New Haven: Yale University Press, 1941.

———. *The Status System of a Modern Community*. ("Yankee City Series," Vol. II.) New Haven: Yale University Press, 1942.

Warner, W. Lloyd, Marchia Meeker, and Kenneth Eells. *Social Class in America: A Manual of Procedure for the Measurement of Social Status*. Chicago: Science Research Associates, Inc., 1949.

Warner, W. Lloyd, and Leo Srole. *The Social Systems of American Ethnic Groups*. ("Yankee City Series," Vol. III.) New Haven: Yale University Press, 1945.

Weber, Max. *Ancient Judaism.* Hans H. Gerth and Don Martindale, trans. & eds. New York: The Free Press of Glencoe, 1952.

———. *From Max Weber: Essays in Sociology.* Hans H. Gerth and C. Wright Mills, trans. & eds. New York: Oxford University Press, 1946.

———. *The Protestant Ethic and the Spirit of Capitalism.* Talcott Parsons, ed. London: G. Allen and Unwin, Ltd., 1930.

———. *The Rational and Social Foundations of Music.* Don Martindale, Johannes Riedel, and Gertrude Neuwirth, trans. and eds. Carbondale: Southern Illinois University Press, 1958.

———. *The Religion of India: The Sociology of Hinduism and Buddhism.* Hans H. Gerth and Don Martindale, trans. & eds. New York: The Free Press of Glencoe, 1958.

———. *The Theory of Social and Economic Organization.* A. M. Henderson and Talcott Parsons, trans. New York: The Free Press of Glencoe and The Falcon's Wing Press, 1947.

Whyte, William Foote. *Street Corner Society.* Chicago: University of Chicago Press, 1955.

Wirth, Louis. *The Ghetto.* Chicago: University of Chicago Press, 1928.

Woods, Frances J. *Cultural Values of American Ethnic Groups.* New York: Harper & Bros., 1956.

Young, Pauline V. *The Pilgrims of Russian-Town.* Chicago: University of Chicago Press, 1932.

Zeligs, R., and G. Hendrickson. "Racial Attitudes of 200 Sixth-Grade Children," *Sociology and Social Research,* September-October, 1933, pp. 26–36.

SPECIALIZED

Annual Report of the City of Minneapolis for the Year 1905, courtesy of Mr. Earl W. Eggers, Minneapolis Fire Department. Letter to Alex Simirenko, February 24, 1961.

Articles of Incorporation of the Russian Orthodox Catholic Brotherhood of St. John the Baptist and Mutual Benefit Association, Document No. 457307; Certificate of Amendment of Certificate of Incorporation of Russian Orthodox Catholic Brotherhood of St. John the Baptist and Mutual Benefit Association, Document No. 1398984.

Articles of Incorporation of St. Mary's Russian Orthodox Greek Catholic Church in Minneapolis, Minnesota, Book 265, p. 489, Document No. 1421343.

Articles of Incorporation of St. Mary's Veterans Association, Book 828, p. 389, Document No. 3171175, filed April 15, 1959.

Benjamin, Bishop. "St. Mary's Russian Orthodox Church and the Parish of Minneapolis," *Golden Jubilee Album of St. Mary's Russian Orthodox Greek Catholic Church.* Minneapolis: 1937.

Benzin, Basil M. "My Recollections of the North American Ecclesiastical Seminary, 1905 and 1906," *Golden Jubilee Album of St. Mary's Russian Orthodox Greek Catholic Church.* Minneapolis: 1937.

Certificate of Organization of the Russian Orthodox Cemetery Association. Unpublished document, Manuscript Division, Minneapolis Historical Society.

"Church Club Plans Fair—Helping Hands Are Sometimes Battle-Scarred," *The Minneapolis Star,* Oct. 26, 1960.

"D.P. Group Gets Own Church," *The Minneapolis Star,* April 21, 1956; *The Minneapolis Sunday Tribune,* April 22, 1956.

Dzubay, Rev. John, ed. "20th Anniversary of St. Mary's 'R' Club, Chapter 94 (1936–1956)." Minneapolis: 1956.

Dzubay, Rev. John. "The Light of Orthodoxy," The 66th Anniversary of St. Mary's Russian Orthodox Greek Catholic Church. Minneapolis: 1953.

———. "Orthodoxy in America." Minneapolis: 1955.

———. "St. Mary's 73d Anniversary," in"73d Anniversary Souvenir Book, Summer Festival and Picnic," St. Mary's Russian Orthodox Greek Catholic Church. Minneapolis: 1960.

Gilman, Cathryn Cooke. "Neighbors United through Social Settlement Services at the North East Neighborhood House, Minneapolis, Minnesota, 1914–1948," 3 vols. Unpublished manuscript, Minnesota Historical Society, courtesy of Mr. Logan Gilman.

Gilman, Robbins, to Governor Luther Youngdahl, January 2, 1947. Robbins Gilman and Family Papers, 1899–1952, Box 20, Manuscript Division, Minnesota Historical Society, St. Paul.

Golden Anniversary Souvenir Album of the St. Mary's Russian Orthodox Greek Catholic Church a capella Choir, Minneapolis, Minnesota. Minneapolis: 1941.

Golden Jubilee Album of St. Mary's Russian Orthodox Greek Catholic Church. Minneapolis: 1937.

Grigorieff, Dimitry. "The Historical Background of Orthodoxy in America," *St. Vladimir's Seminary Quarterly,* V, No. 1–2 (1961). 3–53.

Historical Magazine of the Protestant Episcopal Church, Ethelbert Tabbot issue (June, 1953).

Jalma, George Michael, "The Church of St. Mary the Protectorate," *The Russian Orthodox Journal*, XXV, No. 3 (July, 1951). 5–6.

Kochanik, P. *Yubileyny sbornik soyuza pravoslavnykh sviashchenikov v Amerike* (New York: 1936).
Kohler, Katherine M., and Walker A. Anderson. "A Social Survey of 20,000 Families Residing in the Ten Minneapolis Settlement House Districts." Minneapolis: Adult Education Department, 1934. (With the Gilman Papers, Box 50, Manuscript Division, Minnesota Historical Society.)
Kolesnikoff, Rev. Vasily. "The Parish of Minneapolis Thirty Years Ago," *Golden Jubilee Album of St. Mary's Russian Orthodox Greek Catholic Church*. Minneapolis: 1937.

Manna, Charles. "Moses of New Land Recalls Tribulations of the Old," *The Minneapolis Morning Tribune*, June 22, 1959.
Masica, J. F. (Kaniewski-Loss Post No. 1852, Veterans of Foreign Wars of the U.S.), letter to Alex Simirenko, January 18, 1961.
Minneapolis Star and Tribune Library. "Biographical Information for Use in the 1947 Municipal Campaign of Paul J. Jaroscak."
———. "Biographical Information on Harold Kalina."
———. *The Minneapolis Tribune*, Oct. 31, 1952;
———. *The Minneapolis Star*, Sept. 3, 1951; Oct. 8, 1954; Nov. 11, 1954; March 18, 1955; Dec. 1, 1956; Oct. 17, 1957; Feb. 20, 1958.
———. "Jaroscak is District Judge," *The Minneapolis Star*, May 28, 1951.
———. "Jaroscak Wins County Bar Vote," *The Minneapolis Star*, Sept. 8, 1952.
———. G. Aaron Youngquist, "Appraising a District Judge," *The Minneapolis Star*, Oct. 27, 1952.
———. Editorial. "The Judgeship Contest," The Minneapolis Star, Oct. 27, 1952.
———. "A.F.L. Delegates Reject Move to Ditch Julkowski," *The Minneapolis Tribune*, October 14, 1954.
———. "N.E. Neighborhood House Picks Head," *The Minneapolis Star*, Feb. 16, 1955.
———. "Legislator Praises Settlement Work," *The Minneapolis Star*, Oct. 21, 1957.
———. "Sen. Kalina," *The Minneapolis Star*, Dec. 11, 1958.
———. "U.S. Bar Association Names City Lawyer," *The Minneapolis Tribune*, Dec. 20, 1953.

------. "William G. Kohlan," *The Minneapolis Star,* Jan. 18, 1954.
------. "Air Vets Elect," *The Minneapolis Star,* Feb. 26, 1954.
------. "Forget-Me-Not Drive to Open," *The Minneapolis Star,* Sept. 15, 1955.
------. "Attorney Elected to State D.F.L. Committee," *The Minneapolis Tribune,* Nov. 29, 1955.
------. "Andrew G. Kohlan," *The Minneapolis Star,* July 3, 1956.
------. "City Lawyer to Oppose Wier in D.F.L. Primary," *The Minneapolis Tribune,* July 18, 1958.
------. "Words Fly over Renaming Attorney," *The Minneapolis Star,* Jan. 21, 1960.
Minnesota Census Bureau. Forth Decennial Census of Minnesota, 1895. St. Paul: Minnesota State Documents.
------. Fifth Decennial Census of Minnesota, 1905. St. Paul: Minnesota State Documents.
Mlinar, John W. "One of the Pioneers of the Minneapolis Russian Community" Tape-recorded interview by Alex Simirenko with Rev. Vladimir Borichevsky, Jan. 20, 1958.

Nedzelnitsky, Rev. John. "The 50th Anniversary of the Russian Orthodox Colony in Minneapolis," *Golden Jubilee Album of St. Mary's Russian Orthodox Greek Catholic Church.* Minneapolis: 1937.

"Pastor Butchers 'Tito' and 'Stalin': Finds Peace," *The Minneapolis Tribune,* Aug. 4, 1952.
Popoff, Rev. Constantine. "Memories of St. Mary's Parish in Minneapolis," *Golden Jubilee Album of St. Mary's Russian Orthodox Greek Catholic Church.* Minneapolis: 1937.

Rogers, May Wyon. "Our New Americans," *Minneapolis Sunday Tribune,* August 6, 1916.
Russky Pravoslavny Kalendar. Pittsburgh: 1934.
The Russian-American Orthodox Kalendar for 1950. Wilkes-Barre, Pa.: Svet, 1950.

Simirenko, Alex. "Aspect of the Social and Ideological Adjustment of the Russian Community in Minneapolis." Unpublished M.A. thesis, University of Minnesota, 1958.
------. "A Case Study: The Minneapolis Russian Community in Transition," *St. Vladimir's Seminary Quarterly,* V, No. 1–2 (1961), 88–100.
------. "The Social Structure of the Minneapolis Russian Community,"

Proceedings of the Minnesota Academy of Science for 1959. Minneapolis) XXVII (1960).

Sorenson, C. A. (Director of Administrative Research, Census and Attendance, Minneapolis Public Schools), letter to Alex Simirenko, March 14, 1961.

St. Mary's Russian Orthodox Greek Catholic Church. "73d Anniversary Souvenir Book, Summer Festival and Picnic." Minneapolis: 1960.

———. "1959 Financial Report." Minneapolis: 1959.

———. "1960 Financial Report." Minneapolis: 1960.

———. "Souvenir Book of the 64th Anniversary Summer Festival and Picnic." Minneapolis: 1951.

"Survey of the East District of Minneapolis Prepared to Show the Sources of Constructive and Destructive Influences Affecting Youth," (1923). Gilman Papers, 1899–1952, Box 35, Manuscript Division, Minnesota Historical Society.

Thorkelson, Willmar. "Church Will Build on Site of Landmark," *The Minneapolis Star,* Dec. 13, 1956; Oct. 21, 1957.

U.S. Bureau of the Census. *U.S. Census of Population: 1890,* Part 1. Washington: Government Printing Office, 1895.

———. *U.S. Census of Population: 1900,* Vol. I, Part 1. Washington: Government Printing Office, 1901.

———. *U.S. Census of Population: 1920,* Vol. II. Washington: Government Printing Office, 1922.

———. *U.S. Census of Population: 1930,* Vol. III, Part. I. Washington: Government Printing Office, 1932.

———. *U.S. Census of Population: 1940,* Vol. II, Part 4. Washington: Government Printing Office, 1943.

———. *U.S. Census of Population: 1950,* Vol. XI, Part 23. Washington: Government Printing Office, 1952.

———. *U.S. Census of Population: 1950,* Special Report P-E No. 3A. Washington: Government Printing Office, 1954.

———. *U.S. Census of Population: 1960,* PC (1) 25C. Washington: Government Printing Office, 1961.

———. *U.S. Census of Housing: 1960,* HC (3) – 224, and HC (1) No. 25. Washington: Government Printing Office, 1961.

———. *Statistical Abstract of the U.S.: 1961.* Washington: Government Printing Office, 1961.

1960 Year Book and Church Directory of the Russian Orthodox Greek Catholic Church of America. New York: Metropolitan Council Publications Committee, 1960.

Zaichenko, Paul. "For the 50th Anniversary of the Parish of Minneapolis," *Golden Jubilee Album of St. Mary's Russian Orthodox Greek Catholic Church*. Minneapolis: 1937.

———. "My Twelve Years of Service in Minneapolis," *Golden Anniversary Souvenir Album of St. Mary's Russian Orthodox Greek Catholic Church a capella Choir*. Minneapolis: 1941.

Index